D1481887

GLOBAL PERSPECTIVES
ON ARMS CONTROL

Foreign Policy Issues
A Foreign Policy Research Institute Series

Series Editor
NILS H. WESSELL

Managing Editor
ELIZABETH D. DUNLAP

GLOBAL PERSPECTIVES
ON ARMS CONTROL

Edited by
Adam M. Garfinkle

PRAEGER SPECIAL STUDIES • PRAEGER SCIENTIFIC

New York • Philadelphia • Eastbourne, UK
Toronto • Hong Kong • Tokyo • Sydney

Library of Congress Cataloging in Publication Data

Main entry under title:

Global perspectives on arms control.

(Foreign policy issues)
"Updated versions of papers originally prepared for
the Seventh International Arms Control Symposium, hosted
by the Foreign Policy Research Institute at Philadelphia
in May 1982"—Foreword.
Includes index.
1. Arms Control—Addresses, essays, lectures.
2. Atomic weapons and disarmament—Addresses, essays,
lectures. 3. Europe—Defenses—Addresses, essays,
lectures. 4. Asia—Defenses—Addresses, essays, lectures.

5. Security, International—Addresses, essays, lectures.
I. Garfinkle, Adam M., 1951–   II. International
Arms Control Symposium (7th : 1982 : Philadelphia, Pa.)
III. Series.
JX1974.G474 1984   327.1′74   83-21094
ISBN 0-03-069658-5

Published in 1984 by Praeger Publishers
CBS Educational and Professional Publishing
A Division of CBS, Inc.
521 Fifth Avenue, New York, New York 10175 U.S.A.

© 1984 by Praeger Publishers

23456789 052 987654321

Printed in the United States of America on acid-free paper.

FOREIGN POLICY RESEARCH INSTITUTE

The Foreign Policy Research Institute is a nonprofit organization devoted to scholarly research and analysis of international developments affecting the national security interests of the United States. The Institute's major activities include a broad-based research program; an internationally recognized publications program; seminars, workshops, and conferences for business, government, and academic leaders; and a fellowship program that provides training in policy analysis to promising scholars.

The Institute's research and publications programs are designed to:
- Identify, explore, and forecast political, military, and economic trends in the international system;
- Analyze the fundamental issues facing U.S. foreign policy;
- Suggest guidelines for U.S. foreign policy that contribute both to American security and to the development of a stable international order.

To accomplish these purposes, the Institute:
- Maintains a staff of specialists in the field of international relations as well as an extensive library of pertinent periodicals, books, and information files. The Institute's library is open to use by scholars, students, and the general public;
- Draws upon the expertise of leading academicians and persons in public life who are concerned with international affairs;
- Convenes and publishes the results of conferences and symposia of U.S. and foreign experts on contemporary international problems.

The products of the Institute's research program include the following publications:
- **ORBIS:** a quarterly journal of world affairs, widely recognized as a leading forum for research in the field of international and strategic studies;
- **Foreign Policy Issues:** a book series (in cooperation with Praeger Publishers) of important studies written by authorities in the field of international and strategic studies;
- **Philadelphia Policy Papers:** analyses of timely issues and developments having serious implications for U.S. foreign and defense policy;
- **Research Reports:** sponsored by various institutions, including agencies of the U.S. government.

The opinions expressed in publications of the Foreign Policy Research Institute are those of the authors and should not be construed as representing those of the Institute.

Foreword

The Foreign Policy Research Institute has a long tradition of interest in arms control. This volume, *Global Perspectives on Arms Control*, edited by Dr. Adam M. Garfinkle, is the latest in a series of books the Institute has published over the years on arms control and strategic nuclear issues.

Global Perspectives on Arms Control brings together the diverse perspectives of scholars from several countries. It does so at a time when nuclear strategy and arms control have become a source of concern to the broad publics of many of these countries. One wishes that the positive impact of such concern might extend from the democratic nations where public opinion is the ultimate determinant of policy to those states where popular support for peace and disarmament is channeled through officially sanctioned organizations toward predetermined ends. Such a development would, indeed, mark a breakthrough in the long and tortuous history of arms control negotiations.

The book includes updated versions of papers originally prepared for the Seventh International Arms Control Symposium, hosted by the Foreign Policy Research Institute at Philadelphia in May 1982. Cosponsors included the Centre for the Study of Arms Control and International Security (United Kingdom), the Centre d'Etudes Politiques de Défense (France), the Konrad Adenauer Foundation (Federal Republic of Germany), the Research Institute for Peace and Security (Japan), and the Institute for Defense Studies and Analyses (India). Also participating in the symposium were delegations from the Soviet Institute of the USA and Canada and the Chinese International Strategic Studies Institute. In addition, the World Affairs Council of Philadelphia joined the Foreign Policy Research Institute in sponsoring the symposium, as did the city of Philadelphia, which designated the symposium an official event in the city's Fourth Century Celebration.

Applying characteristic energy and imagination, Alan Ned Sebrosky was principally responsible for conceptualizing and organizing the symposium. Charles B. Purrenhage and Elizabeth D. Dunlap ably performed the preliminary editing on several of the manuscripts making up this volume. Dr. Adam M. Garfinkle, research associate at the Foreign Policy Research Institute conceived the volume and nurtured it from the beginning. To him the reader owes the greatest debt.

Nils H. Wessell
Series Editor
Foreign Policy Issues
A Foreign Policy Research Institute Series

Preface

On May 6–8, 1982, prominent scholars, policy makers, and journalists from Great Britain, France, West Germany, Japan, China, India, the Soviet Union, and the United States participated in the Seventh International Arms Control Symposium (SIACS), which was hosted by the Foreign Policy Research Institute (FPRI). This volume represents the formal proceedings of the symposium: eight essays presented at plenary sessions and the keynote address by Eugene V. Rostow, who was at the time director of the U.S. Arms Control and Disarmament Agency. As coordinator of the symposium and editor of this volume, it is my pleasure to bring these essays to the general public.

SIACS, held at the Bellevue Stratford Hotel in Philadelphia, was one of a series of such gatherings presented by the FPRI over the past quarter century to examine issues pertinent to the national security of the United States and its allies and, more broadly, the political health of this small planet. The first of these meetings was held at Ann Arbor, Michigan, in December 1962; the second, sponsored by seven Philadelphia-area colleges and universities, convened at Philadelphia in March 1964. Both of these conferences examined the major arms control issues of the early 1960s. The first conference, which occurred less than two months after the Cuban missile crisis, was understandably concerned with the headiest of issues. The second, which took place shortly after the signing of the Test Ban Treaty, was somewhat more relaxed, if not completely optimistic about the future.

The Third International Arms Control Conference met in April 1966 under the sponsorship of the University of Pennsylvania, St. Joseph's College, and the

Bendix Corporation. Major topics of analysis included nonproliferation regimes, the ballistic missile defense controversy, and the implications of the Sino-Soviet dispute for the political and military strategies of the major powers. From this third conference, *Arms Control for the Late Sixties*, coedited by James E. Dougherty and John F. Lehman, Jr. (Princeton: D. Van Nostrand Company, 1967), emerged. It follows a volume also coedited by Messrs. Dougherty and Lehman, *The Prospects for Arms Control*, published after the second seminar.

The Fourth International Arms Control Symposium, which met in October 1969, focused on the soon-to-commence Strategic Arms Limitation Talks (SALT) and the issues surrounding these negotiations. Some of the topics examined included verification and inspection requisites, domestic and bureaucratic constraints in the negotiations, bargaining and communication techniques, implications of SALT for superpower-ally relationships, and, of course, the impact of SALT on the strategic balance. Symposium papers were published in such journals as *Asia Survey, War/Peace Report, Freedom at Issue,* and *Arms Control and National Security.* In retrospect, what is notable about these essays is the cautious and dispassionate attitudes they displayed toward SALT. This contrasted sharply with the general sense of euphoria prevalent in many academic circles at the time.

The Fifth International Arms Control Symposium, held at Philadelphia in October 1971, examined the evolution of SALT since November 1969, when the talks began. The symposium, which met less than a year before the signing of SALT I, considered a wide range of pertinent topics, including the rationale for superpower arms control, the implications of technological innovation for arms control and the strategic balance, the character of the bargaining process in SALT, the implications of SALT for non-proliferation efforts and international security writ large, and the implications for international diplomacy of SALT's success or failure. The fifth symposium resulted in a very well received volume entitled *SALT: Implications for Arms Control in the 1970s,* edited by William R. Kintner and Robert L. Pfaltzgraff, Jr., and published by the University of Pittsburgh Press. This volume featured a keynote address by Walt W. Rostow and included essays by Thomas Wolfe, Robert Bowie, Robert Scalapino, J. I. Coffey, Geoffrey Kemp and Ian Smart, William R. Van Cleave, and others.

The Sixth International Arms Control Symposium, was held at Philadelphia in November 1973. It was jointly sponsored by the University of Pennsylvania, the Fletcher School of Law and Diplomacy of Tufts University, the University of Chicago, Beaver College, St. Joseph's College, the University of Pittsburgh, and the FPRI. Standing between the consummation of SALT I and the still-to-be-negotiated SALT II, the meeting focused on both the past and the future. Of special interest in this symposium was the emerging dissociation of interests and perspectives of the United States and its allies over détente and its arms control "centerpiece." Convened in the wake of the Yom Kippur War, the sixth symposium gave voice to the premonition that, if détente had not proved to be all that some had hoped it could be, perhaps SALT would result in similar disappointments. The sixth symposium featured a keynote address by Dr. Fred I. Iklé, then the director of the Arms Control and Disarmament Agency, and essays by James Dougherty, George Quester, Gaston Sigur, Graham Allison, Morton Kaplan, and others. The proceedings edited by Robert L. Pfaltzgraff, Jr., were published by D. C. Heath and Company under the title *Contrasting Approaches to Strategic Arms Control.*

In preparing for SIACS, FPRI decided to encourage the participation of representatives of foreign institutions to a greater extent than had previously been the case. To this end, cosponsors from abroad were sought and brought together under the aegis of FPRI. As a result, only two plenary papers were given by U.S. citizens; the others were delivered by representatives from France, Great Britain, West Germany, Japan, India, and the Soviet Union.

SIACS met just as the Reagan administration was putting the finishing touches on its proposals for Strategic Arms Reduction Talks (START) amid a burgeoning nuclear "freeze" movement and ongoing negotiations with the Soviet Union over intermediate-range nuclear forces in Europe. In one respect SIACS proved to be too timely: its two keynote speakers, the director of the Arms Control and Disarmament Agency, Eugene V. Rostow, and the director of the State Department's Bureau of Politico-Military Affairs, Richard Burt, were both forced to cancel their talks at the last minute in order to attend lengthy late-night sessions in Washington. Robert Dean, deputy director of the Bureau of Politico-Military Affairs, and Robert Grey, then deputy director-designate of the U.S. Arms Control and Disarmament Agency, addressed the symposium instead. Other participants from U.S. government agencies included Gunning Butler, Jr., director, START and Arms Control, Office of the Undersecretary of Defense, Research and Engineering; Michael Mobbs, representative to START of the Office of the Secretary of Defense; Victor Gilinsky, commissioner of the Nuclear Regulatory Commission; Paula Dobriansky of the National Security Council; and Marian Leighton of the Central Intelligence Agency. A full list of participants is given in Appendix II of this volume.

During the course of the symposium, participants attended four plenary sessions and five working group sessions, each featuring four panels. The following broad themes were addressed in the sessions: arms control, strategic instability, and international security; arms control and European security; arms control and Asian security; and strategic threats of the future. A complete list of working group topics is provided in the conference program included in Appendix I.

During the initial plenary session, papers were presented by William Van Cleave of the Defense and Strategic Studies Center of the University of Southern California; Genrikh Trofimenko of the Institute of the USA and Canada, Soviet Academy of Sciences; and Yves Boyer of the Centre d'Etudes Politiques de Défense.

According to Trofimenko, the major challenges to global stability in the 1980s are the inability of the United States and its allies to accept socioeconomic change in the Third World, the obstinacy of Western diplomacy, and the West's dangerous and anachronistic obsession with the use of force. In his view, the superpowers should put aside their parochial differences and launch détente into a new and more ambitious phase. Van Cleave, on the other hand, identified the major challenge to global stability as the political ambitions and military expansionism of the Soviet Union. Van Cleave was careful to point out, however, that questions of stability involve at least two parties. The relative complacency of the Western community of nations is, therefore, partially responsible for the dangerous challenges the world is currently facing. While Van Cleave praised the Reagan administration for recognizing the problem, he urged that still more be done to meet the challenges.

Yves Boyer's comments focused on the problems of definition in arms control discourse. The ambiguity in the meaning of such terms as "equality," "stability," and "parity," stemming from divergences in differing political cultures, is one source of the major failings of the SALT process to date. Boyer also discussed the technological momentum of the arms race that has continually defied and outstripped the process of negotiation.

The first two working-group sessions, chaired by such scholars as Martin Edmonds, W. Scott Thompson, Derek Leebaert, Richard Betts, Pierre Dabezies, and Robert Legvold, examined a number of important issues related to the plenary theme. What was perhaps most striking about these discussions was the widespread disenchantment expressed with the intellectual rules of thumb that have heretofore guided much thinking about these subjects. The underlying causes of the willingness to redefine basic terms were the unstable character of the current U.S.-Soviet strategic equation and the sense of novelty occasioned by a still-new administration trying to put U.S. arms control and strategic policies in some order.

The second and third plenary sessions sought to gain an understanding of superpower rivalries and negotiations as they occur in specific regional political contexts. Plenary II featured presentations by Philip Williams of the University of Southampton and Col. Wolfgang Schreiber of the Konrad Adenauer Foundation. Williams presented a valuable taxonomy of European attitudes toward arms control on three levels: strategic, theater, and conventional. The analysis revealed underlying assumptions about U.S.-Soviet relations and the current international system held by cynics, realists, proponents of arms control, "disarmers," and others. Williams then linked together many attitudes and issues in current European debates and pointed out the implications for U.S. policy as its NATO and arms control components meet.

Colonel Schreiber's paper took up the underlying differences between Western and Soviet concepts of security, détente, and arms control, particularly as related to Europe. He argued for a "forward" political and moral challenge to Soviet hegemonic ambitions in Europe.

Working group discussions, led by analysts such as Michael Dillon, Jean Klein, and Steven L. Canby, concentrated on the various military and political implications of the NATO dual-track decision of December 12, 1979, on theater nuclear modernization. Discussion pointed out the political linkages between intermediate nuclear forces (INF) talks on the one hand and START and the Mutual and Balanced Force Reductions (MBFR) negotiations on the other, and the symbolic "coupling" impact of the U.S. "zero option" as against its strategic rationale—or lack thereof.

Presentations of Asian security issues were delivered by Hiroshi Kimura of the Slavic Research Center, Hokkaido University, and K. Subrahmanyam of the Institute for Defence Studies and Analyses. Each author approached the security issues of his respective Asian region from a candidly national perspective. Subrahmanyam's analysis concentrated on the dangers to India of Pakistani nuclear armament and implied possible Indian countermeasures. Kimura made the point that, despite the European-centered nature of current arms control negotiations, the consequences could affect East Asia as well. What if, he asked, the INF negotiations succeed in removing Soviet SS-20 missiles from the European theater, only to have them redeployed in Asia?

Subsequent discussions, led by Allen S. Whiting, Ambassador William H. Sullivan, George Quester, and others, were united by a geopolitical reality: the fact that U.S., Soviet, Chinese, and Japanese security concerns merge in Asia as in no other area of the globe. It was evident that the intersection of so many powerful interests and the heterogeneity of Asian political cultures posed formidable barriers to the sort of institutionalized arms control forums we see in Europe. Arms control and national security in Asia seem to be dependent on an array of forces in the political environment that can only be described by traditional balance-of-power models.

The final plenary session featured presentations by Fabienne Luchaire of the Centre d'Etudes Politiques de Défense and Colin S. Gray, president of the National Institute for Public Policy. Ms. Luchaire, who spoke on the topic of nuclear proliferation and terrorism, pointed out the phases in the development of terrorist tactics over the years. Of particular interest was the point that in addition to the use of nuclear devices by terrorist groups on the one hand, and the terroristic use of nuclear weapons by states on the other, there are other, more dangerous and probable possibilities. States could disintegrate, leaving perhaps desperate factions in command of nuclear weapons or facilities, or a state could "use" terrorist groups to engage in nuclear blackmail in order to minimize direct risks to itself. Ms. Luchaire suggested that the threat of nuclear terrorism is neither as simple nor as remote as is sometimes thought.

Colin Gray's discussion of the military uses of space was both technically enlightening and provocative. Gray asserted that, despite the popular tendency to link together the military uses of space and arms control regimes specifically designed to deal with them, the two are not necessarily linked in the minds of high-level decision makers in Moscow and Washington. Both the Soviet Union and the United States will exploit these new technologies to the fullest, and the United States, according to Gray, should do its best to win this new competition.

The real question has less to do with arms control per se than with the future of the strategic balance and the implications for superpower doctrines, strategies, and the arms control interests that flow from them.

Subsequent working groups, chaired by Richard Bissell, Donald Snow, Philip Towle, and Manfred Hamm, illustrated the "strained" limits of national power before the onslaught of technological dynamism. The discussants agreed that we are on the verge of dangerous and unpredictable times. Challenges to sovereignty range along a spectrum from subnational proliferation and terrorism to high-technology defenses that only a small, select group of nations can exploit. While the military uses of space are likely to benefit some nations at the expense of others, terrorism, nuclear and otherwise, erodes the power of all states, especially the most advanced and complex.

With cosponsoring and participating institutions spread over eight countries and attendees from a great many more, the Seventh International Arms Control Symposium was a logistical and organizational nightmare that could easily have become a waking calamity had it not been for the saving labors of many at the Foreign Policy Research Institute. Included in this rather large group are Kenneth Warner, Richard Smith, Michael Dorfman, Belinda Quan, Roy Kim, Alvin Z. Rubinstein, Dorothy Greenwood, Alan Luxenberg, Alan N. Sabrosky, who was the Institute's director at the time, and Nils H. Wessell, its current director. Special recognition must be given to Richard Porth, FPRI's conference coordinator, who has transformed dealing with travel agents, hoteliers, printers, and restauranteurs into an art.

As was the case with the symposium itself, this volume has had its share of helpers. Typists, forever patient and forgiving of afterthoughts, include Saundra Bailey, Donna Hill, Dorothy Greenwood, and Mary Tate. I am also indebted to Dorothy Breitbart, the political science editor at Praeger Publishers, and Susan Goodman Alkana, the project editor, whose administrative skills facilitated the production of the volume. Finally, a debt of gratitude is owed to the production staff at Praeger, whose efforts produced this handsome object-in-time, standing for the intellectual labor of many.

Adam M. Garfinkle
Philadelphia, Pennsylvania
June 1983

Contents

Foreword
by *Nils H. Wessell*   vi

Preface
by *Adam M. Garfinkle*   viii

List of Acronyms   xvii

Introduction: The Great Nuclear Debate
by *Eugene V. Rostow*   1

PART I: ARMS CONTROL, STRATEGIC
INSTABILITY, AND INTERNATIONAL SECURITY

1. **Challenges to Global Stability in the 1980s**
   by *William R. Van Cleave*   15

   Introduction: The Major Challenge   15
   Soviet Ambitions and Motivations   17
   The Military Balance   20
   The Western Contribution to Instability   23
   What Is to Be Done?   27
   Notes   30

2. **Challenges to Global Stability in the 1980s: A Soviet View**
   by *Genrikh Trofimenko*   33

   On Global Stability   33
   The Challenge of Change   35
   Diplomatic Problems and Economic Crisis   37
   The Use of Force in the Nuclear Age   38
   Soviet-American Détente: Key to Global Stability   40
   Beyond Power Politics   45
   Notes   45

PART II: ARMS CONTROL
AND EUROPEAN SECURITY

3. Arms Control and West European Security in the 1980s
by *Philip Williams*   **49**

The Uncertainties of Arms Control   49
Competing Conceptions   51
Conventional Arms Control   58
Intermediate Nuclear Forces and Arms Control   61
Competing Conceptions Revisited   64
Notes   67

4. Superpower Competition, Détente, and European Security
by *Wolfgang Schreiber*   **69**

Superpower Competition   69
Security: East and West   73
Détente   75
Conclusions   78
Notes   79

PART III: ARMS CONTROL
AND ASIAN SECURITY

5. Arms Control in East Asia
by *Hiroshi Kimura*   **83**

Introduction   83
The Military Situation   84
Three Interpretations   86
Arms Control Proposals: Motives and Responses   88
Obstacles to Arms Control in East Asia   90
Notes   93

6. Nuclear Proliferation and the Balance of Power in South Asia
by *K. Subrahmanyam*   **95**

Redefining Proliferation   95
Defining South Asia   97
The Regional Balance of Power   101
Conclusions   109
Notes   109

PART IV: STRATEGIC THREATS OF THE FUTURE

7. Subnational Proliferation, Technology Transfers, and Terrorism
by *Fabienne Luchaire*   **113**

Introduction   113
Psychological Factors of Terrorism and the Use of Nuclear Weapons   116
Technical Factors and the Risk of Subnational Proliferation   122
Dangers Inherent in Transfers of Technology   127
Conclusions   131
Notes   132

8. U.S. Military Space Policy
by *Colin S. Gray*   **133**

In Search of Coherence   133
ASAT and Arms Control   135
Ballistic Missile Defense and Strategic Dogma   136
Space Policy and National Security   138
Asking the Right Questions   141
Notes   143

Appendixes
I Symposium Plenary and Working Group Organization   147

II List of Participants   153

Index   **165**

About the Contributors   **171**

List of Acronyms

ABM	Antiballistic missile
ASAT	Anti-satellite
BMD	Ballistic missile defense
CBM	Confidence-building measure
CERCA	Compagnie pour l'Etudes et la Realisation de Combustibles Atomiques
C³I	Command, Control, Communications and Intelligence
CSCE	Conference on Security and Cooperation in Europe
DSAT	Defense of Satellite
EDC	European Defense Community
FPRI	Foreign Policy Research Institute
HEL	high energy laser
IAEA	International Atomic Energy Agency
ICBM	Intercontinental ballistic missile
INF	Intermediate nuclear forces
MBFR	Mutual and Balanced Force Reductions
NPT	Nonproliferation Treaty
SALT	Strategic Arms Limitation Talks
SIACS	Seventh International Arms Control Symposium
SLBM	Submarine-launched ballistic missile
SSBN	Nuclear-powered submarine missile launcher (Soviet designation)
START	Strategic Arms Reduction Talks

GLOBAL PERSPECTIVES
ON ARMS CONTROL

Introduction: The Great Nuclear Debate

Eugene V. Rostow

The period 1981–1982 has witnessed a healthy increase in public concern about the state of our security in general and about nuclear arms and nuclear arms control agreements in particular. Since I have tried for years to stir up popular interest in these matters, I can only cheer. We cannot hope to restore a strong, confident, bipartisan foreign policy—a national objective of primordial importance—until there has been a thorough, civil, and disciplined debate about what our foreign policy is for, what it is supposed to accomplish, and by what means. Such a debate should produce a new state of public opinion, the only legitimate source of policy in a democracy.

Before commenting on some of the issues that have lately attracted so much attention on the arms control front, let us review a few fundamental propositions on this subject and, by doing so, establish a framework for further observations.

The first principle of President Reagan's approach to arms control and disarmament has been to insist that arms control be viewed as an integral part of our foreign and defense policy as a whole. Arms control is not a magical activity that can produce peace by incantation, without pain and without tears. The other day one of my children sent me a cartoon of the 1930s by the famous British cartoonist David Low. The cartoon makes President Reagan's point perfectly. Low never drew a figure for "Disarmament" without a twin figure labeled "Collective Security." Unless collective security is fully and visibly restored, American negotiators and policy makers are going to wear out the seats of a good many pairs of pants during the next couple of years. Arms control negotiations can be a useful element in a strategy for achieving peace. But they are not a substitute

---

When this was written, Dr. Rostow was director of the U.S. Arms Control and Disarmament Agency.

for such a strategy, nor, equally, are they a substitute for programs designed to restore the military balance with the Soviet Union.

Second, we must guard against the illusion that Senator Edmund Muskie expressed on March 18, 1981—that negotiating with the Soviet Union about arms control is in itself "a restraining influence" on Soviet behavior. This view is wishful thinking and nothing more. We negotiated about arms control with the Soviet Union throughout the 1970s. It was a disastrous period in the history of the cold war in Southeast Asia, the Middle East, Afghanistan, and Africa, and it also witnessed the development and deployment of many new and improved Soviet weapons systems. Of course, the United States is in favor of negotiating with the Soviet Union about arms control and every other aspect of foreign policy. Indeed, we are doing so now in Geneva about intermediate-range nuclear weapons and longer-range central strategic systems. But we must not confuse hope with reality. And we must not fall into the treaty trap: negotiating with the Soviet Union is not like playing croquet.

Third, it must be stressed once more that nuclear arms do not exist in a vacuum. The secret is out of the laboratory, and there is no way to put it back. Mankind has eaten the apple and must live with the consequences. Any industrialized country can make nuclear weapons. The West must therefore retain the weapon, if only to prevent its possible use by others. Moreover, there is a close and fundamental connection between the nuclear weapon and the use of conventional forces, as the Cuban missile crisis demonstrated in 1962.[1]

We must design both our military and diplomatic policies, and our arms control policies, on the basis of these inescapable facts. There is no way to build an impermeable wall between the use of nuclear and conventional weapons. Just as small nuclear wars may become big ones, so small or large conventional wars can escalate to the nuclear level if nuclear powers are involved. We cannot be sure that we can keep the demon in its cage forever. In order to prevent the horror of nuclear war, therefore, we and our allies, and other nations devoted to peace, must take responsibility for the agreed rules of world public order against all forms of aggression, both conventional and nuclear. The effectiveness of these rules has declined since the American withdrawal from Vietnam. Until their influence is restored, there is little chance for achieving meaningful arms control.

The United States must be prepared, too, to deter the possibility of political coercion based on the threat to use nuclear weapons, which is by far the greatest of the nuclear dangers we face—not nuclear war but nuclear blackmail. The president of the United States must never be put in a position where he would have to choose between abandoning a vital American interest and launching nuclear war. That is the essence of the policy of deterrence, which has worked successfully since 1945. It must continue to be the goal of our security and our arms control policies.

The fourth preliminary point is a simple one: the ground swell of concern about the nuclear problem throughout the Western world is not a mysterious phenomenon, a plague visited on us from the heavens, or a hobgoblin created by Soviet propaganda. It has a perfectly natural cause. The Soviet Union has pulled out all the stops of a great propaganda campaign to persuade us that the cause of our anxiety is a nuclear arms race. This clearly is not the case. Wars are not caused by arms races or the activities of "merchants of death." They are caused by predation, fear, or the faith of zealots and crusaders. In any event, there has been no nuclear arms race. For ten years or more the Soviet military establishment has increased at the rate of some 4 percent a year in real terms—8 percent a year in the nuclear area. During the same period the armed forces of the West have remained stable or fallen behind. Now the West is trying to modernize its forces after the long pause of the 1970s, and to close certain critical gaps that have developed. But the Western effort to restore the military balance with the Soviet Union is not the cause of the current concern about war throughout the West. It is a symptom of that concern and a response to it. The West is not seeking nuclear superiority in any sense of the term. The United States is trying only to reestablish its second-strike capacity so that we and our allies can deter Soviet aggression and nuclear blackmail against the United States, its allies, and their supreme interests.

The cause of the recent increase in anxiety about war throughout the West is the Soviet program of expansion, based on a formidable and continuing military buildup, and a willingness to use aggressive war as an instrument of national policy. There is no way in which Soviet behavior can be explained as defensive or reconciled with the rules of world public order. The process of Soviet expansion no longer concerns remote coaling stations. It affects areas of great and immediate strategic importance like the Middle East, the Caribbean, and the approaches to Europe and Japan. The Soviet Union's use of aggression as a tool of policy has weakened the taboos against the use of force and encouraged other nations to follow its example, as we have seen in the South Atlantic and the Persian Gulf. As a result, the state system has been slipping toward chaos.

Naturally, the Soviet drive for hegemony and its consequences have touched sensitive nerves throughout the West. And our people—and people throughout the world—are responding. A U.S. senator told me the other day that what his constituents are saying on these matters is something altogether familiar to a politician, and of the utmost importance: "Do something." Our people are not committed to any particular solution, he said—a freeze at current levels, a no-first-use pledge, or any other formula—and they certainly do not support either unilateral disarmament or unilateral nuclear disarmament. But they emphatically want their government to do whatever is prudent and reasonable to protect the interests of the nation and to prevent war. As usual, the people are absolutely right.

Actually, public opinion and national policy have moved a long way from the post-Vietnam panic and paralysis of the mid-1970s. We are already more than halfway back to "collective security." Of course, the post-Vietnam retreat to isolationalism is not over. One could hardly say that after the publication of the article by Robert McNamara, Gerard Smith, McGeorge Bundy, and George Kennan advocating a no-first-use-policy and other manifestations of the isolationist spirit.[2] But the post-Vietnam foreign policy debate in the United States is now in its second stage. The four years of debate that culminated in the election of President Reagan and his first year in office have accomplished a good deal. Americans now recognize the imperial character of Soviet foreign policy and the magnitude of the military buildup on which it is based. They understand that Soviet expansion has proceeded too far—that it has become a threat to the balance of world power and the system of public order that necessarily depends upon it. And they have concluded that the United States made a mistake during the 1970s in allowing the Soviet Union to catch up in military power, and then forge ahead.

There is a solid American consensus in favor of restoring the conventional and nuclear military balance so that we and our allies can protect our interests in peace, by the methods of alliance diplomacy backed by adequate deterrent force. But now we face the next set of security problems, those requiring us to define those interests in detail, and to develop a strategy for safeguarding them. What is the role of nuclear weapons in our arsenal and in the Soviet arsenal? What is the relation between nuclear and conventional weapons? What are our objectives in arms control negotiations with the Soviet Union, and what are the objectives of the Soviet Union? On these questions, consensus does not yet exist. It is the task of the political process during the next few years to attain it.

The answers President Reagan has given to these questions are firmly rooted in the history of our experience since 1945. He has made it clear that we will not retreat to Fortress America, but will defend our alliances and our interests throughout the world. He has said that we can no longer tolerate a "double standard" with regard to Soviet aggression. Both we and the Soviet Union must obey the same rules with regard to the international use of force—the rules to which we both agreed when we signed the United Nations Charter. This is the only acceptable meaning for the elusive word "détente." And for the first time we are approaching the task of arms control negotiation with the Soviet Union on the basis of the realistic view that we and the Soviet Union have different doctrines about the role of nuclear weapons, and therefore different conceptions of arms control.

For us, nuclear weapons exist to deter the use of nuclear weapons and other forms of aggression against our supreme interests as a nation. Our weapons are exclusively defensive in character, and the mission of our nuclear arsenal is to deter aggression by presenting a visible and credible capacity to retaliate as the conclusive deterrent.

It is now clear that the Soviet Union has an entirely different military doctrine. For the Soviet military the nuclear weapon is the ultimate sanction behind a program of endless expansion conducted by the aggressive use of conventional forces, subversion, and terrorism. The Soviet nuclear weapon is deployed to deter our deterrent by threatening to overwhelm it, and thus make Soviet aggression possible. Some 75 percent or 80 percent of the Soviet nuclear force consists of intercontinental ballistic missiles (ICBMs)—swift, accurate, and extremely destructive first-strike weapons that could destroy missiles deployed in hardened silos. No defenses yet qualify their power to destroy, and no American weapon compares with the heavy Soviet missiles in destructive power. The large Soviet ballistic missiles are weapons of intimidation, and they already exist in such numbers, and with such capabilities, as to cast doubt on the ability of U.S. forces to survive and retaliate—that is, they cast doubt on our nuclear guarantees.

The Soviet lead in ground-based intermediate-range and intercontinental ballistic missiles is the most serious foreign policy problem we face. This advantage gives the Soviet Union the potential to improve its military and political position through a first strike against our ICBM force, our submarines in port, and our bombers on the ground. The menace of nuclear imbalance in that sense is being translated into political currents of great power, as we have seen during the last few years. The deployment of vast numbers of warheads on Soviet intermediate-range SS-20s and on ICBMs is designed to make our flesh crawl, and to induce acute political anxiety in Europe and elsewhere at a time when the American intercontinental nuclear guaranty is being questioned.

The combination of these pressures is a recipe for nuclear coercion. Henry Kissinger deepened Western anxiety about the nuclear imbalance a few years ago with his celebrated comment that great powers did not commit suicide on behalf of their allies. But political anxieties about the nuclear umbrella would have existed even if Dr. Kissinger had not spoken. They are what former Chancellor Helmut Schmidt has called "subliminal" emanations of the Soviet nuclear arsenal.[3] They are there.

The pressures of Soviet nuclear mobilization have other effects. There has been a conspicuous increase in the number of Americans who are seriously advocating an American return to neutrality and isolation, as if that approach to foreign policy were an available option for the United States. Such American voices have their inevitable echo in Europe, Japan, and other parts of the world dependent upon American protection: the chorus advocating American isolation and accommodation to Soviet power is answered abroad by advocates of neutrality on the one hand, and of nuclear armament on the other.

In light of these considerations, President Reagan decided to make the removal of the destabilizing Soviet advantage in ground-based ballistic missiles the first goal of our arms control effort, and the first aspect of the problem for us to take up with the Soviet Union. We were slightly ahead of the Soviet Union in the number of warheads on deployed ICBMs in 1972. In 1982 the Soviets have a lead in this crucial area of approximately three to one. It follows that they have the capacity to destroy our ICBMs and other nuclear forces with a fraction of their forces, holding the rest in an ominous reserve that could paralyze our remaining strategic forces. Until this Soviet bulge in nuclear power is eliminated, either by arms control or by American modernization efforts—until, that is, a presumptive Soviet first strike ceases to be plausible, and the Soviet strategic arsenal is confined to the role of deterrence—it will not be possible to restore political stability.

The *New York Times* put the issue well in an editorial entitled "How Much Is Enough?" The task of arms control diplomacy, the *Times* said, is to allow the United States to maintain deterrence, "which has kept the industrial world at peace for the longest stretch in history," and "to forbid the weapons which defy deterrence . . . . That done, the arms race can subside. Unless it is done, there will never be enough."[4]

This view of the matter is the basis for our approach both to the intermediate nuclear forces (INF) talks now going on in Geneva and the Stategic Arms Reduction Talks (START) talks the President proposed at Eureka College on May 9, 1982.[5] In these talks we sharply distinguish purely retaliatory weapons from those with first-strike potentialities. What we are seeking in these talks, which are closely related in subject matter, is to achieve stability at equal and much lower levels of force—a posture on each side that would permit us to deter both nuclear war and other forms of aggression against our supreme interests. Such a policy would deny the Soviet Union the capacity for nuclear blackmail based on superiority in ground-based intermediate-range and intercontinental ballistic missiles.

In the INF talks we proposed initially that all the Soviet SS-4, SS-5, and SS-20 missiles be dismantled. In exchange we would not deploy our 572 Pershing II and ground-based cruise missiles in Europe, pursuant to the NATO decision of 1979.

The Soviet Union bitterly attacked our INF proposal as unfair, on the ground that it would require the Soviets to make a larger reduction than we would be called upon to make. This is hardly the case, since the sacrifice of future weapons is not really different from dismantling existing arsenals. But even if it were true, it would be irrelevant. Arms control negotiations are not bargains among peasants haggling over the price of potatoes at a country fair. The Soviet Union and the United States, the two leading nuclear powers, are trustees for humanity, and should do whatever is necessary to help lift the cloud of war from the horizon of the future. This is reflected in the fact that since President Reagan's speech of November 18, 1981, on intermediate-range missiles, European and American opinion, and opinion throughout the Western world, has solidly supported the principle of our INF proposals as altogether fair and equitable. After all, no state should expect us to acknowledge the right to build a military force that could be used only for purposes of aggression.

The president's proposals for the START negotiations are equally sound and equitable. They propose equal ceilings at much lower levels of force—ceilings that would strengthen deterrence and promote stability by significantly reducing the Soviet lead in ICBMs. Coupled with the dismantling of the Soviet intermediate-range ballistic missiles, such a result would enable us to maintain an overall level of strategic nuclear capability sufficient to deter conflict, safeguard our national security, and meet our commitments to allies and friends.

To achieve this goal, the president announced a practical, phased approach to the negotiation, like the procedure being used in the INF talks. It is based on the number of weapons and in their destructive capacity. "The focus of our efforts," the president said, "will be to reduce significantly the most destabilizing systems—ballistic missiles—the number of warheads they carry and their overall destructive potential." While no aspect of the problem is excluded from consideration, the United States proposed that the first phase of the negotiation should reduce ballistic missile warheads to equal levels at least one-third below current numbers. Furthermore, to enhance stability, we have proposed that no more than half these warheads be deployed on land-based missiles. This provision alone should achieve substantial reductions in missile throw-weight. Our proposal calls for these warhead reductions, as well as significant reductions in the number of deployed missiles to be achieved as quickly as possible.

In a second phase, closely linked to the first, we will seek equal ceilings on other elements of U. S. and Soviet strategic forces, including equal limits on ballistic missile throw-weight at less than current U. S. levels.

In both phases of the START talks, we insist on verification measures capable of assuring compliance. In the case of provisions that cannot be monitored effectively by national technical means of verification, we propose cooperative measures, data exchanges, and collateral constraints that can provide the necessary confidence in compliance. The Soviet Union has indicated—and Mr. Brezhnev said it publicly—that it will consider reasonable verification procedures of this kind to supplement national technical means of verification.

The Soviet Union attacked our START proposals as unfair, on the ground that they call for unequal reductions—indeed, that they call for "unilateral Soviet disarmament." It is hardly obvious why this is the case. Each side now has approximately 7,500 ballistic missile warheads. Under the American proposal each side would have to reduce to no more than 5,000, of which no more than 2,500 could be on ICBMs. True, the Soviet Union would have to dismantle more ICBM warheads than we would in order to comply with the ICBM sublimit, while we might have to dismantle more submarine-based missiles. But this is the point: there is nothing inequitable about an equal ceiling that strengthens deterrent stability.

The significance of this approach as a step toward stabilizing the relationship between the United States and the Soviet Union highlights the shortcomings of the familiar popular outcry that there is nuclear "overkill," that there are enough weapons on each side to destroy the world many times over. Many use this assertion to support the claim that no more nuclear weapons are required and that a freeze at current levels could do us no harm. It may be that a rose is a rose is a rose (although as a gardener I have never believed that Gertrude Stein's famous sentence made sense), but all nuclear weapons are not equal. Some are more accurate and destructive than others, and some must cope with defenses. Until we make the Soviet first-strike scenario inconceivable, our nuclear guaranty to our allies in Europe, Asia, and the Middle East will remain in some doubt. A state of doubt on this crucial point increases the risk to our security.

These aspects of the nuclear problem expose the fallacies of the argument recently put forward in favor of accepting the Soviet Union's frequent proposal for a pledge that we not use nuclear weapons first even if Soviet tanks were rolling across the German plains toward the English Channel. The American pledge to use nuclear weapons if necessary to defend our allies against Soviet aggression has been the basis for the recovery and cultural renaissance of Western Europe, Japan, and many other parts of the world since 1945. For more than thirty-five years it has been the counterweight to Soviet superiority in manpower, tanks, and other conventional arms. In Ambassador Paul Nitze's words, it would be tempting fate "to remove the essential prop of nuclear deterrence before rectifying the conditions that led to its fashioning in the first place." Such a step would deprive NATO of credibility. And it would give a new and terrifying impetus to the process of nuclear weapons proliferation. For countries threatened with destruction, doubt about the American nuclear guaranty is an invitation to take the nuclear option. To propose, in effect, the abrogation of NATO and the other security treaties on which our safety as a nation depends cannot be a serious or credible policy. It would inevitably result in a retreat to the dangerous isolationism of bygone days.

It is difficult to follow the argument for a no-first-use pledge made in the *Foreign Affairs* article by Bundy et al.[6] The authors concede that we would have no way to be confident that the Soviet Union would in fact fight only with conventional weapons. After all, Soviet doctrine and Soviet equipment are based on the full integration of nuclear and chemical weapons into the battlefield tactics of the Soviet armed forces. And Soviet tactical doctrine relies on preemption, not passive defense. Of course, proponents of the no-first-use principle tell us, we should have to be ready to reply in kind if the Soviet Union should use nuclear weapons first. But if we have to be prepared to use nuclear weapons after all, what has been gained by the no-first-use pledge, except to make nuclear war more likely?

But our security treaties with Europe, Japan, and other key countries are not gestures of sentiment or philanthropy, to be abandoned if the going gets rough. They represent bedrock security interests of the United States. One has only to consider where we would be if we accepted the no-first-use argument and abandoned Europe to its fate. For more than 20 years Soviet military and political strategy has been based on the concept that the nation that controls the Eurasian landmass controls the world. If the Soviet Union could gain control of Western Europe, the Soviet leaders believe, it would automatically control the Middle East and Africa as well. Japan, China, and many other countries would draw the necessary conclusions, and accommodate to the power of the Soviets. The United States would be left isolated and impotent.

Proposals for a nuclear freeze at current levels would be almost as devastating in their effect as the thesis of Mr. McNamara and his friends. By halting our current modernization efforts, such a freeze would leave our nuclear guaranty in doubt, and therefore reduce our capacity to protect Europe, Japan, and other supreme national interests. It would remove any incentive the Soviets might have to accept the substantial reductions we are seeking in both START and INF. And it would constitute, in effect, a unilateral American renunciation of the joint NATO decision of 1979 to modernize Western intermediate-range forces. It would therefore adversely affect allied confidence in our leadership and stead-fastness.

Some students of the security problem are urging President Reagan to ask the Senate to consent to the ratification of SALT II, preferably with four or five amendments, before we proceed with START. Advocates of this position point out that both the Soviet Union and the United States are respecting the limits on deployed launchers provided for in that treaty. They ask why we shouldn't ratify the treaty and get on with its successor.

It is quite true that both nations are, in general, observing the limits on deployment provided for in SALT II. It is a normal diplomatic procedure not to rock the boat unduly during negotiations; for the moment the SALT II limits are in the interests of both nations. But the formal ratification of SALT II would be an altogether different matter.

In the first place, if we should ratify SALT II, amended or unamended, the SALT Treaty would inevitably constitute the starting point and baseline for the START negotiations. That fact would almost surely force us to use the wrong unit of account in negotiating a new agreement. The interim agreement of SALT I and SALT II are based on deployed launchers as the unit of account. It is now obvious that counting only deployed launchers is an inadequate way to measure and compare the destructive capacity of nuclear weapons. President Reagan has decided to base the START treaty directly on the number of missile warheads and their destructive potential. That is the only sensible way to compare the military and political significance of ballistic missiles. To ratify SALT II now would simply perpetuate what turned out to be a costly error.

One of the worst consequences of that error is that neither the interim agreement of 1972 nor SALT II succeeded in preventing the emergence of Soviet superiority in ground-based ballistic missiles that threaten the survivability of our ICBMs. To prevent, and now to eliminate, that Soviet advantage has always been a major U.S. interest and objective in nuclear arms limitation agreements. The ratification of SALT II would codify and confirm both the present high ceilings and the Soviet position of superiority in this area.

As Senator Henry Jackson has pointed out, it would be "a profound mistake" to legitimize the nuclear status quo. Such a step would lock the United States into a position of strategic inferiority, and make it impossible for us to escape. It would therefore make it nearly impossible for the United States to solve its most urgent security problem: to end the growing doubts about the American nuclear guaranty for Europe, Japan, and other vital American interests. As a result, ratifying SALT II would eliminate any possible motive the Soviet Union might have to agree to reductions.

There is another pitfall in the SALT II ratification proposal. The Soviet Union could also propose amendments, and we could spend the next few years renegotiating SALT II rather than attempting to persuade the Soviet Union to accept a treaty that would help stabilize the political and military relationship between the two countries.

These reasons alone are sufficient justification for refusing to ratify SALT II. There are many lesser reasons for reaching the same conclusion: the failure to include the Backfire bomber, to eliminate the Soviet heavy missiles, or to prevent the encryption of telemetry.

In the end, however, those who advocate ratifying SALT II now are motivated by altogether different reasons, which have nothing to do with the actual provisions of the treaty. Some believe that the overall political and military situation of the United States is hopeless, and that we should make a nuclear arms agreement with the Soviet Union as an act of submission, on the best terms we can get. There is no need for me to characterize this pernicious outlook. Others subscribe to the view that even a bad agreement with the Soviet Union somehow contributes to peace and reduces the risk of war. The bitter history of the 1970s should teach us that there is no substance in this view. If the Soviet Union should ever conclude, however, that this opinion dominates American policy, whether out of mistaken conviction or for reasons of electoral politics, the prospects for negotiation would be dim indeed. Those who favor a few quick cosmetic amendments for SALT II and calling the result START I are not advancing the interests of the nation.

President Reagan is eager to reach a sound agreement with the Soviet Union—an agreement that contributes to our security and furthers the cause of peace. But he will never approve a poor agreement for the sake of having an agreement.

There has been much talk in the press and in Congress about the "acceptability" or "negotiability" of the principles and guidelines President Reagan had proposed. Predicting Soviet behavior is not easy, and I admire people who tell us with assurance exactly what the Soviet Union will and will not do. On this arcane subject, however, one simple observation is in order.

The Soviet Union did not achieve its advantage in ground-launched ballistic missiles in a fit of absentmindedness. It spent years of effort and billions of dollars in doing so. And it will give this advantage up only when it is convinced that the alternatives are worse. That is why we say that arms control agreements can be understood and negotiated only in the context of our foreign and defense policy as a whole. The president's speech at Eureka College offered the Soviet Union a far-reaching and permanent program of cooperation, as have other of his statements of policy. It also announced our unshakable determination to defend our interests and to insist on the fundamental principle, *pacta sunt servanda* (treaties must be kept), as the bedrock on which peaceful international society is built. Without the effective implementation of this policy, the essence of our national interest, we may make agreements but there will be no peace. As former Secretary of State Alexander Haig once commented, it must be understood that arms control agreements are of no use if they make the world safe for conventional aggression.

The menace of the nuclear weapon is so great that it should lead the nations at long last to realize that there is no rational alternative to peace. Sound, equitable, and verifiable nuclear arms agreements could reduce the risk of war. In themselves they cannot guarantee peace, or even the absence of nuclear war. But arms control agreements should be viewed as stepping-stones to a much greater goal, peace itself. When the Soviet Union proposes that we sign a no-first-use pledge, the proper answer for the United States is that both nations, and all other nations, should rededicate themselves fundamentally to policies of full and reciprocal respect for the rules of the United Nations Charter against all forms of aggression, nuclear and nonnuclear alike. In the nuclear world no lesser goal can suffice. Peace really has become indivisible.

The United States, its allies, and other nations that accept the principles of peace have more than enough power and potential power to achieve this goal, if they muster up the will to do so. It is time for the Soviet Union to realize that its policies of expansion have passed their peak, and produced not bread but a stone. There are many objective reasons why the Soviet Union should want a period of stability in its relations with the West—its troubles in Poland and Eastern Europe, the state of its economy, and many social problems that have become manifest in recent years. Above all, the Soviet Union, like every other country, should understand the truth behind Nikita Khrushchev's famous comment: "The nuclear weapon threatens socialist and capitalist states alike."

Many are offering quick fixes and miraculous cures for the ills that afflict mankind. Others have lost their nerve and are looking for escape hatches. The medicine men and the escapists should be recognized for what they are. There are no quick fixes nor escape hatches.

But the American people and their leaders are not going to lose their nerve or bend their knees. The threat we face can be countered by the methods of steady diplomacy backed by adequate deterrent force. President Reagan has made it clear many times that the tragic lesson of the 1930s is burned into his mind and into his memory. The statesmen of that time failed to prevent World War II because they refused to accept the superobvious facts. In the setting of nuclear weapons, it is imperative that the statesmen of the West succeed this time, not only in preventing war but also in establishing peace.

NOTES

1. Editor's note: For an elaboration of this point, see Rostow's interview in *Encounter*, April 1983, p. 79.

2. "Nuclear Weapons and the Atlantic Alliance," *Foreign Affairs*, Spring 1982, pp. 753–68.

3. Editor's note: Again, for elaboration see the *Encounter* interview, April 1983, p. 78.

4. *New York Times*, April 11, 1983, p. A20.

5. For the text of the Eureka speech, see *Presidential Documents*, vol. 18, no. 19, Monday, May 17, 1982, pp. 599–604.

6. "Nuclear Weapons and the Atlantic Alliance."

Part I:

Arms Control, Strategic Instability, And International Security

1

Challenges to Global Stability in the 1980s

William R. Van Cleave

INTRODUCTION: THE MAJOR CHALLENGE

Latent challenges to global stability in the 1980s are undoubtedly many, as the Argentine aggression against the British Falkland Islands has demonstrated; and not all are predictable with any confidence, as that event also has demonstrated.

The "Third World," a term of apparent unity manifest only in U.N. votes against the United States and Israel, contains a diversity of social and economic sources of instability, and a variety of political-military rivalries, any of which may prove "destabilizing." Many disputes exist over boundaries and territories, and may at any time flare politically or erupt in violence. Some of these may be resolvable by peaceful means; others will prove more volatile. Some—such as the chronic Arab-PLO threat to Israel—are deep-seated.

In addition, competition for control of and access to valuable natural resources will likely grow in coming years and will contain the seeds of armed conflict. The seeds will be more nourished than starved if a U.N. majority attempts to impose unrealistic regulations concerning these resources, as it has with the adoption of the Law of the Sea Treaty.

However contentious and challenging such sources of instability may become, they are minor compared with the major challenge to global stability in the 1980s. The free world is faced with the challenge of an aggressive, massively armed totalitarian state that would impose its system, by force of arms if necessary, on others. Rather than conducting a *tour d'horizon* of potential trouble spots, we should focus attention on this most present and pressing danger: the Soviet Union.

Secretary of State Alexander Haig warned of "the emergence of the Soviet Union as a global military power, increasingly bold in the use of its might to promote violence, notably in areas of stategic significance to the West."[1]

This emergence has taken place since the early 1970s, as Soviet military power has grown in support of an adventurous policy, contrary to the interests of global stability. Since its support and manipulation of the October 1973 Middle East war,[2] we have seen the Soviet Union first help undermine the Paris Peace Accords, and then support Vietnamese aggression throughout Southeast Asia. We have witnessed Soviet threats to stability in central Africa and the Horn of Africa; in the Middle East, where the Soviets are encircling the Persian Gulf; and in the Caribbean and Central America. We have witnessed the brutal invasion and occupation of Afghanistan, and the imposition of martial law in Poland under the threat of Soviet invasion. We have proof of Soviet support for terrorism worldwide. As former Secretary of State Henry Kissinger testified to Congress, "the fact is that since 1975 there has been an unprecedented Soviet assault on the international equilibrium."[3]

There is, however, another potential source of instability. That is the failure of the challenged to confront the challenger with enough strength and determination to dissuade the overt, armed challenges that must raise the risk of war.

It is the conjunction of the two—as history has repeatedly shown—that is most destabilizing. The history of forceful expansion of empires, and of aggression by individual states, is one of opportunities opened or foreclosed to expansionist powers. We must realize that failure of the Western alliances to marshal the military capability and political resolve to contain the Soviet Union could undermine global stability, for it would open tempting opportunities to a Soviet Union that is looking balefuly outward.

The overriding threat of the 1980s, then, is not the existence of nuclear weapons per se, or of indigenous social and economic problems; it is the Soviet Union, an expansionist state with insatiable "security" demands supported by an extensive and still-growing military capability. As Eugene Rostow emphasized:

> The situation we confront resembles that of the Thirties in many ways. But it is significantly different too—more dangerous; more volatile; and far more difficult to control by the polite warnings and veiled threats of old-fashioned European diplomacy.
>
> There is no blinking the fact that the Soviet Union risks war in its campaigns of expansion all over the world. Those campaigns use aggressive war as an instrument of national policy; they are carried on by methods which violate the rules of the Charter governing the international use of force. No one claims that the Soviet Union initiates all the trouble in the world. But it does take advantage of trouble in order to expand its sphere of influence.[4]

The apex of this challenge will emerge precisely in the 1980s. This is because of an unfortunate concatenation of factors: Soviet military strength will be at a peak while the West remains comparatively weak in its military defenses. This will present a great temptation to Moscow to use the excessive military strength it has acquired. And that temptation will be heightened by pressing Soviet domestic problems and by a fear that time may be against the Soviets.

Soviet strength is almost entirely military; there is nothing else the Soviet system offers that would influence others to adopt Soviet practices or to conform to Soviet policies and objectives. The flaws and weaknesses inherent in the Soviet system must, in time, take a toll on Soviet strength. In time, it is possible—although the prospect does not now seem compelling—that the free world can rally its superior assets to negate Soviet military power. Time, then, must seem to any Soviet leaders given to honest reflection to be against the Soviet Union. But we must shorten that time as much as possible to reduce the period and extent of Soviet military advantage, and give Soviet leaders less time to grow confident.

It is the combination of these factors—the nature of the Soviet system and its hegemonic ambitions, the military balance, opportunity, and timing—that make the coming years exceedingly dangerous. Yet, too few of us appreciate the gravity of the situation.

The irony of a conspicuous threat that so many refuse to see until nearly too late is hardly a new phenomenon in democratic societies. The initial Athenian reaction to reports of Sparta's military buildup and hostile intentions, according to Thucydides, was that they "would not believe the charge, giving too much weight to their wish that it might not be true." Winston Churchill in *The Gathering Storm* and Walter Lippmann in *The Public Philosophy* were eloquent in their anguish over the same phenomenon. Lippmann wrote:

> . . . the American people were as unprepared in their minds as in their military establishment. . . . They had refused to take in what they saw, they had refused to believe what they heard, they had wished and they had waited, hoping against hope.[5]

In the late 1950s Dean Acheson observed this same psychology at work in the United States:

> No matter how plainly the Russians talk and act, we simply refuse to believe what they say and to understand the meaning of what they do. President Eisenhower and Secretary Dulles keep insisting that the test must be deeds, not words. *Floods of deeds follow, amply explained by torrents of words.* Yet our leaders and, indeed, our people cannot believe what they see and hear.[6]

SOVIET AMBITIONS AND MOTIVATIONS

It is often necessary to explain, even to otherwise well-educated people, that the most fundamental differences exist between the Soviet and Western political systems. It is easy to share the simple bewilderment of "Blackford Oakes" about anyone who, directly or indirectly, "would choose to work for the people who operated Gulag, rather than for the people who wanted to confine Gulag's boundaries."[7]

The first fundamental difference between the free world collective defense system and the Soviet international system is that the former is a voluntary association of free states, while the latter is an empire held together by force and subservience. Alexis de Tocqueville recognized the fundamental difference when he pointed out that the American system is based upon the principle of freedom, and the Russian system on the principle of servitude.[8] The next difference is that the Soviet military empire would expand at the expense of the free world, while the free world is interested only in remaining free.

The Soviet regime maintains its incumbency through systematic coercion and the suppression of liberties. To such a repressive, imperialist regime the existence of healthy, free-world democracies is a constant threat. This is not only because they stand in the way of further expansion of the Soviet system, but also because of the example they provide to people under Soviet control of a contrasting quality of life and of superior political and economic institutions. Successful democracy and open market economies are per se a threat to Soviet totalitarianism and Communism.

Soviet imperial urges are based not only on the holy faith of a "historic mandate" but also on a unique concept of "security," which dictates endless conflict. According to this view, the Soviet regime can be secure only to the extent its neighbors and rivals become insecure. As Zbigniew Brzezinski has written, "the Soviet conception of their own security is inherently offensive." This means that international stability at the present time is anathema to the Soviets. As Professor Brzezinski has also pointed out, "the Soviet leaders are compelled to view any effort to stabilize or to normalize the international situation as a hostile design."[9]

Political rivals must be weakened. Strategic areas must progressively be brought under Soviet domination. The sources of raw materials that fuel the West must eventually be controlled by the USSR. Defenses that stand in the way of the expansion of Soviet hegemony must be neutralized by superior Soviet military forces.

Domestic considerations intensify the compulsion for expansion. Foreign victories and the continuous enhancement of Soviet international power are necessary to allay domestic dissatisfaction and to bolster the patriotism and loyalty of the population. What else could divert the attention of the Russian people from what Charles Wolf, Jr., has termed "the brutishness with which the Soviet system crushes political dissent?"[10] In addition, there are now salient economic motivations for expansion. The Soviet economy is experiencing a serious decline in growth, and its productivity is not meeting basic requirements. If military power can be used to expand Soviet political influence, it can also be used for economic gain. As Professor Patrick Parker and I wrote in 1979:

> The Soviet Union, as it accumulates excessive military power, may at the same time be increasingly driven to look outward to ameliorate growing economic problems. While it is frequently argued that these economic problems will even-

tually dampen military expenditures, it is less frequently recognized that military forces might be used to overcome the problems.[11]

This, quite obviously, draws our attention to the Middle East, and oil; to Africa and Southeast Asia, and the strategic minerals located there. As Professor Parker and I also noted:

> All Russian military spending since World War II would pay for itself if the Russians could bring Iran, the Persian Gulf, and possibly Saudi Arabia under the Red Banner, militarily, or politically, through forced accommodation to the Soviets. This cannot have escaped the attention of Soviet leaders, nor is it reasonable to believe that they have failed to think very hard about it.
>
> Middle East oil could do many things for the Russians. It would solve their domestic oil problem and provide them with much needed hard currency; it would make increasing dependence on agricultural imports much less hazardous; it would relieve a good deal of the expected economic problems; it would provide tremendous leverage over Western Europe and Japan and could be used to weaken and possibly destroy those U.S. alliances. In short, it would keep the Soviet Union economically strong, militarily powerful, and strategically in control of Europe, the Middle East, and through Japan, possibly the Far East as well.[12]

While these compulsions to expand exist, the key to the actual threat they may pose for international stability is the military balance or, more broadly, what the Soviets call "the correlation of forces."

The Soviet view of the world is strategic and adversarial, but, operationally, actions depend upon the correlation of forces. To the Soviets the correlation of forces is the major determinant of international relations; it determines opportunities and timing. It is more than a balance sheet of global power; it is also a guide to action. A correct calculation of the correlation of forces requires a net assessment of all aspects of relative national power in play at any point in time. It encompasses, therefore, relative tangibles and intangibles, nonmilitary as well as military. But the core is the military balance; and as the military balance is central to the correlation of forces, so the nuclear balance is central to the military balance. Politically, superiority over the United States in nuclear capability is expected to be the key in influencing policies and attitudes among Western countries. Militarily, it means control over escalation, which determines relative ability to threaten, and greatly influences the decision to use military force of any kind. Soviet leaders probably believe this advantage will be particularly relevant in crises and confrontations.[13]

The Soviets clearly believe that a major shift in the correlation of forces, based upon a major shift in their favor in the military balance, has occurred. It is, of course, this shift that has had the highest priority in Soviet national objectives.

And a major change in the military balance, highly detrimental to international stability and the security of the West, has taken place. It is this unfortunate situation in which Soviet imperial impulses are supported by a balance of military power that seems favorable to their implementation, that poses the principal challenge to stability in the eighties.

What are the realities of the military balance?

The Military Balance[14]

President Reagan created something of a domestic political storm when he stated candidly what official reports had been warning for a number of years: "The truth of the matter is that on balance the Soviet Union does have a margin of superiority."[15] And Secretary of Defense Caspar Weinberger acknowledged, "Unfortunately it is true."[16]

Before addressing the military balance, we should frankly face the fact that the two sides arm, and maintain nuclear stockpiles, for very different purposes. The Soviets have been engaged in a determined arms race to gain military superiority over the West, in order to further imperial ambitions. It has nothing to do with "security" in the Western sense of the term. As former President Nixon succinctly summarized it: "In the West arms are maintained as a necessity of defense; in the East arms are maintained to achieve the expansion of Soviet power."[17] Or in the words of Eugene Rostow:

> Our purpose in having nuclear weapons is defense and deterrence, to prevent aggression against our vital interests. The Soviet purpose . . . is to serve as the ultimate engine of a process of nuclear blackmail—a process of expansion involving the use of or the credible threat to use propaganda, terrorism, proxy wars, subversion, or Soviet troops under the sanction and protection of Soviet nuclear superiority.[18]

The likelihood of Soviet military superiority over the West by the early 1980s has been in authoritative open literature for some time; it was a major issue in the aftermath of the "B Team" experiment in competitive intelligence in 1976, in the debate over SALT II, and in the 1980 presidential campaign. The annual reports to Congress of the secretary of defense and of the joint chiefs of staff not only have contained charts and statistics pointing precisely to such a situation, but also have explicitly warned of it. In 1979 Secretary of Defense Harold Brown said, "Our most serious concerns which we need to act now to meet are about the period of early- to mid-1980s."[19]

In 1980, General David C. Jones testified: "We face an adversary at least our equal in strategic nuclear power and possessing substantial advantages in theater nuclear power and conventional forces." Moreover, he added, "the trends for the future are adverse. In many areas, they have already surpassed us, and I am concerned because their momentum will allow them to gain an advantage over the United States in most of the major indicators of strategic force by the early

1980s. Moreover, because of lead times in modern weapons programs, this progressive shift in the strategic balance will continue into the latter part of the 1980s."[20] The Chief of Naval Operations in 1979, Admiral Thomas B. Hayward was even more direct:

> With respect to essential equivalence it is my view that without any question, the Soviets will have a first strike capability over the next few years. If that is not a loss of essential equivalence, I do not know what is. . . .[21]

Given the disparity in the military efforts of the two sides since the late 1960s none of this should come as any surprise. The Soviets have been willing to devote enormous resources in a concentrated effort to amass military power; the West has not. Our direction has been quite nearly the opposite. We must acknowledge that it has been the combination of these two decidedly dissimilar approaches that has produced the unprecedented and ominous change in the military balance that has taken place. The change could not have occurred had it rested on the Soviet effort alone; it required a lack of Western vigilance and resolve as well. That this disparate combination developed and has been allowed to persist over several years is a product of intellectual and political failure in the West.

Between 1969 and 1979, the decade of SALT and détente, American defense spending fell from nearly 9 percent of gross national product (GNP) to 5 percent or less. During the same period Soviet military spending grew to perhaps 15 percent or more. According to some experts, it may be 20 percent of GNP in 1982.[22] During that period Soviet military spending increased annually, at a steady rate variously estimated at 4–5 percent or as much as 8–10 percent; American spending actually *declined*.[23] As a result, since 1969, when Soviet military spending first surpassed that of the United States, the annual and cumulative gap between the two military efforts has steadily widened.

By 1981 Soviet annual military investment (research and development, production, and construction) had reached nearly double that of the United States, capping a cumulative investment difference over the preceding decade estimated by Secretary of Defense Weinberger to be more than $400 billion.[24] Because of this, the impressive advantages already achieved by the Soviet Union in the military balance will increase and expand over the next several years as these investment differences result in operational military forces.

The differences in weapons production between the two sides are nearly unimaginable. To take but a few examples: Each and every year the Soviet Union produces at least twice as many ICBMs as the United States tentatively plans to produce in 1982–92. Each and every year the Soviet Union produces more submarine-launched ballistic missiles (SLBMs) than the United States plans to produce in 1982–87. The Soviets produce some 1,300 fighter or fighter-bomber aircraft per year, to what has recently been fewer than 300 for the United States; and some 3,000 tanks per year, to fewer than 400 for us. (Non-Soviet Warsaw

Pact countries have for several years produced about twice as many tanks as the United States).[25] While we are only starting on a modest submarine-launched cruise missile (SLCM) production program, the Soviets have for a number of years been producing 600–700 per year. While we have withdrawn from European deployment some 1,000 nuclear warheads, the Soviets have added a far greater number of SS-20s, 21s, and 23s, all new-generation delivery systems. Operational SS-20 launchers now exceed 300, each with at least one additional refire missile, each with three warheads—nearly 2,000 warheads there alone.

In strategic nuclear offensive forces the Soviets have outspent the United States by over three times since the early 1970s; in strategic defense forces there is no meaningful comparison. Since SALT I was signed—an agreement, it was argued, that would arrest the momentum of Soviet strategic arms programs—the Soviets have deployed some dozen and a half new or modified strategic ballistic missile systems—to one for the United States. They have introduced a dozen variants of three (possibly four) new ICBMs, the smallest of which has about the throw weight of the proposed MX, and have equaled or bettered the accuracy of U.S. ICBMs. They have introduced four new types of ballistic missile submarines, to one for the United States. And they have, by now, surpassed the United States in numbers of ballistic missile launchers, ballistic missiles, ICBM (and even total missile) warheads, and megatonnage, equivalent megatonnage, throw-weight, and countermilitary potential. Furthermore, they have several new types of ICBMs and SLBMs under development.

Even in the area of strategic bombers, where it is often argued that the United States holds an advantage, the Soviets have been far more active. The numbers of Backfire bombers, which remain in active production, already exceed the numbers of operational B-52G and B-52H aircraft; and new strategic bombers are under development. One we have recently seen—a B-1-like aircraft, only larger—may well be in the Soviet force before the B-1 is in the U.S. force.

In the nuclear balance, then, we have seen a steady deterioration in all indexes of capability, both static and dynamic, relative to Soviet capabilities.[26] In all indexes Soviet superiority exists, will emerge, or will grow during the next few years.

It is noteworthy that the preattack comparison chart for strategic forces, presented to Congress by the joint chiefs of staff, shows U.S. inferiority in three of the four measures used as far ahead as the chart projects—1992, twelve years after the election of Ronald Reagan.[27] The lone index where the curve approximates parity is numbers of "on-line" warheads. This is largely fictitious, however, because SALT counting rules are followed, which exaggerate our numbers and artificially depress Soviet numbers—for instance, Backfire is excluded, but our bombers are credited with maximum payloads; our projected cruise missiles are included, but not the more numerous Soviet cruise missiles; and Soviet additional ICBMs are ignored. For these same reasons the curves that still show Soviet advantages are clearly understatements.

Unless more extensive and time-urgent measures are taken than are now planned by the Reagan administration, the United States faces a period of several years in which likely surviving and deliverable U.S. strategic forces not only will be inadequate to support official strategy (which is already the case), but also will carry high risk in their ability to promote crisis stability and to deter plausible threats.

This is what, in its broadest sense, is meant by the term "window of vulnerability." In its more narrow sense it refers specifically to the vulnerability of key components of our strategic nuclear retaliatory forces, whose survivability has been severely eroded by a combination of Soviet action and relative U.S. inaction. This window of vulnerability for American strategic forces is, in my view, the most serious and urgent military problem we face. It is upon us now. We cannot afford to live with it during the 1980s while we plan improvements that will have effect in the 1990s.

The strategic nuclear deterrent may be directly applicable to a fairly narrow range of threats, but the strategic nuclear balance is the high ground that overshadows all other uses of military force involving the Soviet Union or the United States. Such Soviet superiority at this higher level of escalation creates a situation in which the threat of escalation could weigh against the United States. If Soviet dominance of the strategic nuclear level is permitted to continue, Soviet leaders may feel freer to use force at lower levels, in the belief that the United States and its allies would shy away from military opposition out of a fear of escalation. Even if this confidence should prove misplaced, the situation would nevertheless invite a military challenge that should have been deterred in the first place. It is exactly such miscalculations that we should prevent if we are to promote global stability.

The implications of the adverse strategic balance for stability are even more sobering when one considers how thinly stretched Western general-purpose forces have become. During 1980 the Army chief of staff referred to a "hollow army," while the chief of naval operations reported that he had a "one-and-a-half ocean navy for a three-ocean world." The United States has for several years grossly underfunded both the readiness and the modernization of its general-purpose forces. In many instances procurement has been below peacetime attrition rates. At the same time the Soviets have massively equipped and modernized their general-purpose forces. They have now developed a considerable power projection capability that can threaten Western interests in various areas of the world. With the brutal Soviet invasion and forceful occupation of Afghanistan, Soviet willingness to use military force for imperial purposes was again demonstrated.

THE WESTERN CONTRIBUTION TO INSTABILITY

The West has itself contributed much to this unstable situation. Lulled by the rhetoric of détente and the still unfulfilled promises of arms control, it has allowed its military strength to erode. In the late 1960s the United States was willing deliberately to allow the Soviet Union to reach "parity" with it in strategic arms, believing this to be the key to successful strategic arms limitation talks. SALT was then to help bring order to the strategic competition between the two sides and to help stabilize the strategic balance. Successful SALT was also to be the centerpiece of détente.

The SALT process, however, turned out to have a dynamic of its own that was not appreciated at the start. SALT exerted an inhibiting effect on American responses to the developing Soviet threat that went well beyond the terms of any agreements. There was a reluctance to proceed with programs or activities that seemed to run counter to anticipated, or even hoped-for, terms of agreements still in the process of being negotiated. Consequently, actions that should have been taken to improve our strategic position and to hedge against the failure of the arms control effort were salted away. Strategic arms limitation activity, therefore, must bear a measure of the responsibility for the unfavorable situation we are in today.

As Henry Kissinger admitted to the Senate Foreign Relations Committee:

> I am conscience-bound to point out that—against all previous hopes—the SALT process does not seem to have slowed down Soviet strategic competition, and in some sense may have accelerated it. . . . We will not draw the appropriate conclusion if we do not also admit that SALT may have had a perverse effect on the willingness of some in the Congress, key opinion makers, and even Administration offices to face fully the relentless Soviet military buildup.[28]

Strategic trends during the SALT decade have been decidedly adverse to the United States. The trends have been toward Soviet superiority, not essential equivalence; toward reduced, not enhanced, strategic stability; toward increased and critical vulnerability of our deterrent forces, not improved survivability; toward the need to spend more on our strategic forces, not less; toward a worsening political relationship with the Soviet Union, not more cooperative Soviet behavior; and toward poorer, not better, prospects for effective arms limitation agreements in the future. There is, then, little basis for regarding the SALT process itself as beneficial, much less worthwhile enough to cause us to accept bad agreements in order to preserve the process.

Détente joined the SALT process in inhibiting appropriate American responses to the Soviet buildup. Originally it was intended—at least in President Nixon's mind—that for détente to work, containment of the Soviet Union must remain American policy, and that the United States would, at a minimum, keep pace with the Soviet Union militarily. Détente would not, in this image, result in reduced American vigilance and preparedness. Unfortunately, even when the magnitude of Soviet arms programs and international behavior became more than suspect, détente led us to rationalize away the evidence. Military laxation, not military vigilance, became part of détente—whether through wishful thinking that the Soviets would eventually reciprocate, or through resignation and skepticism about our ability to compete with determined Soviet military programs. In short, détente dulled our ability to recognize a clear and present danger.

U.S. détente policy was to be a mixture of cooperation and competition, a delicate balancing of rewards and penalties to be applied as Soviet behavior dictated. The penalties we would threaten were largely the withholding of rewards, such as trade, technology transfer, and credits. We would reward the Soviets for behaving as they should anyway if they were seriously interested in détente, international stability, and meaningful arms control. We would penalize them by withholding those rewards if they behaved outrageously.

Whatever its theoretical merit, détente can never provide a practical basis for a policy that can safeguard American interests against determined Soviet transgression. The Soviets are willing to accept the rewards offered by détente, but not to pay a price for them. And the penalties we threaten are unpersuasive, since they were not resolutely invoked when warranted, while at the same time Western behavior offers opportunity after opportunity for the Soviets to exploit.

By 1982 it should be clear to objective observers that this policy has not worked. Détente has been discredited by Soviet actions in the Middle East, Africa, and the Caribbean; by armed aggression and brutal repression in Afghanistan; by the imposition of martial law in Poland; by Soviet violations of international agreements; and by the threatening Soviet military buildup.

While the United States, joined by other Western democracies, pursued the will-o'-the-wisp of Soviet moderation, the Soviets remained intent upon altering the military balance and the global "correlation of forces" in their favor. Seeing Soviet concessions where none existed, our leaders, in pursuit of SALT and in an effort to defend the policy they had devised, permitted the atrophy of Western military power and political will. The ten-year SALT process, during which the Soviets moved from massive strategic nuclear inferiority to superiority, has typified détente's "accomplishments."

The original idea of arms control was that political hostility need not preclude cooperation in military areas, provided there was common interest in such cooperation. Arms control agreements could be reached between political adversaries if that were the case.

We have come to see, however, especially in SALT, that the Soviets have not shared our arms control concepts or objectives, but have exploited the arms control process for unilateral advantage. Arms control, to the Soviets, was merely another instrument in waging war with the West, in acquiring and protecting military superiority. International political reality may always have been at odds with the original concept of arms control—that it could be conducted almost regardless of the political context and the differences in political objectives of the parties. Perhaps not, but Soviet behavior and the Soviet arms control approach have certainly shaken the original premise.

This raises the basic question of linkage between arms control and the political-strategic behavior of the parties to arms control negotiations. There is clearly a limit on the extent to which the two can be dissociated, and Soviet behavior must make us sensitive to this limit.

The reality of linkage is simply that a Soviet Union seeking unilateral advantage everywhere in the world will pursue similar goals in arms control negotiations. A Soviet Union seeking superiority in arms cannot possibly be a true believer in the arms control principles and aspirations fervently held in the West. In that respect arms control intentions and international political intentions cannot be dissimilar. That is the reality of arms control and of linkage.

The Republican Party platform of July 1980 expressed this clearly: ". . . arms control negotiations, once entered, represent an important political and military undertaking that cannot be divorced from the broader political and military behavior of the parties."

After his election President Reagan reaffirmed this basic point:

I have made it plain that I believe in legitimate negotiations that are aimed at reducing the strategic nuclear weapons in the world. I just think you cannot sit down at the negotiating table and ignore the policies of the Soviet Union, when you're talking disarmament, while they're carrying on as they are in Afghanistan and Africa and so forth.[29]

Or, as he succinctly put it in his first presidential news conference: "In other words, I believe in linkage."[30]

Secretary of State Haig told the Foreign Policy Association:

Such "linkage" is not the creation of U.S. policy: It is a fact of life. A policy of pretending that there is no linkage promotes reverse linkage. It ends up by saying that in order to preserve arms control, we have to tolerate Soviet aggression. This Administration will never accept such an appalling conclusion.[31]

Linkage may be "a fact of life," and the Reagan administration may vow not to tolerate Soviet aggression in order to preserve the arms control process, but the administration has still chosen to continue the Geneva intermediate nuclear forces (INF) negotiations, without so much as an interruption due to Poland, to remove the grain embargo, and to begin Strategic Arms Reduction Talks (START) despite such aggression.

Nonetheless, what both linkage and our arms control experience tell us is that the prospects for those negotiations are not good while the Soviet Union continues to covet military superiority and international hegemony.

Eugene Rostow underscored this reality in his report to Congress on the Geneva negotiations:

The Soviet Union has not yet demonstrated that it is convinced of the need to negotiate seriously. Until it comes to accept that necessity, . . . it will continue to conduct the INF negotiations not as a part of a quest for stability and peace . . . but as a tactical effort to divide the United States from Europe, from Japan, and from its other allies and vital interests; to prevent American and Allied military modernization; and to destroy the credibility of the American nuclear guaranty. In short, the Soviet Union is not yet negotiating. It is playing to the galleries of public opinion in the NATO countries, Japan, ANZUS, and other Western nations. I am sorry I must report this to you. . . . But I have no progress to report.[32]

WHAT IS TO BE DONE?

Soviet leaders must recognize that a determined Western effort to stop the erosion of our defenses and to restore a safe military balance would succeed—in time. They are probably not convinced that the West is capable of such timely, resolute, and sustained action—and time is certainly against us, since we have let the trends continue too long—but they must still be concerned about the prospect. And we must expect that they will do their best to interfere.

Soviet propaganda is already at work on this task, attempting to strengthen the anti-rearmament forces in Western societies. The Soviets understand the appeal of arms control and the distaste for high levels of military spending in the West. They particularly understand the fear and other emotions that nuclear weapons can evoke in the West, and they are seeking to promote and exploit those emotions, hoping to paralyze Western efforts to correct the nuclear balance before they get under way.

What must be done is to counter these efforts and revitalize the consensus, demonstrated in the 1980 presidential election, for a firm foreign policy and a strong national defense. If we are now to come to grips with reality and to restore the "margin of safety" in the military balance, we must abandon the unrealistic views and uncertain policies that have placed us in this situation. The task before us is not only to formulate sound foreign, defense, and arms control policies, but also to explain them clearly to the public and win public support for them. This requires a better job of political leadership and public education—a better job of frankly addressing realities—than Western governments, including the American one, have yet demonstrated.

While seeking to preserve the facade of détente for the benefit of Western publics, the Soviets have been progressively testing the West, and they have undoubtedly been satisfied with the results. Anger has occasionally been raised over the more outrageous Soviet actions, but no effective responses have resulted.

The problem is clear. In 1980 Ronald Reagan said:

> The prerequisite for taking even the first step to redress the shifting balance against the United States is to formulate a coherent, consistent, and principled grand strategy; our plan for action, our agenda for the 1980s. And that strategy must be clearly understood at home and abroad, by friends and enemies and those who are neither.[33]

So far, such a comprehensive strategy has not emerged. The American government speaks forcefully about the Soviet threat in the 1980s, but has not produced a consistent foreign policy, a comprehensive strategy, or an adequate defense plan to counter the threat it describes. Issues are raised and then dropped. Actions contradict words. Accommodation and resistance are kaleidoscopically intermixed. Foreign policy seems reactive, sometimes inconsistent, and frequently confused as to priorities.

In the area of defense policy it is a mixed picture. The three principal Republican defense pledges of the 1980 campaign were the following:

—A comprehensive military strategy: "elaboration of such a strategy will be the first priority of a Republican Administration," stated the platform

—Immediate and sustained increases in defense spending, sufficient to restore military strength across the board

—Timely action to correct the major vulnerabilities and deficiencies in our military forces, particularly in making our nuclear deterrent forces "survivable as rapidly as possible to close the window of vulnerability before it opens any wider."

Of these, we have yet to see a comprehensive military strategy clearly enunciated. The annual *Defense Report to Congress* for fiscal year (FY) 1983 is markedly deficient when it comes to strategy; indeed, it seems to shy away from the subject. Without such a strategy to explain, link, and justify the separate defense programs, there will remain problems with acquiring adequate defense funding. It is much easier for critics of specific programs to chip away at the funding for them when there is no clear strategic plan to relate them to the totality of the defense program.

The Reagan administration has twice (in FY 1982 and FY 1983) proposed real increases in the defense budget, and the current five-year defense plan would move spending from roughly 5 percent to about 7 percent of GNP. And both the president and the secretary of defense have been strong in resisting major cuts, despite substantial political pressure (some from Republican members of Congress who supported the party platform on defense).

Let there be no mistake: after the years of gross underfunding, compared with the constantly increasing Soviet effort, there is no way to provide for national security save through substantial and sustained increases in defense spending. Compared with the need, the proposed increases are modest. They are more than modest; they are inadequate.

I do not suggest that all proposed expenditures necessarily deserve support. But there is a great difference between having professional doubts about particular programs and seeking defense spending cuts for the sake of cuts. The latter must be avoided. Money not spent on specific programs should be shifted to other programs, or to operations and maintenance. The needs are great, greater than the amounts being made available. Cutting already modest increases would hurt defense far more than it would help balance the federal budget, and would be entirely the wrong signal for Congress to send the Soviets or our allies.

In my view it is necessary to move the U.S. defense budget to a minimum of 8 percent of GNP (and 9–10 percent would be more appropriate), and to do so rapidly, to make up for lost time. There is no question of being able to "afford" it; what is at question is only whether our politicians have the courage to demand it.[34]

As to the third pledge, to close the window of vulnerability in an expeditious manner, the failure to do this is perhaps the most disappointing, even alarming, failure in the defense program. In fact, the strategic force modernization program of the Reagan administration extends the duration of the window of vulnerability. As Senator Sam Nunn exclaimed after being briefed on that program: "The window of vulnerability is really being expanded by this program."

If this window of vulnerability is not firmly and expeditiously closed, no adequate, comprehensive military strategy is possible. No such strategy can be based on the vulnerabilities we face at the highest level of deterrence. And without such a military strategy, no grand strategy for the 1980s is possible.

Finally, as to arms control, Secretary of State Haig emphasized the obvious in 1981:

> There is little prospect of agreements with the Soviet Union that will help solve such a basic security problem as the vulnerability of our land-based missiles until we demonstrate that we have the will and capacity to solve them without arms control should that be necessary.[35]

We have not done that, so it follows that there is little prospect of such agreements, and I think we should not expect them.

There is a more general problem as well. We are still proceeding with the development of arms control positions without the guidance of a clear strategy, or even a clear vision of arms control. This does not necessarily mean that there is no strategic doctrine in the Department of Defense, but that it is not very clear and that it does not guide arms control. There is no obvious relationship between the administration's START proposals and what is publicly known of U.S. strategic doctrine, or the force requirements of that doctrine. To the contrary, they seem contradictory.

We know that we should blend arms control into the more comprehensive goals of foreign policy and strategy; and the more clearly these goals can be defined, the more accurately arms control proposals can be judged. So far, however, it is not at all clear that we have yet learned from past mistakes in this regard. Viewing it from the periphery, at least, it seems that many of these mistakes are being repeated.

These problems will not be simple to resolve, but neither are they impossible to resolve. It will, however, require a major change of effort and new direction. But what is at stake is stability in the 1980s.

It must be understood that the more uncertain Western foreign policy, the more inadequate the collective Western defense effort; or the more feeble the responses to Soviet challenges, the more Soviet confidence will grow and the more assertive the Soviets will become. As William Odum has pointed out, the United States must now decide whether to engage the Soviet Union competitively or to retire strategically.[36] That is what is at stake.

NOTES

1. Address to the annual meeting of the U.S. Chamber of Commerce. "Excerpts from Haig's Speech on Foreign Policy," *New York Times*, April 28, 1982, p. A12.

2. Or, in the words of the director of the U.S. Arms Control and Disarmament Agency, "supplying, planning, encouraging, and even participating in the Arab aggression against Israel." Eugene V. Rostow, "The Case Against SALT II," *Commentary*, February 1979, p. 24.

3. Henry Kissinger, statement before Senate Foreign Relations Committee, July 31, 1979 in *The SALT II Treaty Hearings*, part 3, p. 171.

4. Eugene Rostow, "The Unnecessary War," the Winston Churchill Lecture of the English Speaking Union, London, November 30, 1981. (Available from U.S. Arms Control and Disarmament Agency.)

5. Walter Lippmann, The Public Philosophy (Boston: Little, Brown, 1955), p. 40.

6. Dean Acheson, *Power and Diplomacy* (Cambridge, Mass.: Harvard University Press, 1958), p. 9. Emphasis added.

7. William F. Buckley, *Marco Polo, if You Can* (Garden City, N.Y.: Doubleday, 1982), p. 181.

8. See Alexis de Tocqueville, *Democracy in America* (New York: Knopf, 1945) I, 434.

9. Zbigniew Brzezinski, *Ideology and Power in Soviet Policies* (New York: Frederick A. Praeger, 1962), p. 108.

10. Charles Wolf, Jr., "Soviet Empire-Builders Push on," *Los Angeles Times*, February 24, 1981, part II, Editorial page.

11. William R. Van Cleave and Patrick J. Parker, "Political, Economic, and International Security Aspects," in Van Cleave and W. Scott Thompson, eds. *Stategic Options for the Early Eighties: What Can Be Done?* (New York: National Strategy Information Center, 1979), p. 161.

12. Ibid., p. 165.

13. This is hardly surprising. They have experienced confrontations with the United States in which the superiority of U.S. military power forced the Soviet Union to abandon its objectives. Berlin and Cuba in the early 1960s illustrate the point.

14. For a recent assessment of the military balance and an evaluation of U.S. military programs, see Committee on the Present Danger, *Has America Become Number Two?* (Washington, D.C., Committee on the Present Danger 1982).

15. News conference, March 31, 1982. *New York Times*, April 1, 1982, p. 1.

16. Michael Getler, "Senators Skeptical About President's Claim of Superiority, *Washington Post*, April 30, 1982, p. A20.

17. Richard M. Nixon, *The Real War* (New York: Warner Books, 1980), p. 152.

18. Statement before a joint hearing of the subcommittees of the Committee on Foreign Relations, U.S. House of Representatives, February 23, 1982. *ACDA Arms Control Bulletin*, February 23, 1982, p. 1.

19. Harold Brown, Secretary of Defense, *Department of Defense Annual Report to Congress*, FY 1979, p. 5.

20. Joint Chiefs of Staff, *United States Military Posture for FY 1981*, p. v.

21. Senate Armed Services Committee, *Military Implications of the Treaty on the Limitation of Strategic Offensive Arms and Protocol Thereto* (SALT II Treaty), Hearings before the Committee on Armed Services, part I (Washington: U.S. Government Printing Office, 1979), p. 177.

22. William T. Lee, Steven Rosefielde, and Patrick J. Parker reach these conclusions. See, for instance, William T. Lee, *Understanding the Soviet Military Threat*, Agenda Paper 6 (New York: National Strategy Information Center, 1977); and Steven Rosefielde and Patrick J. Parker in Steven Rosefielde, ed., *World Communism at the Crossroads* (Boston: Martinus Nijhoff, 1980), esp. ch. 2. See also Igor Birman, "Who Is Stronger and Why," *Crossroads* (Jerusalem), Winter–Spring 1981, pp. 117–26.

23. From FY 1969 through FY 1979, in total obligational authority, the U.S. defense budget declined in real terms in every year but two. Caspar W. Weinberger, Secretary of Defense, *Annual Report to Congress*, FY 1983, Table IV.E.1. (Table IV.G.1 presents GNP percentages), pp. IV-7, IV-10.

24. Testimony of Secretary of Defense Caspar Weinberger, March 21, 1982 cited in *Soviet Aerospace*, March 27, 1982.

25. See Caspar W. Weinberger *Soviet Military Power* (Washington: U.S. Government Printing Office, 1982), pp. 12–13.

26. A study conducted in 1978 for the Defense Nuclear Agency traced 41 indexes of comparison between U.S. and Soviet strategic nuclear forces from 1962 to 1982. In 1962 all favored the United States, most by a wide margin. In 1978 all but a few favored the USSR. By 1982, according to the study, virtually all would favor the USSR, most by a wide margin.

27. Joint Chiefs of Staff, *United States Military Posture*, FY 1983, Chart II-8, p. 23.

28. Henry Kissinger, prepared statement before the Committee on Foreign Relations, U.S. Senate. *Hearings, The SALT II Treaty*, 96th Cong. 1st sess., July 31, 1979, part 3, p. 165.

29. "An Interview with Ronald Reagan," *Time* Magazine, January 5, 1981, p. 31.

30. "Transcript of President's First News Conference on Foreign and Domestic Topics," *New York Times*, January 30, 1981, p. A10.

31. Alexander Haig, address to Foreign Policy Association, New York, July 14, 1981. Reprinted in "Excerpts from Haig's Speech on Administration's Policy on Arms Control" *New York Times*, July 15.

32. Statement of Eugene V. Rostow before a joint hearing of the Subcommittees on International Security and Europe and the Middle East of the Committee on Foreign Affairs, U.S. House of Representatives, February 23, 1982, reprinted in *ACDA Arms Control Bulletin*, February 23, 1982.

33. "Excerpts from Speech by Ronald Reagan, February 15, 1980," campaign press release. (Mimeographed.)

34. Some may question this. I would remind them that the United States has in the past supported defense budgets of this proportion of GNP, and in times of prosperity. In the last year that the United States had a balanced budget (1969), defense commanded nearly 9 percent of GNP. For further discussion see Committee on the Present Danger, "Is the Reagan Defense Program Adequate?" Washington: Committee on the Present Danger, 1982 esp. "Appendix: The Economics of Defense."

35. Alexander Haig Foreign Policy Association address, July 14, 1981.

36. William Odum, "Whither the Soviet Union," *Washington Quarterly*, Spring 1981, pp. 31–48.

2

Challenges to Global Stability in the 1980s: A Soviet View

Genrikh Trofimenko

ON GLOBAL STABILITY

Before entering into a discussion of the contemporary threat to global stability, it is first necessary to clarify the term itself. What do we mean when we speak of "global stability"? Indeed, is there a universally accepted definition of the term? I would argue, to state my own position very clearly from the start, that at present there is no such consensus.

In the Soviet Union politicians and academicians as a general rule do not use the term "global stability." They usually refer instead to the global "balance of forces." Soviet leaders and specialists in international relations emphasize that the USSR is satisfied with the existing balance of military forces in the world and does not aim at tilting that balance in its favor. From this point of view, "global stability" implies both sustaining the existing world balance and opposing those factors that might undermine it, thereby leading to instability and a drift toward war. In the Soviet Union notions of "stability" and "instability" are viewed first and foremost as indicators of the state of peace on our planet, its strength (stability) or its weakness (instability).

To ensure and consolidate world peace in the nuclear age, it is of primary importance that all countries abide in good faith by the norms and principles of international intercourse. These are enshrined in such fundamental documents as the United Nations Charter, the Final Act of the Helsinki Conference on Security and Cooperation in Europe, and many other multilateral and bilateral agreements concluded between the countries of East and West during the 1960s and 1970s. These instruments have developed and embodied the code of détente, the principles of peaceful coexistence and cooperation among states, regardless of social system, in the nuclear age.

It stands to reason that preserving peace in the world requires not only that we maintain global stability (in the sense just described) but also that we enhance it by reducing the heat of the military confrontation—both at the global level (between the largest states of the world and the principal military-political groupings) and at the regional and local levels (by elaborating and implementing confidence-building measures, limiting and radically reducing nuclear and conventional armaments, and developing mutually advantageous cooperation, including economic, between states).

Apparently, however, the U.S. approach to "global stability," both official and unofficial, does not coincide—or at least fails to coincide in many respects—with the foregoing approach. For the United States global stability means not so much maintaining and preserving the existing global balance of forces as it does a desire to change the parameters of the strategic picture in its favor and to maintain and bolster a pro-U.S. social and political status quo throughout the non-socialist world.

An extreme exposition of this perspective was offered by former U.S. Secretary of Defense James Schlesinger in 1980. Speaking at the annual conference of the International Institute for Strategic Studies in London, Schlesinger provided this explanation of the basic cause of "instability for the balance of the century": "The basic reason is . . . simple: the relative decline of American power and, associated with it, the reduced will of the American people to play a combined role as international guardian and self-appointed moral perceptor—in short—the end of *Pax Americana*."[1] An especially fatal role with respect to "enhancing global instability," said Schlesinger, was played by "the partial dissolution of the security framework provided by the United States for a quarter of a century after World War II."[2] A similar view of the issue of world stability is held by the present U.S. leadership, which emphasizes, to quote President Reagan, that U.S. "military strength is a prerequisite to peace."[3]

Thus, we find ourselves at the outset taking rather divergent approaches to a key notion. For the Soviet Union, sustaining global stability means maintaining the present balance of military forces in the world, though possibly lowering armaments levels. At the same time the Soviet Union accepts the possibility of changes in the sociopolitical status quo, so long as such changes result not from outside military interference, but from the internal processes of the various states in the world community. For the United States, on the other hand, it seems that the "preservation of global stability" amounts to freezing the social status quo, using every means—including armed interference—to prevent further erosion of U.S. positions in the Third World. At the same time Washington, as seen by its position on SALT II and by its new military programs, strives not to maintain the current strategic military balance, but to tip the existing balance in its favor. Thus Washington presses on in the arms race (both strategic and conventional), continues its "bloc building" activities, expands its armed forces outside the

United States, and even expresses a willingness to use those forces in "favorable circumstances."[4] Given these different approaches to the notion of global stability, one is justified in assuming that the views of Soviet and most U.S. theoreticians concerning the factors that destabilize the international situation will hardly prove to be compatible.

It is with some reluctance that I start out by stressing possible divergences in views at a time when, in my opinion, the search for ways and means to safeguard global stability would be far better served by attempts to identify a common ground of approach. Yet, it is necessary to define our differences in interpreting the concept of global stability precisely to help us, by accounting for these differences, identify points of agreement on how best to guarantee global stability, however conceived. The important thing is to put an end to the continued deterioration of the international situation and to control those rising tensions that threaten to spark a global military conflict.

THE CHALLENGE OF CHANGE

What are the current challenges to global stability, understood as a more or less stable strategic military balance between the present-day centers of world power? First and foremost, in my view, is the attempts to oppose the natural processes of change stemming from the inevitable sociopolitical evolution of the world. When one speaks about the principal tendency and chief features of change at the present stage, one must mention the further consolidation of national statehood by countries that have only recently freed themselves from colonialism: their struggle to complement their formal political independence and with continued societal change.

The view that the socioeconomic processes and armed conflicts in the Third World now pose the greatest threat to world stability is also held by American politicians and scholars—with one important difference. They tend to describe these processes as unnatural—as "upheavals" or "turmoil"—caused by artificial influences from outside, rather than as a natural stage in the ongoing sociopolitical evolution of the world.

There was a time, in the recent past, when American statesmen and political scientists took a different view of events in the Third World—welcoming the process of change and to some extent, albeit cautiously, supporting it. This was the period, immediately following World War II, that saw the beginnings of a powerful upsurge in the anticolonial struggle of the peoples of Asia, Africa, and the Middle East, and that eventually forced the colonial powers to give up their possessions. This suited the United States, for it enabled Washington to go all-out in the pursuit of the Open Door Policy. Formulated at the dawn of the twentieth century, that doctrine proclaimed the necessity and feasibility of replacing the traditional administrative and policeman colonialism with economic influence and domination. Now, as President William Howard Taft was wont to say, dollars would be substituted for bullets.

The United States, then, supported the process of decolonization because that support would enable Washington to fill the vacuum that, according to John Foster Dulles, was being created by the exit of the European powers, and to build up a vast American economic empire—the *Pax Americana* that U.S. theoreticians and politicians still long for. With the 1970s, however, came a new stage in the liberation of the developing world—the struggle by newly free states to create a new international economic order. This struggle against neocolonialism turned out to be directed above all against U.S. economic hegemonism, and it brought a sharp reaction from the United States.

Washington's willingness to go to any length to perpetuate in the Third World a state of affairs favoring the United States was to manifest itself in highly diverse forms. Among these one might mention the attempt to preserve for many more years, through some minor, pro forma concessions to the young states, an unequal system of global economic relations (it is this U.S. desire to preserve the status quo that is the chief cause of the failure of the North–South dialogue); efforts to "engage" the Soviet Union and the other socialist countries in consolidating this pro-American socioeconomic status quo;[5] the doctrine of "regional policemen," whereby the more conservative of the developing countries stabilize a pro-U.S. system in a region because their interests coincide with those of the United States; and the twists and turns of the Brzezinski Doctrine regarding the need to be on the side of change in order to direct it. This last doctrine, though, as Jeane Kirkpatrick shrewdly noted, was an unnatural one from the viewpoint of today's American leadership.[6]

Since none of the foregoing approaches brought the United States the desired result, it now feels increasingly constrained, both in doctrine and in practice, to resort to instruments of military might. This line originated in the Carter Doctrine, preceded and accompanied by the establishment of the Rapid Deployment Force. The same line is being pursued by the Reagan administration, which is beefing up U.S. military positions in the Middle East, Asia, and Central America as well as acting through its proxies (Israel, Thailand, Honduras, and others) to achieve a "stabilization" or restoration of a pro-American status quo in those areas.

This use of U.S. military might to halt any sociopolitical change that runs against its interests, together with the expanding presence of U.S. armed forces outside the United States, constitutes one major factor undermining global stability in the 1980s. Global and regional destabilization will continue because the force of arms can only exacerbate, never resolve, the socioeconomic problems that underlie local unrest and uprisings, and cause confrontations between the developing countries and international monopolies that plunder their wealth, protected by the Western powers.

DIPLOMATIC PROBLEMS AND ECONOMIC CRISIS

Another destabilizing factor is the diplomacy that aims at setting the countries of a particular region against one another in order to capitalize on the resultant tensions by offers to arbitrate or "guarantee peace." We are witnessing this sort of diplomacy worldwide—in the Middle East, where the United States is trying to maneuver between Israel and the Arab countries, using for its own ends the "fruits" of Israel's aggressive policy; in Africa, where U.S. policy is contributing to the explosive situation on the Horn of Africa and in the southern part of the continent; in Asia, where Washington systematically nudges the ASEAN countries toward confrontation with those countries of Indochina that have taken the road of socialism; and in Central America, where the military regimes of Honduras and Guatemala are being used to exert pressure on Nicaragua and to interfere in El Salvador's struggle. This "crisis diplomacy" cannot but sharpen regional tensions and, in the end, increases the danger that local crisis will get out of control.

There are no fewer potential conflicts in the world of the 1980s than in the world of the 1970s or 1960s. One need only glance at any region of the world to see frictions spawned by national, political, or economic contradictions, or by the expansionist claims of some states. Even in Europe, the most stable region in the world, recent years have seen a rise in tensions, owing to Washington's rejection of the policy of détente and NATO's military buildup.

Still, Europe is a region where in the 1970s major steps toward stabilization were taken: numerous treaties were signed between countries of Western and Eastern Europe; an agreement was concluded on West Berlin; and the Final Act of the Conference on Security and Cooperation in Europe was signed at Helsinki, laying down the principles of peaceful coexistence and a set confidence-building measures. All this contributed in no small measure to a situation in which, despite the increase of tensions in many regions of the world and even in Europe itself, détente on the European continent remains a fact of life, facilitating constructive solutions to such problems as nuclear and conventional arms reductions. Elsewhere in the world, however, the United States and its partners refuse to resolve crisis situations on the basis of comprehensive solutions in which all concerned parties participate, a posture that creates the conditions for a deepening of those crises and for their spillover into armed conflict.

The separate Camp David deal paved the way for fresh Israeli aggressions— first against Iraq, then against Lebanon. The lack of a comprehensive settlement between the countries of Indochina and the ASEAN states, including Thailand, helps sustain a hotbed of tension in Southeast Asia. The absence of a settlement between Afghanistan, on the one hand, and Iran and Pakistan, on the other, does nothing to reduce tensions in South Asia and, indeed, makes it necessary for the Soviet Union to keep its troops in Afghanistan to help that country's government repel invasions from without. The same is true in regard to the situation in southern Africa, where the Republic of South Africa, relying on the support of the Western powers, strives to prevent by force of arms a political settlement of the Namibian question. In short, the renunciation of comprehensive settlements and the determination to obtain unilateral advantages from crisis situations in the developing world constitute yet another factor exacerbating international instability and generating the threat of escalation to international clashes involving the participation of the great powers.

The international situation is further destabilized by arms transfers, which have increased dramatically in recent years. This phenomenon not only increases the number of civilian casualties in any given Third World conflict, but also intensifies and widens the conflicts themselves. Having begun in December 1977, the Soviet-American talks on conventional arms transfers—negotiations that might have led to bilateral limitations and, eventually, to more comprehensive international agreements—were broken off by the United States without any grounds for such a step.

A further proliferation of nuclear weapons in the world would, without a doubt, be another destabilizing factor. In this respect the Reagan administration's relaxation of controls on exports of fissionable materials and related equipment, established by the U.S. Nuclear Nonproliferation Act of 1978, is hardly conducive to a strengthening of the nonproliferation regime. Nor can the situation have been helped by Washington's refusal to follow through with the three-power talks (United States, Great Britain, and the Soviet Union) whose aim was to impose a total ban on nuclear weapons tests.

Growing economic troubles, both national and worldwide, can also be counted among the major factors destabilizing global politics in the 1980s. The economic crisis that has been developing for years in so many Western countries is attributable, of course, to a large set of causes. In no small measure, however, the deterioration of the economic situation in the United States and many other industrial nations is a product of chronic budget deficits stemming from exorbitant arms spending. Since economic relations in the modern world are intertwined and global in their impact, protracted national economic crises contribute to a general worsening of the world economic situation, resulting in more intense economic competition between states and causing trade and monetary wars—which, in turn, heat up the international political situation and increase the danger of military conflict.

THE USE OF FORCE IN THE NUCLEAR AGE

Today the "scramble for critical raw materials" is generating in the West a host of theories that seek to justify a priori the resort to armed force in order to gain access to such commodities. More than that, Washington now offcially proclaims that one of the main reasons for the new buildup of American military power and the increase in the U.S. military presence abroad is "to protect access to foreign markets and overseas resources in order to maintain the strength of the United States' industrial, agricultural, and technological base. . . ."[7] To any impartial observer this sounds like the most blunt proclamation of the "classical" colonialist doctrine. It seems that in a reversal of the Open Door Policy bullets are being again substituted for dollars.

But the shortage of a particular commodity is often generated by an excessive buildup of military material requiring large quantities of that commodity for its production. Thus, a vicious circle is created: raw materials are needed to prepare for war, and war is needed to gain control over the sources of those materials. It is also clear that, given the ongoing industrialization of the world, the raw materials shortage will worsen even if military arsenals are reduced. It is evident, moreover, that the policy of acquiring raw materials by armed force—that is, the policy of imperialism—if it continues to be practiced by the strongest of states, can lead only to a world military conflagration. That is why, in the present age, nations must acquire needed raw materials and resolve their disputes by peaceful means. We have now arrived at the principal threat to world stability: that war, in the opinion of many politicians and strategists, is still the chief means of resolving disputes between states and realizing a nation's "vital interests."

Although even those who advocate the use of military force recognize the devastating nature of nuclear war and its unacceptability as a universal instrument (reserving it, so to speak, for certain emergency situations), they still refuse to renounce war as a matter of principle. That is why they ignore warnings that a nuclear war could lead to the ultimate "stability" of a global graveyard, dismissing such views as the fantastic exaggerations of alarmists. In a nuclear war—especially a "limited" or "counterforce" war—they say, "only" some 100–200 million (well, perhaps 500 million) will die, but not the whole of mankind. Thus, they argue such a war is both "thinkable" and "survivable"—and, in a certain set of circumstances, even justified.[8]

That such a terrible price might be paid for the triumph of an idea (though, to be sure, a "lofty" and "democratic" one) cannot but cause one to shudder. Really, can anyone in full possession of his faculties regard as an "ideal" or a "political goal" something that demands such a mind-boggling sacrifice of human blood?

Besides, there is some chance that the price will be even higher—that humans will vanish as a biological species from the face of the earth. This prospect is presented quite convincingly by Jonathan Schell in *The Fate of the Earth*. One may assume that this chilling prospect is not very likely, that it is fractional. But if the possibility exists at all, Schell rightly says, it cannot be ignored:

> It is clear that at present, with some twenty thousand megatons of nuclear explosive power in existence, and with more being added every day, we have entered into the zone of uncertainty, which is to say the zone of risk of extinction. . . .

Therefore, although, scientifically speaking, there is all the difference in the world between the mere possibility that a holocaust will bring about extinction and the certainty of it, morally they are the same, and we have no choice but to address the issue of nuclear weapons as though we knew for a certainty that their use would put an end to our species.[9]

The challenge—not just to global stability, but to the integrity of our species—lies in the fact that, having got hold of and amassed colossal stockpiles of weapons capable of wiping out man and his civilization, the world continues to think in prenuclear categories. The instrument of nuclear war is still considered an effective and usable means of settling disputes and attaining political goals. This kind of thinking by strategists and politicians, lagging behind the realities of the nuclear age, constitutes the most flagrant and formidable challenge to stability—indeed, to peace on earth in general. This has been so since the invention of the atomic bomb, and the problem will continue (if we are lucky) for years to come, until nuclear weapons are totally banned and removed from the arsenals of states.

War or aggressiveness is not intrinsic to man biologically. Indeed, U.S. sociobiologists have shown that as a species humans are governed by a genetic altruism. War is a cultural institution that appears at a certain stage of development in human society. Archaeologists, in excavations of ancient human settlements, have found no evidence that war existed at the dawn of civilization. War made its appearance later, and was related to class stratification in the primitive community and to the struggle for territory. Through the millennia the institution of war evolved until it reached its ultimate "perfection": today there is a real possibility that war could destroy not only the enemy, but all combatants and noncombatants. In the face of this horrible prospect, as Teilhard de Chardin said, the same human energies that were previously wasted in bloodshed must be harnessed in a united effort to control forces of nature for a better future—for unleashing new forces of life.[10]

SOVIET–AMERICAN DÉTENTE: KEY TO GLOBAL STABILITY

It is the two superpowers, the USSR and the United States, which together account for 95 percent of the world's stockpile of nuclear explosives, that are being called upon to effect a change in thinking, a change in course from nuclear confrontation to cooperation. The fact is that now, in the 1980s, the fate of the earth depends on whether these two powers will begin cooperating again to prevent nuclear war or whether they will continue to slide toward nuclear catastrophe.

In the 1970s an appreciation of the need to cooperate led the United States and the Soviet Union to détente, and it is worthy of note that the challenges to international stability that exist today also existed then. At the same time, everyone seems to agree that the 1970s on the whole, were a more stable, less tense period than the present one—despite the fact that in the 1970s war dragged on in Vietnam and major fighting occurred in the Middle East. Yet, people throughout the world did not perceive such a serious threat from nuclear war as they do today, which explains the appearance of a vast movement both in Europe and the United States to banish that threat. Why is this so?

The reason lies in the state of relations between Washington and Moscow. Relations were good in the 1970s; now they are bad. Indeed, it has become an axiom of world politics that if relations between the two superpowers are good, or tending to improve, then the world can be optimistic. Conversely if relations are bad, or are tending to deteriorate, then the appropriate response is pessimism. I am of course aware that some will reproach me for looking at the world from the perspective of "great-power policy." But mine is not a great-power outlook; rather, it is a recognition that nuclear conflict between the United States and the Soviet Union would constitute a fatal disaster for mankind. That is why normalization of Soviet-American relations is so important, why our two countries must continue a political dialogue, and why there must be mutual understanding so that we can set an example for others in the field of arms limitation and disarmament. This is not happening, and it is not the Soviet Union that is to blame.

In this respect I should identify two aspects of Soviet–American relations: the psychological and the material. When the Reagan administration took office in January 1981, nothing occurred in a material sense that was capable of causing a further deterioration in relations between our countries. President Reagan even lifted the grain embargo. Nevertheless, not long after, Soviet–American relations became much more tense—in no small measure because of a change in Washington's rhetoric. Even as late as President Carter's administration, some elements of a civilized dialogue still lingered. Under Reagan, though, we are being treated to endless charges of Soviet evildoing, tiresome prophecies of an eventual collapse of the Soviet system, and groundless accusations that the Soviet Union harbors aggressive intentions. Despite unchanging material ties between our two countries, relations deteriorated sharply because of this new, destructive psychological attitude on the part of Washington.

Such an unfriendly approach could only cause a deterioration of material bilateral relations. Thus we see just how great is the role of "atmospherics" in international relations—at times pushing a state irrevocably toward an irrational confrontation. In reference to such bellicose rhetoric and its influence upon politics, the West German newspaper *Frankfurter Rundschau* commented: "Wars have many causes, and the most dangerous of them is the arms race and the constant talk of war through incantations, mostly through grotesque exaggerations, making a 'likely' adversary gradually appear real."[11] This is precisely what is happening now in the United States, where the Soviet Union has come to be referred by U.S. officials as "U.S. Enemy Number One." This sort of propaganda naturally tempts one to respond in kind. But since in the USSR we understand that rhetoric can radically influence the course of events, we deliberately refrain from fanning a war psychosis in our country in response to tough talk from Washington. In contrast with statements by the present U.S. administration, those of the Soviet leaders are characterized by restraint, stressing the constructive elements of cooperation and searching for positive ways to strengthen peace on our planet.

In the sphere of material relations, on the other hand, both sides are concerned mainly about the balance of armaments, especially about strategic weapons. The balance today, as we see it, is in a state of parity—a parity fixed in the SALT II Treaty, signed by President Carter. As I have already pointed out, the Soviet Union is satisfied with the existing parity and, as has been underscored repeatedly by the Soviet leaders, does not strive to gain superiority. The Reagan administration, though it criticizes the SALT II Treaty, does abide by it. That must mean the treaty suits Washington. President Reagan claims that the Soviet Union is outstripping or has already outstripped the United States in strategic arms. But if that is so, all the more reason to register parity contractually, even in some rough form, and then to move beyond, toward a more comprehensive definition of all the parameters of strategic parity and toward reducing strategic arms.

Instead, the Reagan administration has embarked on an arms race unprecedented in peacetime. It even tries to commit future U.S. administrations to long-term military ventures. This is evidenced by the annual difference of $40–$50 billion, envisaged for 1982–87, between the funds earmarked for the Defense Department under "total obligational authority" and current military appropriations. And of the destabilizing factors in the 1980s, this new spiral of the arms race, begun by the Reagan administration, is among the main ones.

What is at issue is not simply a trebling of the U.S. military budget in less than ten years. It is also noteworthy that Washington now strives to extend the arms race into new areas: it wants to destroy the antiballistic missile (ABM) treaty, has already embarked upon unprecedented preparations for waging chemical warfare, and wishes to unleash an arms race in space. All this comes at a time when most people in the world realize that a nuclear arms race is not the way to solve the problems of mankind, or even those of the United States.

We can—if the United States is willing—repeat in regard to the arms race in space the same course we have followed on earth: we can move from a situation of temporary advantage for the country that began the race to a situation of parity. Otherwise, an arms race in space can only lead us to a point at which decisions regarding the use of weapons will be even more divorced from living decision makers and delegated to computers of extreme sophistication and rapid operation. As forecast in some of the world's more nightmarish works of fiction, decisions literally involving global life or death will be wrenched from human hands. The destruction of civilization will then become not just probable but almost certain. Do the U.S. statesmen who threaten the Soviet Union with an arms race in space, and who refuse to discuss proposals to ban military activities in space, think about these consequences?

Now, what should the Soviet Union do in the face of this new American challenge? Is it to follow suit and respond to military preparations with military preparations of its own? Of course, we could do that. In principle, however, we are against maintaining ad infinitum a balance of terror. We want to break out of the vicious circle in which the world finds itself. The world demands new, totally unconventional approaches to resolving the problems of mankind, approaches having nothing to do with the arms race. To develop such approaches, however—and, more important, to implement them—we must stop the arms race—above all the U.S.–Soviet strategic-nuclear arms race—at least at the level of the present balance of terror or, more precisely, at the level of equal vulnerability to a retaliatory strike, and then begin working on how to replace this tenuous balance with something more stable.

In the early 1970s we began thinking about this problem, and with détente, notwithstanding all its shortcomings, we managed to take a number of significant steps to lessen fear and increase confidence. The fact that today, despite rising tensions, the world has not yet slid to the brink of a major war, is also a result of détente—a result of its moral, if not material, potential.

The potential or momentum of détente may also account for the fact that the Reagan administration, which came to power under the slogan of gaining strategic superiority over the USSR, refusing to negotiate with Moscow until gaining a position of strength, rather quickly felt the need to resume negotiations with the Soviet Union on medium-range nuclear missiles in Europe, and then to embark on new negotiations with the Soviet Union on limiting and reducing strategic arms. The reason is that today a government cannot count on domestic support for a foreign policy if that does not include, if only as a declared objective, measures to curtail military confrontation and to limit and reduce the opposing nuclear arsenals.

It is not my intention here to enter into a detailed analysis of the two sides' positions and proposals at the negotiations in progress, although one cannot fail to comment on the futility of the U.S. effort to achieve, through the vehicle of negotiations, a change in its favor in the nuclear-strategic and European balances. This is not a realistic approach. And yet, the very fact that Washington has resumed a dialogue with Moscow on nuclear arms issues, together with the official statement that the United States is in favor of a contractual reduction in nuclear arms, constitutes, in my view, a change in the right direction. The arms race weighs heavy on our two peoples, and the annually projected U.S. budget deficits, to the tune of $200 billion, speak for themselves.

The British philosopher Bertrand Russell, discussing the relation between psychology and politics, stressed that someday psychology might become a powerful new weapon in the hands of government: "If the holders of power desire peace, they will be able to produce a pacific population; if war, a bellicose population."[12] In the United States of today, however, we observe something quite different: although the powers that be try very hard to foster bellicose sentiments, the public at large rejects those sentiments. Broad segments of the public are becoming increasingly resolute in advocating the need for nuclear disarmament and for a nuclear freeze by the USSR and the United States. I consider this to be a direct consequence of détente and of the attractiveness of the foreign policy ideals proclaimed in documents signed during the détente period.

The idea of a reciprocal "freeze"—as a first step toward the reduction and eventual liquidation of our nuclear arsenals—is close to the Soviet view. Indeed, if one complements the stabilization of strategic weapons (laid down in the SALT II Treaty and observed de facto by both parties) with a ban on the production of new weapon systems, an idea long favored by the Soviet Union, that would amount to a freeze. Such a freeze would be the first important step toward ending the nuclear arms race.

In its struggle to make progress along the road of constructive proposals and to reduce the danger of a nuclear clash, the Soviet Union has made a historic decision—officially renouncing the first use of nuclear weapons. With this step we have demonstrated our belief in the power of the human mind, our faith that other nuclear powers are capable of forgetting time-worn stereotypes inherited from the days of the cold war and of taking a fresh look at today's realities.

Speeches and statements by high-level U.S. officials sometimes contain assurances that the United States will not attempt a first strike. U.S. Defense Secretary Weinberger, for instance, has said: "The United States remains committed to a defensive use of military strength; our objective is to deter aggression, or to respond to it should deterrence fail, not to initiate warfare or 'preemptive' attacks."[13] But if this is so, why has the Reagan administration not translated its position into a legal obligation not to resort to first use of nuclear weapons? If the world's two largest powers would make a reciprocal commitment in this regard, quite a substantial and real contribution toward stabilizing the global political situation will have been made. Since there would be no first strikes, there would be no retaliatory strikes. And if a similar commitment were to be assumed by the rest of the nuclear powers, this would be tantamount to a general ban on the use of nuclear weapons.

Besides this principal task for our time—the need to banish the threat of general world war by ending the arms race, disarming, and building confidence among states—it is evident that in the 1980s we shall confront a number of other developments affecting global stability. First, there is the increasing linkage of the world through communications, together and simultaneously with the development of political multipolarity. Second, there is the inevitable impact of economic interdependence. Third, we have the development of peaceful uses for nuclear energy, which, incidentally, could lead to a situation in which even a conventional war, with its destruction of nuclear power plants, might have catastrophic consequences. Finally, there is the industrial world's development of automation and cybernetics, which eventually may create redundant manpower and seriously exacerbate social problems. All this, together with the demographic problems of the developing countries, requires the most serious search for solutions.

BEYOND POWER POLITICS

Under the circumstances there is a very acute need to renounce power politics, to perfect the art of peaceful diplomacy, to improve international mechanisms for the settlement of disputes, and above all to enhance the efficacy of the United Nations and its agencies. What is needed is a resolute end to the psychological atmosphere of the cold war and to the international politics of bluffing.

Banishing the threat of another world war will enable mankind to concentrate on solving those problems whose long-term effects pose an objective threat to human civilization: preservation of the earth's ecosystem, development of new sources of energy, resolving the food problem, and the like. These problems are so formidable that individual countries will not be able to solve them. Problems of this magnitude ought to be tackled collectively by the entire international community. To do this, however, it is necessary that states be given an opportunity to concentrate on these common problems, and not waste their resources and best minds in the invention of still more effective means of mass destruction. As Shelley said in *Prometheus Unbound,* his hymn to man's actually becoming master of his own destiny: "Gentleness, Virtue, Wisdom and Endurance,/These are the seals of that most firm assurance/Which bars the pit over Destruction's strength!"

NOTES

1. James Schlesinger, *Third World Conflict and International Security,* Part 1, Adelphi Paper no. 166 (London: IISS, 1981), p. 5.

2. Ibid., p. 8.

3. President Reagan's address to the British Parliament, *Weekly Compilation of Presidential Documents,* Vol. 18, No. 23, Monday, June 14, 1982, p. 769.

4. The American political scientist Robert W. Tucker, whose views are close to those held by the present U.S. leadership, has written: "If a measure of the respect American power used to command is to be restored, there must be a visible demonstration of this power, and the more impressive the demonstration the better." Robert W. Tucker, *The Purposes of American Power* (New York: Praeger, 1981), p. 106.

5. This led to Washington's unfounded interpretation of détente as a Soviet acceptance of the status quo in the developing world in return for a U.S. acceptance of strategic parity.

6. Jeane Kirkpatrick, then professor of political science at Georgetown University, described the Brzezinski admonition to recognize the inevitability of global change, so that the United States might exert a "constructive influence" on that change, as a result of "Marxist ideas" that had alleg-

edly infiltrated U.S. foreign policy. See Jeane Kirkpatrick, "Dictatorships and Double Standards," *Commentary*, November 1979, pp. 34–45.

7. *Report of the Secretary of Defense Caspar W. Weinberger to the Congress on the FY 1984 Budget, FY 1985 Authorization Request, and FY 1984–88 Defense Programs*, February 1, 1983 (Washington, D.C.: U.S. Government Printing Office, 1983), p. 15.

8. Laurence W. Bielenson, whose works are promoted by President Reagan, asks this question: "Is nuclear war different because of the great damage it will inflict?" He then goes on to say: "Hand to hand combat is as brutal as bombing, and a man killed by a spear is as dead as a man killed by a nuclear missile. A Soviet–American war would leave most of the world unharmed except for deaths from fallout that would kill some but not wipe out populations or civilization." Laurence W. Beilenson, *Survival and Peace in the Nuclear Age* (Chicago: Regnery/Gateway, 1980), pp. 17, 38.

9. Jonathan Schell, *The Fate of the Earth* (New York: Knopf, 1982), p. 95.

10. See Pierre Teilhard de Chardin, *The Future of Man* (New York: Harper and Row, 1964), pp. 154–60.

11. Quoted in *International Affairs* (Moscow), 1982, no. 3: 87.

12. Bertrand Russell, *Sceptical Essays* (London: Unwin, 1961), p. 146.

13. *Report of Secretary of Defense Caspar W. Weinberger to the Congress on the FY 1983 Budget, FY 1984 Authorization Request, and FY 1983–87 Defense Programs*, February 8, 1982 (Washington, D.C.: U.S. Government Printing Office, 1982), pp. 110–11.

Part II:

Arms Control
and European Security

3

Arms Control and West European Security in the 1980s

Philip Williams

THE UNCERTAINTIES OF ARMS CONTROL

In the early 1980s the uncertainties surrounding the future of arms control are perhaps greater than at any time since the notion was seriously developed in the late 1950s and early 1960s as part of what is sometimes described as "the golden era" of strategic analysis. As a result of the experience of arms control in the 1970s, the optimism and apparent certainty that pervaded much of this literature has given way to a new period of pessimism and doubt. Indeed, the principle of arms control, which was once deemed to hold out considerable promise of regulating superpower relations and ameliorating tensions, is now regarded with considerable skepticism and even hostility by observers on both ends of the political spectrum.

Even those who remain faithful to the cause are faced with a formidable set of unanswered, perhaps unanswerable, questions. Attempts to distill specific, positive "lessons" from the arms control experience of the 1960s and 1970s yield little that is conclusive, and insofar as there ever was a consensus on the basic premises of arms control, it has evaporated—with the result that assumptions once taken for granted are now vigorously challenged. Among the outstanding issues and areas of uncertainty are the following:

1. What is the precise nature of the relationship between arms control and East–West accommodation? Is arms control a prerequisite of détente or a consequence of it?

2. Does arms control offer any serious prospect of slowing down, let alone halting, the arms race, or is its contribution merely to make the competition more predictable? And if its impact on the arms race is only marginal, does this really matter: is an unrestrained armaments competition the danger to international peace and security that is often suggested?

3. What is the relationship between arms control and strategic stability? Is the notion of stability itself one that has any relevance or even attraction outside the strategic studies communities of North America and Western Europe?

4. Is arms control a dynamic process? Does one agreement necessarily encourage and facilitate further negotiations and agreements? Is there, as is sometimes suggested, a mad momentum of arms control?

5. Are there inherent tensions and contradictions between bilateral arms control negotiations conducted exclusively by the two superpowers and the obligations of the United States to its overseas allies?

6. Are specific arms control agreements of long-term or only short-term value? Put slightly differently, can what are essentially static and inflexible agreements have continued relevance and utility in a technological environment that is anything but static?

7. What are the causes of the disappointing record of arms control up to the present? Do they lie in inadequate conceptualization and a failure of imagination, or are they inherent in negotiations between adversaries, neither of whom is a monolithic and completely rational actor but a conglomerate of different agencies, departments, and constituencies, all with their own peculiar vulnerabilities and special interests to protect and their particular aspirations to pursue? Do bureaucratic bargaining and domestic political considerations render negotiated and formal arms control negotiations a less promising avenue than more tacit or informal measures?

8. Following from all these other questions, is arms control a goal seriously worth pursuing throughout the 1980s, something that could make an important contribution to international peace and security, or should the forces of the strategic marketplace be allowed to proceed unhindered by any form of cooperative regulation?

Perhaps nowhere are these questions quite so urgent as in Europe, which remains the most heavily armed region of superpower confrontation. Yet the discussion of arms control possibilities in Europe is, if anything, even more complex than elsewhere, complicated by the fact that any but the most basic and insignificant proposals cut deeply into alliance politics. Analysis is also bedeviled by a plethora of conflicting attitudes, contradictory impulses, and highly disparate prescriptions—at all levels. Divisions over arms control in the Atlantic Alliance are accompanied by even more pronounced fissures within individual member states, while academic debate has increasingly been merged into a wider public discussion that, although often emotional, has succeeded in underlining the urgency of the issue. Amid all the arguments and advice, however, it is possible to discern at least five distinct approaches to arms control and European security in the 1980s, and these must now be examined.

COMPETING CONCEPTIONS

There are, of course, considerable dangers in attempting to categorize and summarize what are in some cases highly sophisticated analyses of the arms control possibilities in Europe: subtlety and nuance are inevitably lost in the process. Nevertheless, the effort seems worth making, in part to expose more clearly the divergent political and strategic assumptions underlying much of the debate in Western Europe. What often appear to be arguments over arms control are really arguments over the nature of the "real" threats to European security. Moreover, a carefully drawn taxonomy can provide a sounder basis on which to evaluate both past practice and future prospects.

Anti-Arms Control—a Strategic Appraisal

The first approach is one that goes beyond condemnation of particular agreements or criticism of specific negotiating proposals to challenge the very principle that the United States (at least within the context of the existing strategic balance) and Western Europe should seek arms control agreements with the Soviet Union. To put it crudely, rather than being seen as a solution to some of the security problems common to both East and West, the uncritical search for arms control is identified as a major problem of Western security. Much of the criticism of the SALT II agreement—particularly that emphasizing the "tranquilizer effect" of the negotiations—took this form, as did the papers contributed by Richard Burt, Robin Ranger, and Colin Gray to a symposium on Western security.[1] The theme was developed most forcefully and explicitly by Colin Gray, whose critique revolved around several specific propositions:

1. The dangers of an unresticted arms race are usually grossly exaggerated; far more of a threat are the activities and military programs of the Soviet Union, which have to be offset by corresponding countermeasures from the United States.

2. In arms control negotiations, the Soviet Union, by nature of its closed political system, suffers none of the disadvantages of the West, where democratic debate encourages dangerously optimistic assessments of Soviet intentions.

3. Arms control inhibits U.S. defense planning by encouraging complacency, by excluding serious consideration of war-fighting (as opposed to deterrent) capabilities, and by providing a constituency hostile to what are often essential armament policies. The overall effect is to hinder U.S. military preparedness, and thereby offer potential advantage to the adversary. This is all the more serious because although "stability or equilibrium may be negotiated through arms control, . . . it is enforceable only through competition,"[2] and by concentrating on control rather than competition, the United States has allowed the Soviet

Union to obtain a degree of strategic superiority, which could have far-reaching political consequences.

4. The notion of stability, as emphasized in the U.S. approach to superpower arms control, suffers from two serious defects. In the first place it renders extended deterrence less credible—and in the context of SALT in particular has contributed to the "decoupling" of Europe from the United States by distinguishing so clearly between strategic capabilities and other forces. Second, it is ethnocentric and fails to take into account that the Soviet strategic culture is based on assumptions radically different from those of the West.

The critique is an impressively powerful and incisive one. Yet, in the last analysis, technological expertise and strategic sophistication are less important than the hard-line (and, depending upon one's point of view, alarmist or realist) interpretation of Soviet foreign and military policy and a suspicion that Moscow is rather more adept at getting what it wants out of negotiations than is the West. Two separate strands come together in Gray's analysis: an assessment of the Soviet Union based on what Daniel Yergin termed the "Riga Axioms,"[3] and an evaluation of U.S. diplomacy that goes back to Alexis de Tocqueville's assertion that democracies are ill-suited to the conduct of foreign policy. The prescriptions follow: the United States should eschew arms control talks with the Soviet Union unless these are absolutely unavoidable and the United States can negotiate from strength rather than weakness. The prognosis for arms control in Europe is equally forthright: "Arms control in Europe probably has no future, just as it has no past. There is an insufficient basis of common interest between the Warsaw Pact and NATO for there to be any serious prospect of an agreement that sensible observers would deem worthwhile, let alone 'stabilising' by rigorous Western technical definition."[4]

Cynicism and Survival

In the light of Gray's emphasis on the need to think strategically about arms control, this first assessment can usefully be termed the strategic appraisal. The second approach is perhaps most appropriately described as "cynical." In this perspective there are no illusions about the competitive nature of East–West relations. It differs from the strategic approach, however, in that, although not oblivious to the pitfalls, it regards arms control negotiations as an important and worthwhile political and strategic activity. Negotiations can fulfill several different functions, all of which come down to an understanding of arms control as little more than a continuation of the arms race by other means. The main themes are summarized in the following propositions:

1. Although arms control theory emphasizes the common interest of the participants in reaching an agreement, arms control practice puts more weight on the conflicting interests of the participants in determining the precise details of the outcome. The objective is to maximize military advantages and minimize disadvantages and weaknesses through shrewd and tough bargaining. The precise

terms of the bargain are vital, and if they are not in some way advantageous, the agreement is not worth having.

2. Even if negotiations do not result in formal agreements, they should still be pursued. Negotiations per se are probably indispensable, because they can be used to legitimize both existing programs and projected deployments in the face of domestic pressure for either drawing down forces or holding back on proposed expansion. Thus the "bargaining chip" argument for new weapons may strengthen the case for development or deployment—even though there may be no serious intention of bargaining away the chip. Equally expedient is the argument that certain kinds of force reductions should not be made unilaterally so long as there is a possibility that arms control negotiations might succeed in eliciting a quid pro quo from the adversary. In short, arms control negotiations are an invaluable legitimizing device for arms competition.

3. Following from this, negotiations can have useful propaganda benefits. The kind of gamesmanship identified by Spanier and Nogee as being a major characteristic of the disarmament negotiations of the 1950s is an equally important aspect of arms control talks.[5] The aim may be less to seek an agreement than to maneuver the adversary into a position where he is blamed for the lack of progress or the breakdown of the negotiations.

The "cynical" approach is similar to the "strategic" view in its recognition that the pressures of democracy often pose enormous problems for defense planners concerned with peacetime preparedness. Whereas strategists such as Gray see arms control as part of the problem, however, the cynics see it as part of their response to resource allocation pressures. Rather than inhibiting force planners, arms control provides a necessary weapon in the public relations armory. Another difference is that the second approach, implicitly at least, denies the Soviet Union a monopoly of realpolitik and Machiavellianism, and rejects the contention that there are pronounced inherent assymetries in East–West negotiations. The United States and its allies are much more adept than the strategic perspective acknowledges. Not surprisingly, this leads to prescriptions and prognoses considerably at variance with those of the first approach. The lack of sufficient common interest to make possible a meaningful agreement does not matter. Negotiations have a future not so much for what they can achieve, as for what they can facilitate. Appearances are everything, and so long as one conveys an impression of seriousness and integrity, it is not always crucial that the talks result in formal agreement.

Arms Control as Diplomatic Lubricant

The third approach to arms control is superficially akin to the second in its emphasis on the political importance of arms control negotiations. It differs very radically from it in that the political functions are, above all, symbolically related to the détente process. In this perspective arms control negotiations are less a disguise for continued competition in armaments than a device for political cooperation. Thus, the precise content of negotiations matters less than the fact that the two sides are negotiating seriously. Although they are not always fully articulated, it is possible to discern several distinct propositions central to this approach:

1. Dialogue is to be encouraged as something that promotes greater sensitivity and mutual understanding between adversaries.

2. There is something incongruous about a process of political accommodation that is accompanied by continued and unrestrained military competition, something precariously incomplete about a resolution of tensions that does not encompass any regulation or moderation in the pace and scope of each side's military activities.

3. If détente is to be viable, it must be a dynamic process. Arms control negotiations are a manifestation of that dynamism, in that their very existence signals the desire to establish or perpetuate a necessary modus vivendi between nuclear-armed adversaries.

Once again the underlying judgments are crucial, revealing as they do that what often appear to be differences over arms control are essentially arguments about the nature of the threat. Thus, just as the tendency of the more hawkish strategists to dismiss arms control as a delusion stems from suspicion about the Soviet Union and hostility toward détente, so those who promote arms control as "political symbolism" do so primarily because they attach such a high value to détente. The relaxation of tension in Europe in particular is something that should not be given up lightly—and if this requires restraint in weapons deployment and a continued commitment to negotiations, then it is a price well worth paying.

The major threat is not the Soviet Union, but a reversion to cold war confrontation, with all this implies for states that are not only in the front line, but dependent on the continued restraint of one superpower and the continued security guarantee of the other. Consequently, any major innovation in, or augmentation of, NATO's military posture in Europe has to be assessed primarily for its effect on East–West relations. What the strategists condemn as a manifestation of "Finlandization," giving the Soviet Union an unwarranted influence in Western force planning, the pro-détente school regards as necessary prudence. The Soviet Union, just like the West, has legitimate security concerns that ought to be respected. After all, it is argued, an insecure Soviet Union may be more of a danger than a Soviet Union with marginal military advantage but that, as a result, feels far less threatened.

True Believers

The fourth approach to arms control is that of the true believer—and it is an approach that differs significantly from those outlined above. In contrast with the third alternative, the committed arms controller regards the process as a necessary complement to national defense efforts, not for its symbolic value but for its substantive impact. The emphasis here is less on arms control as a prerequisite for détente than on détente as a prerequisite for arms control. Although it is acknowledged that arms control agreements that, for one reason or another, may be widely regarded as inimical to national security can themselves become "consumers of détente," it remains a major tenet of many arms controllers that the meager results so far obtained stem from an increasingly unfavorable political context and an equally hostile technological environment. The implication is not that arms control should be jettisoned, but that a more imaginative approach is needed.

The experience of the 1970s is recognized as a salutary one, but in shedding the "illusions of arms control," it is important not to disavow the idea itself. As one analyst has put it: "There is little wrong with the principle that, in this dangerous age, superpowers (and their allies) should talk regularly and in detail about their respective force structures, nor with the hope that they can take remedial action to remove sources of disturbance in their strategic relationship."[6] Thus it is worth reiterating, albeit very briefly, those propositions that the committed arms controllers have salvaged from the 1970s:

1. Arms control is not a panacea. It is a substitute neither for national military preparations nor for broader attempts to normalize superpower relations.

2. Nevertheless, arms control as a regulatory concept does have a continuing role in helping to manage the mixed relationship between Washington and Moscow. It does not aspire to transform the "adversary partnership" of the superpowers into either entente or condominium because structural and ideological considerations render this impossible. But it does help to prevent the U.S.–Soviet global engagement from degenerating into one of unmitigated conflict and unrestrained competition. This is not to argue that the arms competition is an independent cause of tension in East–West relations, but it is to suggest that it can exacerbate political difficulties.

3. By building arms control considerations into each side's military planning, the process is made more rational. In both the United States and the Soviet Union there exist powerful groups with a vested interest in perpetuating the arms competition. Thus, it is not a simple action–reaction process. Rather it is a case—in part at least—in which the adversary's actions are used to justify and rationalize programs of one's own that have been developed more or less autonomously. There is an unholy alliance between the military establishments of the rival superpowers. The existence of arms control constituencies within the United States and the Soviet Union—even if they operate from weak political bases—does at least mean that the process does not go unchallenged and that military enthusiasm and zeal are not entirely unrestrained.

4. The financial costs of the arms race give both superpowers an incentive to establish mutually acceptable restraints and limitations on their military prepara-

tions. Although the strength of the economic constraints may differ considerably from Washington to Moscow, criticism of high defense spending as a contribution to major budget deficits in the United States probably does have a counterpart in the impact of declining economic growth in the Soviet Union.

These arguments favoring arms control, of course, are the antithesis of those prepared by the more hawkish strategists. And once again the roots of the conflict lie more in political than in technical judgments, particularly in differing attitudes toward the Soviet Union. Implicit in arms control theory is the belief that nuclear weapons have had a profound effect on the Soviet Union—where they pose the same kind of security concerns and resource allocation dilemmas as those so painfully familiar in the West. In other words, the United States can engage in negotiations with Moscow with a reasonable expectation that the Russians are seriously interested in agreement. This is not to say the Soviet delegates will not engage in hard bargaining, in an attempt to obtain the most advantageous terms possible—but in doing this they will not be behaving very differently from their American counterparts. And there is no reason why the Soviet Union should be markedly superior to the United States in obtaining favorable terms. The implication is that although it is likely to be fraught with difficulty, arms control can make a distinctive and important contribution to European security in the 1980s.

The Disarmers

If the assumptions of the committed arms controllers and those of the strategists are directly opposed, it is one of the ironies of the present debate that the hardliners' distaste for the arms control process is shared by a fifth group of advocates, the disarmers. The study of arms control makes strange bedfellows: E. P. Thompson and Colin Gray have more in common than they may realize, even though they arrive at some remarkably similar conclusions from very different starting points. Another irony is that, in terms of substance, the disarmers' interpretation of arms control is probably closest to that of the cynics, since both groups see it as a political device to legitimize the arms buildup and to divert political pressure for restraint. But what the cynics regard as a positive virtue is seen by the disarmers as a damning indictment. Criticism of SALT II as an "arms escalation" treaty typified an approach that regards existing measures of arms control as essentially fraudulent. If the disarmers have something in common with two of the other approaches, however, in at least one respect they are unique. While all the other perspectives function within the framework of deterrence, disagreeing only about whether arms control enhances or detracts from it, the disarmers reject the framework itself, together with its supporting apparatus. Although the critique is a sweeping one, in the present context there are three propositions worth mentioning:

1. The deterrence system and the arms race that accompanies it are not merely sources of insecurity for both sides but actually make their relationship one of permanent and unremitting hostility. "By maintaining each party in a position of menace to the other, it fixes indefinitely the tensions which make the resolution of differences impossible. It transfixes diplomacies and ideologies into a twilight state; while postponing war, it postpones also the realization of peace."[7] There is, of course, nothing new in this thesis, and in some respects it is simply a variant of the traditional argument of the disarmers that arms are a cause rather than merely a symptom of conflict.

2. An incremental approach is insufficient to break out of the dilemmas and dangers associated with the deterrence systems. Arms control is inadequate because it does not go far enough to make any real contribution to security, and undesirable on the grounds that it makes policy makers and publics alike more willing to tolerate the intolerable.

3. The fact that bargaining chips are rarely bargained away illustrates just how easily defense planners have turned the supposed constraints of arms control to their advantage—a development that further underlies the bankruptcy of arms control in promoting international peace and security.

Although the disarmers share certain judgments and assumptions about the nature of international politics and the sources of conflict, there is less unanimity in their attitudes toward the two superpowers. Some disarmers, for example, see the United States—which after all is a much wealthier and technologically more advanced state than its rival—as the main culprit, a feeling that has been intensified by some of the statements and policies of the Reagan administration. Others see the two superpowers as essentially indistinguishable and equally guilty of pursuing policies inimical to the security of Europe. What unites these groups is the desire that Europe free itself from the tutelage of both Washington and Moscow. The pressures for disarmament in Western Europe in particular stem from an acute sense of impotence and vulnerability, from a recognition, in Stanley Hoffmann's words, that "Western Europe is a frying pan on a stove whose controls are in the hands of others."[8] Thus the demand for disarmament is, in large part, a demand that Western Europe become master of its own destiny rather than remaining a potential battleground for the superpowers.

The existence of these very different approaches has two important and not entirely unrelated consequences, one for policy and the other for assessment. The implications for arms control policy are distressing. The variety of attitudes ensures that the policy pursued by any national government is usually an uneasy compromise among different groups and factions within the executive, the legislative, and the public—all of which have their own expectations and criteria against which the results will be judged. The problem is vastly compounded by the fact that arms control has ceased to be the exclusive preserve of individual states and in the West, especially, has become an alliance responsibility. A composite approach that somehow reconciles demands for preparedness with the desire for restraint, that legitimizes new developments or existing deployments while not excluding their limitation, is formidable; when the members of the Western alliance have divergent assumptions regarding how much or how little is enough and cannot agree on precisely what constitutes either preparedness or restraint, it is exceedingly so.

This is where the problem of policy becomes linked to that of evaluation. The different perspectives yield different criteria whereby arms control initiatives, negotiations, and agreements can be adequately appraised. What from one vantage point may appear very desirable, may be regarded elsewhere as dangerous or destabilizing. The difficulty with agreements that try to satisfy too many criteria is that they may end up provoking disquiet in all corners. This may yet prove to be the fate of negotiations on long-range theater or, as they are now termed, intermediate nuclear, forces. Before examining this possibility, however, it is necessary to look at efforts to obtain conventional arms control in Europe.

CONVENTIONAL ARMS CONTROL

For the committed arms controller the attempts at reducing conventional arms in Europe have been, at best, disappointingly feeble, and at worst, a dismal failure that has done much to discredit the whole arms control enterprise in Europe. The Mutual and Balanced Force Reduction (MBFR) negotiations have been in progress since October 1973, and the NATO and Warsaw Pact negotiators remain almost as far apart today as they were at the outset. Indeed, the talks seem to have become little more than a highly stylized ritual in which the interminable dispute over data is interrupted only by the introduction of new negotiating proposals. Underlying these arguments over data, of course, has been a "fundamental and seemingly irresolvable disagreement over the character of the military balance in Europe."[9] So long as there is no consensus among the participants on whether the talks start from, or are designed to end in, equality, new proposals are likely to be as futile as the old ones. As one commentator has noted: "The West offers terms which require the Soviet Union to give up advantages it now enjoys. The Russians are unlikely to make such a sacrifice. . . . The East offers terms that will perpetuate its advantages."[10] The implication is that both sides have brought to the negotiations the approach of the cynic rather than that of the believer.

Furthermore, from the cynical perspective the failure to bring the negotiations to a productive conclusion does not signify failure. On the contrary, the negotiations do not require an agreement to be deemed successful, since an agreement was not a priority objective. Their main purpose—at least as far as the United States and Western Europe were concerned—was political: they were seen as a way of forestalling or undermining congressional demands for U.S.

troop withdrawals from Western Europe.[11] It is not coincidental that the Nixon administration's enthusiasm for the negotiations increased dramatically in May 1971, when it appeared possible that the Mansfield Amendment designed to reduce the number of U.S. troops in Europe by 50 percent by the end of the year, would receive Senate approval.

From then on, the possibility that unilateral reductions would remove any incentive for the Soviet Union to provide a quid pro quo was a major political asset, skillfully exploited not only by the Nixon and Ford administrations but also by critics of the Mansfield proposal in the Senate. Other considerations, such as the growing antipathy towards détente and the improvement in the U.S. balance of payments, may have contributed more to the decline of the pressure for troop withdrawals after 1974; but the Vienna talks were vital in containing the pressure in 1973 and 1974. It is one of the paradoxes of the MBFR negotiations that their prime purpose was to uphold the status quo by inhibiting unilateral withdrawals by the United States—and insofar as maintaining the U.S. military presence in Western Europe at existing levels was deemed essential to Western European security, then the MBFR negotiations made a major contribution.

The success of the talks as a cynical gambit stemmed from several factors that may be unique to MBFR:

1. The alliance-wide consensus on the need to maintain a substantial American military presence in Europe: the same issue that divided the Senate united the administration and its NATO partners.

2. The Soviet Union's willingness to participate in the negotiations for much the same reason as NATO. Leonid Brezhnev's speech of May 14, 1971, inviting the West to "open the bottle" of negotiations is generally interpreted as an ill-timed gesture that unwittingly contributed to the defeat of the Mansfield Amendment.[12] Yet if it is accepted that the Soviet Union enjoys the comfort of a status quo in which U.S. troops contribute to the containment of the Federal Republic of Germany, then Brezhnev's speech can readily be interpreted as a deliberate intervention to prevent unilateral U.S. withdrawals.

3. For both sides the negotiations had additional symbolic overtones, and were seen as contributing to the momentum of détente. For Moscow this had the advantage of encouraging movement toward the Conference of Security and Cooperation in Europe. For the Europeans it was an opportunity to participate more fully in President Nixon's "era of negotiations."

For the committed arms controller, of course, all this is less important than the failure to obtain an agreement. Furthermore, although the enthusiasts of détente may take some comfort from the continuation of the negotiations at a time when bilateral arms control between the superpowers was moving into political trouble in the United States, they would almost certainly regard some sort of agreement as a timely boost for East–West accommodation. But what are the prospects for agreement at Vienna, or even for further progress on conventional arms control within the framework of the Helsinki Final Agreement? Three considerations seem to be particularly relevant:

1. The contention that agreement may be necessary for détente runs into the problem that a greater degree of détente may be a prerequisite for agreement. The progress of discussions on force reductions and confidence-building measures (CBM) has limited influence on the political context, but is influenced significantly by that context. This asymmetry is sometimes played down, especially by proponents of CBMs. The 1981 *SIPRI Yearbook*, for example, argued that "the role of CBMs is . . . to prepare the ground, politically and psychologically, for real arms control and disarmament measures. To the extent that decision-makers obtain more realistic perceptions of each other's intentions and capabilities and are reassured of the absence of threats some of the driving forces of the arms race will be removed and the possibilities for real disarmament may improve. Thus CBMs should lead from reductions of fears to reduction of objective grounds for such perceptions and it is important that the link between CBMs and efforts to restrain and reduce military capabilities is maintained. Today this link is all too evident in the reverse; the spiralling arms build up has feed-back on the whole CBM enterprise, leaving us essentially at square one."[13] What this assessment fails to acknowledge is that the reverse link is probably far more powerful than the positive spin-off from further CBMs or agreement on mutual force reductions.

2. Although an agreement on limited or token reductions might appear increasingly attractive as a way of preempting what appears to be a resurgence of congressional demands for American troop withdrawals from Europe, too much should not be made of this. Insofar as the revival of such pressure is not a serious possibility, it seems to stem from anti-European feelings that are unlikely to be diminished by anything that happens in Vienna.

3. The emphasis placed in the last few years on "associated measures" of inspection and verification is readily understandable as a Western attempt to obtain reassurance against the possibility of surprise attack.[14] Yet it seems unlikely that these proposals—together with those for more ambitious CBMs discussed at Madrid—will make much headway against traditional Soviet suspicions about intrusive inspection procedures.

In the last analysis, therefore, the failure to make much progress in conventional arms control can only strengthen the demands of those strategic analysts who argue that NATO requires a more stalwart conventional capability and that security in Europe can be enhanced solely through a buildup of NATO forces and not through unattainable aspirations for a reduction in those of the adversary. The same argument is used in relation to nuclear forces, and it is to the issue of nuclear arms control in Europe that attention must now be given.

INTERMEDIATE NUCLEAR FORCES AND ARMS CONTROL

Before attempting to assess the implications of the Geneva negotiations for the security of Western Europe, it is necessary to examine the NATO decision of December 12, 1979, and the subsequent developments that led to the opening of the talks. The decision to deploy cruise missiles and Pershings in Europe stemmed, naturally enough, from the perceived political, strategic, and military needs of the alliance.

In part, of course, this was an attempt to ensure that West European interests were not ignored or jeopardized by the SALT process, particularly the terms of the SALT II Treaty. The omission from SALT II of Soviet "Eurostrategic" systems, coupled with the willingness of the United States to accept temporary restrictions on ground-launched cruise missiles, which were the obvious counter, was controversial in both Europe and the United States. At a time when it was still hoped that the treaty might be ratified, the NATO decision was deemed necessary to ensure that the prohibition clause in the protocol did not have what the Senate Armed Services Committee described as a "precedential effect."

Closely related to this were concerns that the emergence of strategic parity as enshrined in SALT, coupled with the vulnerability of the Minutemen, made the imbalance of nuclear capability in Europe—which was accentuated by the SS-20—increasingly dangerous. On the one hand, it would give the Soviet Union "escalation dominance" in hostilities and a psychological advantage in crises, and, on the other, it would make the United States less willing to use strategic nuclear weapons on Europe's behalf. Indeed, in such circumstances the abandonment of Europe might appear an attractive option.[15] Thus, action had to be taken to restore the credibility of the American nuclear guarantee and thereby repair NATO's deterrent position.

Another consideration was that NATO's theater nuclear forces—short-range as well as long-range—required modernization, irrespective of any augmentation of Soviet capabilities. As Simon Lunn has pointed out, "The initial requirement for LRTNF modernization rested in the military/doctrinal analysis of NATO's own deficiencies. NATO's doctrine of flexible response required systems based in Europe with the capability of striking the Soviet Union. The existing assets for this role, F111 and Vulcans, were getting old, faced penetration problems against improving Soviet air defenses, and were increasingly vulnerable."[16] Furthermore, the Poseidon submarine-launched ballistic missiles (SLBMs) assigned to NATO were not clearly distinguishable from strategic retaliatory capabilities and were not suitable to cover all the targets the alliance might be interested in.

Thus, the decision to deploy cruise and Pershing missiles was intended to provide political and strategic reassurance by the United States and a necessary modernization of NATO capabilities. Whereas the strategic, and to a degree the political, rationale was related to Soviet deployment of the SS-20, the military rationale was essentially independent on NATO's offensive capabilities. If this has been a source of ambiguity in NATO policy, it has been compounded by uncertainty over the relationship between long-range theater nuclear force (LRTNF) deployment and LRTNF arms control. The "second track" of the December 1979 decision can be seen both as a legitimizing device to enhance the prospects for deployment and as an alternative to implementation of the modernization program. Such tensions and potential contradictions have been inherent in the NATO approach to the Soviet Union since the Harmel Report of 1967 established the goals of deterrence and détente with little regard to possible incompatibilities between them; but they have been dramatically underlined by developments and events since 1979.

The political rationale for deployment was undermined by domestic changes in the United States that meant "the context of the decision evaporated almost as soon as the decision was taken."[17] The result was that European fears of a sellout receded, only to be replaced by a concern that both European détente and the arms control component of the decision would be destroyed by the hardline stance of the United States. Paradoxically, it was this same hard-line stance that intensified public anxiety and protest over the deployment element of the decision.

Part of this protest stemmed from the fact that many Europeans found the strategic rationale for cruise and Pershing not only less than compelling, but also one with disturbing implications. Although the decision made it less likely that the United States would abandon Western Europe, it may have increased rather than diminished the likelihood of "decoupling" and of a nuclear war being confined to Europe. Indeed, it is only if this is admitted as a serious possibility that the deployment makes strategic sense for the United States. If the weapons are genuinely Russostrategic, in the sense that they are intended to hit targets within the Soviet Union, then they are really no different from the strategic capabilities deployed within the United States and in the submarine forces—and in the event of a Soviet nuclear attack on Western Europe, an American president would face exactly the same dilemma as if the weapons did not exist.

The crucial variable is not the location of the weapon but the location of its target. As McGeorge Bundy has pointed out, "Whether they are based in Germany, or at sea, or in Nebraska, there will always be the same awful magnitude in any Presidential decision to use these weapons against anyone, and in particular against the Soviet Union, whose leaders know as well as we do whose command would send them, and where to direct the reply."[18] In other words, the deployment of cruise and Pershing makes sense for the United States only if the weapons are intended for use against Eastern Euope, thereby giving the United States the capacity to match the Soviet Union, option for option, below the level at which superpower homelands become involved.

Whether this would enhance or detract from the credibility of extended deterrence is highly debatable. In the final analysis, the argument revolves around the relationship among options, thresholds, and escalation, with its elements of both deliberation and inadvertence. Adding options, whether they be conventional or nuclear, can in certain senses be seen as increasing the likelihood of escalation. The greater the number of steps on the escalation ladder, the higher the probability that the United States would be prepared to climb at least some of them because each step may appear less awesome. Thus a comprehensive range of options providing for both gradual and graduated escalation may enhance credibility. On the other hand, the availability of options, each of which is designed for a particular level of hostilities, may increase the number of potential stopping places and improve the prospects for halting or resolving the conflict before the higher levels are reached and the more drastic alternatives considered.

This is complicated, of course, by the fact that escalation may be unintended or inadvertent as well as deliberate. Thus even genuine, mutual attempts to limit hostilities to one level may not succeed. "Hence the essential ambiguity of every threshold which, as Albert Wohlstetter has written about tactical nuclear weapons, can be interpreted either as a firebreak or as a bridge to a higher level."[19] Wohlstetter's term "firebridge" reflects this duality.[20] The implication is that there are no ideal solutions or answers. Extended deterrence in Europe is full of tensions, paradoxes, and contradictions that cruise and Pershing accentuate as much as they dispel. Strategic ambiguity rules.

In the light of this, West European reticence about the implementation of the December 1979 decision is understandable. The United States, however, has turned the issue into a test of loyalty for the Europeans. This has also been done with other problems, such as burden sharing and the pledge to a 3 percent per annum real increase in defense budgets. It adds a particularly ironic twist to an episode that began with concerns over the U.S. commitment: stemming partly from growing European doubts about U.S. credibility and fidelity to the alliance, the deployment of cruise and Pershing has become a crisis over the West European commitment both to its own defense and to the Atlantic framework.

Just as it did in 1954 over the European Defense Committee (EDC) and in 1973–74 over European assertiveness on economic issues, the United States has once again begun to hint at possible reappraisals of its security guarantee to Western Europe—unless the Europeans go ahead with implementation as planned. Nowhere has this been more explicit than in a statement of the U.S. ambassador to Bonn that described the nuclear debate as "a battle for the soul of Europe with clear alternatives. On the one hand, the West can reaffirm unequivocally its determination to achieve sufficient collective security to deter Soviet aggression even as the United States seeks through negotiations with the Soviet Union to achieve major reductions of nuclear weapons. On the other hand, if such reaffirmation is long postponed or becomes uncertain, there may well be a growing sentiment in America to turn back upon itself and let Europe depend for its security and freedom upon its own resources or upon Soviet good will."[21]

With this kind of pressure from the United States on the one side and the growth of the European nuclear disarmament movement on the other, the arms control component of the December 1979 decision took on even greater political significance. It has become a way of sidestepping, if not defusing, what could be termed the politics of symbolism, in which the United States has demanded agreement in the absence of consensus and urged implementation of the deployment decision, almost irrespective of the problems this would precipitate for several European governments. At the same time it has avoided—if perhaps only temporarily—a head-on clash with the protest movement.

It is hardly surprising, therefore, that former Chancellor Helmut Schmidt, supported by other European governments, made great efforts to ensure that some progress was made along the arms control track. Indeed, it was only as a result of the demands of the Federal Republic of Germany that arms control in Europe was reinstated as a goal of American foreign policy under the Reagan administration. Chancellor Schmidt was also influential in persuading Brezhnev to moderate the Soviet position and agree to negotiations. As well as helping to bring the superpowers to the negotiating table, the Federal Republic contributed significantly to the U.S. negotiating stance: the "zero option" whereby the United States would refrain from deployment of cruise and Pershing in return for Soviet agreement to dismantle all its SS-20s, as well as its SS-4s and SS-5s, owes much to the German chancellor. Although this approach will almost certainly be modified as the United States gradually adopts a more realistic negotiating position, it does provide a basis on which to make at least a preliminary appraisal of the contibution the Geneva talks might make to West European security.[22] This can now be done in relation to the five perspectives on arms control outlined above.

COMPETING CONCEPTIONS REVISITED

From the strategic perspective, cruise and Pershing are essential. Although not a numerical match for Soviet systems, they add significantly to the survivability and penetration capability of NATO's intermediate-range nuclear force. As such, they help to ensure that Soviet leaders do not attempt to turn military advantage into political gain—as they might be tempted to do if faced with an empty NATO strategy of flexible response that failed to provide the comprehensive repertoire of options implied by its name. Consequently, the missiles are not negotiable, and the alliance has made a major blunder in allowing weapons that are vital to West European security to be presented as "bargaining chips." In this perspective the initial "two track" decision was a mistake, and one that was perpetuated by the "zero option," which is incompatible with NATO's strategic requirements. By making the deployment conditional upon negotiation, the alliance has given hostages to fortune; by linking modernization so closely to the SS-20, it has made itself potentially vulnerable to Soviet propaganda initiatives such as the offers of a "moratorium" or freeze on any new deployments.

From the cynical perspective the negotiations are essentially a means to an end, and are valuable only so far as they succeed in legitimizing the deployment. Insofar as the "two track" nature of the initial decision was necessary to get alliance agreement, then it was a price that had to be paid—and if it is necessary to engage in a charade for the subsequent implementation to go ahead, then so be it. Thus, although cruise and Pershing appear as "bargaining chips," this is for presentational purposes only. President Reagan's dramatic announcement of the "zero option" was a blatant but necessary exercise in gamesmanship. The difficulty with this, of course, is that the more transparent it becomes, the less likely is it to succeed. This is why the State Department's insistence on a negotiating posture with several fallback positions makes far more sense than the Pentagon's demand for a take-it-or-leave-it approach.

From the détente or political symbolism perspective, the negotiations are welcome—both as a means of revitalizing the arms control dialogue after the SALT II setback and as a way of reiterating the principle that détente in Europe *can* be insulated from the breakdown of détente elsewhere. There is also a sensitivity to what are accepted as legitimate Soviet security concerns. After all, cruise and Pershing will add substantially to the U.S. capacity to hit the Soviet homeland. Furthermore, the speed of Pershing inevitably raises concerns over some form of preemptive action by NATO. The danger is that the added insecurities, by making the Soviet Union more, rather than less, assertive and willing to take risks, might jeopardize the political accommodation that has been carefully developed over the last decade or so. Discussions on limiting intermediate nuclear forces (INF) can thus be seen not only as a way of promoting further relaxation in Europe but also as a means of holding on to the gains that have already been made. At some stage, though, an agreement that goes beyond mere tokenism may be essential.

The committed arms controllers are also anxious that the Geneva talks yield concrete results—and are unhappy about what has appeared, in the intitial stages of the negotiations, to be a rather cavalier approach by both superpowers. At the same time, the most salient feature of the talks, from the arms control perspective, must be their sheer intractability—even assuming goodwill and serious intent on both sides. The problem of which systems are to be included, the familiar question of whether the negotiations are designed to start from or end in parity, the geographical scope that any agreement might cover, and the problem of verification, the vexatious issue of British and French nuclear capabilities all militate against easy progress and an early conclusion to the negotiations. At best the talks can hardly fail to be long, complex, and arduous.

If this were not enough, there is also the problem of their relationship to discussions on intercontinental systems. Some arms controllers have argued that discussions on INF alone are so artificial that they should be merged into broader talks encompassing the superpower armories as a whole. The great advantage held up for this option is that it would render asymmetries at the regional level less consequential, because the European balance would be "coupled" much more directly to the strategic capabilities of the two superpowers.[23] Trade-offs between the two levels might also be easier. Yet if deep cuts are to be made in intercontinental forces, as proposed by the United States at the opening of the Strategic Arms Reduction Talks (START), this could magnify rather than reduce the significance of any remaining imbalance in Europe. The merger could also have a disruptive effect on NATO because it would be much more uncertain on which aspects of the talks the Europeans could legitimately attempt to influence the United States. Nor would a merger necessarily make either set of negotiations more manageable. On the contrary, it could complicate further the already complex issues. The continuation of two closely related, but essentially distinct, sets of negotiations, therefore, may be the preferable alternative. This is not to suggest that it is completely satisfactory, of course. Indeed, questions about the optimum relationship between START and the INF negotiations highlight some of the many dilemmas confronting the committed arms controller, and reveal how proposals designed to overcome one set of problems often succeed only in precipitating others.

For the disarmers, of course, the failure of arms control in Europe stems less from the intrinsic difficulties than the lack of enthusiasm and seriousness with which agreement is pursued. The Geneva negotiations in particular are seen as a fraud because they are not intended to produce an alternative to deployment of cruise and Pershing. What makes this all the more unpalatable for many disarmers is that the weapons themselves are deemed unnecessary. This stems partly from a belief that NATO typically exaggerates the Soviet threat and has exaggerated the threat from the SS-20 in particular. After all, it is argued, their deployment has not created any new vulnerabilities in Western Europe. The NATO systems, in contrast, are "so advanced by comparison with the old systems they may in themselves destabilize the whole deterrence system in Europe."[24]

Opposition to cruise and Pershing also results from the inherent ambiguity that, along with several ill-chosen remarks from members of the Reagan administration, has fueled anxieties about U.S. willingness to contemplate a limited nuclear war in Europe. Although President Reagan's emphasis on the "zero option" may have defused the issue somewhat, this is unlikely to be more than a temporary fix. Indeed, there are several differences between the INF negotiations and those on conventional forces that make it unlikely that a cynical approach in Geneva will work as effectively as it did in Vienna:

1. The consensus in NATO on the need for U.S. troops is absent in relation to cruise and Pershing. This was reflected in the nature of the initial decision of December 1979, and the ambivalence has become more, rather than less, pronounced. As Henry Kissinger has noted, there are some who want the negotiations as a pretext to avoid deploying these weapons; there are others who want the negotiations in order to deploy them.[25]

2. The Soviet Union is strongly against cruise and Pershing—and, as Christoph Bertram has pointed out, will be tempted to use the negotiations to delay deployment rather than to reach agreement, in the hope that the opposition movement in Western Europe will prove irresistible. "The anti-nuclear forces in Europe are, in this respect, also anti-arms control forces: the more effective their opposition to the LRTNF programme, the bleaker the prospects for agreement."[26]

3. To state the obvious, the European nuclear disarmament (END) movement is not the U.S. Senate. Whereas the strongest advocates of troop withdrawals regarded MBFR as a stalling tactic, less committed senators were more gullible. END is unlikely to prove so malleable, especially because increasing tensions between the superpowers—which hurt the troop withdrawal lobby after 1973— tend to strengthen the peace movement.

4. There is a critical difference between maintaining the conventional status quo, which was done through MBFR, and deploying new and much more controversial nuclear weapons—which NATO is in the unenviable position of attempting to do.

In other words, although the 1979 decision helped to postpone highly divisive choices for the alliance, this cannot be done indefinitely, given the projected date for deployment. Hard decisions still have to be made. If the negotiations can soften these decisions, and thereby restore and maintain a higher degree of political cohesion in Atlantic relations, then they will contribute significantly to West European security. It is equally plausible, though, that they will yet become a major source of discord. This would not be surprising, for, as we have seen, differences over arms control are essentially differences over other things. And these "other" differences seem as emotionally intractable as they are resistant to logical closure.

NOTES

1. L.S. Hagen, ed., *The Crisis in Western Security* (London: Croom Helm, 1982).
2. See Colin S. Gray, "Arms Control and European Security: Some Basic Issues," in L. S. Hagen, ed., *The Crisis in Western Security* (London: Croom Helm, 1982), pp. 94–120 at p. 108.
3. Daniel Yergin, *Shattered Peace: The Origins of the Cold War and the National Security State* (Boston: Houghton Mifflin, 1977), pp. 17–41.
4. Gray, "Arms Control and European Security," p. 99.
5. J. W. Spanier and J. L. Nogee, *The Politics of Disarmament: A Study in Soviet-American Gamesmanship* (New York: Praeger, 1962).
6. L. Freedman, "Arms Control: The Possibility of a Second Coming," in L. S. Hagen, ed., *The Crisis in Western Security* (London: Croom Helm, 1982), pp. 41–55 at p. 52.
7. E. P. Thompson, "Deterrence and Addiction," in C. F. Barnaby and G. P. Thomas, eds., *The Nuclear Arms Race: Control or Catastrophe* (London: Frances Pinter, 1982), pp. 49–72 at p. 50.
8. Stanley Hoffmann, "NATO and Nuclear Weapons: Reasons and Unreason," *Foreign Affairs* 60, no. 2 (Winter 1981–82): 327–46 at 343.
9. J. Record, *Force Reductions in Europe: Starting Over* (Cambridge, Mass.: IFPA, 1980), p. 65.
10. W. B. Prendergast, *Mutual and Balanced Force Reduction: Issues and Prospects* (Washington, D.C.: American Enterprise Institute, 1978), p. 74.

11. This is dealt with further in Philip Williams, *The Senate and US Troops in Europe 1947–1977* (forthcoming).

12. See, for example, Henry A. Kissinger, *The White House Years* (London: Weidenfeld and Nicolson, 1979), pp. 946–47.

13. *World Armaments and Disarmament: SIPRI Yearbook 1981* (London: Taylor and Francis, 1981), p. 484.

14. See Record, *Force Reductions in Europe*, pp. 63–77.

15. Stanley Hoffmann, "New Variations on Old Themes," *International Security* 4, no. 1 (Summer 1978). Contains an excellent analysis of the dangers of both decoupling and abandonment. See pp. 90–91 in particular.

16. Simon Lunn, "Cruise Missiles and the Prospects for Arms Control," *ADIU Report* 3, no. 5 (Sept./Oct. 1981): 3.

17. Hoffmann, "NATO and Nuclear Weapons," p. 340.

18. McGeorge Bundy, "America in the 1980s: Reframing Our Relations with Our Friends and Among Our Allies," *Survival* 24, no. 1 (Jan./Feb. 1982): 24–28 at 27.

19. P. Hassner, "Who Is Decoupling from Whom?," in L. S. Hagen, ed., *The Crisis in Western Security* (London: Croom Helm, 1982), pp. 168–85 at p. 178.

20. Albert Wohlstetter, "Threats and Promises of Peace," *Orbis*, Winter 1974, pp. 1107–1144 quoted in L.S. Hagen, ed., *The Crisis in Western Security* (London: Croom Helm, 1982), p. 185, note 9.

21. A. F. Burns, address in Bonn, Federal Republic of Germany, December 1, 1981, reproduced in *AEI Foreign Policy and Defense Review* 3, no. 6 (Feb. 1982): 2–5, see 4 in particular.

22. I have benefited considerably from a paper by Simon Lunn entitled "Intermediate Range Nuclear Forces—A Status Report" in developing the argument at this point.

23. See L. Freedman, "The Dilemma of Theatre Nuclear Arms Control," *Survival* 23, no. 1 (Jan./Feb. 1981): 2–10.

24. M. Clarke and M. Mowlan, eds., *Debate on Disarmament* (London: Routledge and Kegan Paul, 1982), p. 4.

25. Henry A. Kissinger, "The Realities of Security," *AEI Foreign Policy and Defense Review* 3, no. 6 (Feb. 1982): 11–16 at 14.

26. Christoph Bertram, "The Implications of Theatre Nuclear Weapons in Europe," *Foreign Affairs* 60, no. 2 (Winter 1981–82): 305–26 at 323.

4

Superpower Competition, Détente and European Security

Wolfgang Schreiber

What is one to make of a title like "Superpower Competition, Détente, and European Security"? It could be taken to imply the existence of a historical political process leading from competition to security, with "détente" acting somehow as a "hinge" or conductor between the two. This is a loaded and probably dubious interpretation, however. A more useful approach, and a more neutral one, would be to examine the analytic interpenetration of these three general concepts, all of which beg for better definition in their own right. This chapter will define and discuss these subject terms both individually and together, in order to make some observations about them and to draw certain conclusions about current problems of European security and arms control.

By taking a definitional approach to the problem, I doubtless belie a German predilection. This may limit somewhat this chapter's appeal, but it will also confer an advantage for, in the words of Clausewitz, "Only from one point of view can we perceive the sum of appearances in their homogeneity and only the homogeneity of our point of view can secure us from contradictions."

SUPERPOWER COMPETITION

The first question we might ask is, What constitutes a superpower? A superpower in the historical context of the European-dominated ancien régime was a power that critically influenced the balance of forces within a particular region at a certain time. It could exert its influence on other areas of the world, but not on the area or claims of another superpower. Concern for balance was thus a predominant characteristic of a world inhabited by many great powers, and caution was another. Political risks were taken with the understanding that if probing should fail, there was a possibility of retreat. Defeat in battle, as well, presumed punishment but not the loss of sovereignty, and certainly not the extinction of society itself.

In the European context, at least, such a world of almost genteel great power conduct ended with World War I. But a new world order had not yet been born. Many inconsistencies remained. Europe was still the planet's geopolitical center of gravity, but its shattered confidence and humbled hubris conveyed an uneasy sense about the future. Even if one cannot sense this in the public diplomacy of the interwar period, one can certainly see it in the literature and art of Europe in the 1930s. World War II brought an end to the reigning view of Europe as the center of global political and economic strength. Instead, Europe became, and remains, the center not of power but of uncertainty in the future on the East–West conflict. The very future of Europe may now rest in the hands of the world's only real superpowers—the United States and the Soviet Union.

While the actions and interactions of the United States and the Soviet Union influence the global future in disproportion to other sovereignties in the present international system, the superpowers still do not monopolize global influence. There are economic powers such as Japan, the European Community, and the wealthy oil-exporting states of the Arab world that exert considerable influence on the world's financial condition, and hence on its politics. There are also countries whose potential growth in population and economy, along with the possession of important natural resources, render them specially placed. Such states include China, Nigeria, India, Brazil, and South Africa. Nevertheless, at the present time the military and geopolitical power of the United States and the Soviet Union, and their mastery of the technological accoutrements of global influence, place them in a special category.

A second question to be posed by way of definition is, What constitutes competition? According to *Webster's New Dictionary of Synonyms*, to "compete implies to struggle to overcome or get the better of in an activity requiring two or more participants and involving rivalry." The term need not imply any agreed set of rules or any agreed set of conditions that would signify the end of the competition. Nevertheless, certain tacit rules have developed over the years that do regularize superpower competition to some degree. Acknowledgment and acceptance of such tacit rules were seemingly implied by the originator of the "peaceful coexistence" in its modern incarnation–Nikita Khrushchev. In 1959 the Soviet premier explained:

> Peaceful coexistence can and should develop into peaceful competition for the purpose of satisfying man's needs in the best possible way. We say to the leaders of the capitalist states: Let us try out in practice whose system is better, let us compete without war. This is much better than competing in who will produce more arms and who will smash whom. We stand and always will stand for such competition as will help raise the well-being of the people to a higher level.
>
> The principle of peaceful competition does not at all demand that one or another state abandon the system and ideology adopted by it.[1]

Three rules or parameters of gaming are implied within Khrushchev's remarks. First, the purpose of competition is to satisfy human needs. Second, the principle of such competition does not demand the abandonment of the ideology or social system adopted by a state. Together, these two "rules" of purpose and principle concern internal policy. They imply a benign and voluntary stance and, in theory, they allow for reversibility, for there is nothing inevitable about particular means for advancing the needs of mankind or adherence to one ideology or another. The third gaming rule implied by Khrushchev's remark concerns the character of U.S.-Soviet relations: that this competition should exclude an unbridled arms race.

The truth of the matter is that U.S.-Soviet competition in the postwar world has not resembled Khrushchev's vision of peaceful coexistence, largely because of Soviet policy itself. If Soviet policy has aimed at the satisfaction of human needs first and foremost, it has done so in a curious way. Unless human needs are defined solely by grotesquely procrustean Marxist categories, it is difficult to see how Soviet policies, from the Gulag to Gdansk, have benefited humanity. As far as the second principle is concerned—that no state is obligated to abandon its social system—it is evident that what the Soviets have persistently meant by such a remark is that whereas their social system and ideology need not be abandoned, those of the non-Marxist world are fair game for propaganda campaigns, subversion, and outright occupation by the Soviet army, within Europe and without.

As to the avoidance of an arms race between the United States and the Soviet Union, here we have a more complex issue. After World War II the Soviet Union under Stalin took full advantage of the immense power vacuum to its east and west created by the collapse of Europe and Japan and the prostration of China. This expansion was in keeping not only with the tradition of Russian imperialism but also with Lenin's sympathetic interpretation of Clausewitz. Khrushchev's intimation that the Soviet Union was ready to separate military from other means of competition flew in the face of Leninist principles and, even if Khrushchev himself believed that such a separation was possible, it never typified Soviet policies.

Given the inherent historicism of the Marxist interpretation of international politics, one can easily imagine how the Soviet leadership today perceives the flow of events since World War II. Those states that fell under the direct control of the Soviet army naturally adopted a Leninist political system and Marxist ideology: this was the contribution of Soviet power in helping along the historically inevitable. Superpower competition for the next 25 years can be defined in retrospect as the struggle from geopolitical inferiority to equality and "equal security" for the Soviet Union, notwithstanding the legacy of unsuccessful resistance to it. Certainly, as the logic would run, the decolonization of former European empires was important in this process, as was the contribution of the capitalist powers themselves by way of their recognition of Soviet strength.

But the most important element in this transition, according to the Soviet interpretation, must be the neutralization of the military advantages of the capitalist world by dint of a difficult and costly, but tireless and ultimately successful, military buildup. And while that buildup was accomplished by Leonid Brezhnev, it must be remembered that it was conceived and commenced under Nikita Khrushchev.

The approach taken by the United States and its allies to the problem of international competition has been both more diffuse and more erratic than the Soviet approach. The West has always approached the problem of competition with the Soviet Union from a defensive perspective. It became the policy of the United States early on to "contain" Soviet expansionism, but not to roll it back or attack the legitimacy and power of the Soviet state itself. All the while, the declared aim of the Soviets was to undermine and bring down Western political institutions. With its pluralist political tradition came the assumption in the West that the world was not too small for a variety of political systems. The advent of nuclear weapons, marking a qualitative contrast with the prenuclear era, reinforced the belief that different systems must learn to coexist.

It was this attitude, of course, that gave birth to the Western understanding of détente. It was assumed, further, that the Soviet leadership would have to acccept the logic of new circumstances and come to similar conclusions. Thus it was that Khrushchevian testaments such as those offered in his *Foreign Affairs* article were interpreted by many as genuine, sincere manifestations of real change in the Soviet political system. Such notions led, too, to the postulation by Western academics of a variety of "convergence" theories. These theories rested on the belief that modern technology and the constraints of the nuclear age would force the U.S. and Soviet political systems closer together and, ultimately, reduce tensions between them.

Such theories were joined, in the 1960s and early 1970s, by theories of "multipolarity," which postulated that new centers of power, and new forms of international power, were eroding the superpowers' domination of the international system. These new theories gave détente a new geopolitical rationale. It was argued that the diffusion of international power to many states, and especially the diminution of the significance of military power, would serve to constrain Soviet ambitions and limit the USSR's capacity to meddle in the affairs of weaker states. This new version of the balance of power, like its predecessors, had as its central metaphor a servomechanism—a self-regulating constellation of forces whose ebb and flow would keep international competition from getting too far out of hand. The appeal of the various multipolarity models was so great that the Nixon administration adopted a version of it and made it the theoretical centerpiece of its foreign policy—or at least the public version of it.

One can argue the extent to which such ideas were sincerely believed by the Nixon administration's foreign policy principals, but the general distinctions between Soviet and Western conceptions of competition can not be denied. These distinctions may flow from equally distinct conceptions of security.

SECURITY: EAST AND WEST

Before the subject of this chapter can be understood coherently, it must be established whether there is at least a marginally common understanding of "security"
between East and West, between the Soviet Union and the United States. If
there is not, it must be assumed that the differences are significant, for conceptions of security are the backbone of foreign policy.

The Soviet Russian perception—and here we must admit that when we
speak of the Soviet Union, we speak at the same time of its domination by ethnic
Russians—of security may be approached semantically. The Russian language
translates "security" into "without danger" (bezopánostj). Instead of expressing
security as a positive value, it expresses it as the absence of a negative value (the
absence of fear, danger, risk, and so forth). At least in the philosophical sense,
this term may be said to possess the quality of expressing movement from the
insecure to the secure. The expression of a motivation to escape danger carries
with it, perhaps, the sense of striving and competition needed for its achievement.

This very Russian notion of security is reinforced by aspects of Soviet Marxist ideology, in which the world is divided into two camps—socialist and capitalist. Security for Russians derives from the progressive transformation of the
capitalist camp into the socialist camp. The ultimate security, therefore, is a fully
Communist world. It is for this reason that the Soviets consistently described
détente not as a permanent condition of peaceful coexistence between two
camps, but as a transition period.

In Soviet thinking security is not only a "vector" pointing toward world revolution and Communist domination in the future; it is also a determining factor
for all social, economic, and military aspects of present conditions. Everything
that coincides with Communist theory about security, as interpreted by the Soviet leadership, will improve actual social, economic, and military security. This
is true canonically, even if, as is visible in the economic field, security and efficiency are in practical contradiction.

Western analysts must be very careful when they attempt to label Soviet motivations in the security field as expansionist or defensive. A sense of defensiveness is not, in the first place, incompatible with an expansionist zeal; certainly it
is not in the Russian case. Viewed from the socialist perspective, the liberation
and consequent inclusion of one country after another in the socialist camp
proves the irreversible trend of history and leads to greater security. This somewhat counterintuitive conception of security befuddles many Western statesmen, yet it is with this conception that we must come to grips if our policies are to
be based on solid ground.

According to Webster's New Dictionary of Synonyms again, "often the term
secure suggests not only a freedom from fear or danger but a position, conditions, or situation free from all hazards." At least in English, to be "secure" implies more an end result than a process or "vector" toward it. A door is secure,

for example, when it is closed or locked tight. Security, in this sense, implies a certain rigidity or finality.

Moreover, in English and other European languages, security is linked to organizations. A trade union can be responsible for the security of income and employment, a bank for the security of money deposited. A government is responsible for providing security from external encroachment. In the Western conception, security is almost a "thing" or an object, instead of an evolving condition. It can also be seen as more of an absolute concept—one can have it or not have it—than as a relative concept, wherein one can never be totally secure.

It may be said, then, that Western perceptions of security are grounded in a concern for stability. Democracies, in a sense, are based on controlled instability, a condition where the alternation of government between coalitions and political forces can take place within an agreed framework. Governmental centers of gravity, so to speak, can be shifted by elections without casting suspicions of illegitimacy on the entire political system. The price of such stability is that to be legitimate, political actors must agree to the rules of the game, which generally eliminates extremism of all sorts from contention. Liberty, therefore, is one pillar of democratic politics, and prudence is another. A Western foreign policy of realpolitik must take both of these considerations to heart if it is to succeed in its purposes; it must not violate its domestic underpinning.

The Western perception of security, as it has evolved since World War II, has tended to favor a more mechanistic approach to democratic politics. Liberty is less important—democracy is more "administered" by huge state apparatuses than it is exercised. This has engendered a certain alienation in the body politic, especially in Europe, and contributed to the decline of the effectiveness of political parties. Individuals, and even party leaders, have lost their passion; they look at their own government, and at the alliance, as means for the attainment of security to be judged impartially. Thus, the means used by governments to ensure security have alienated the citizen from the ends of security.

What do these differences between Eastern and Western notions of security tell us? The Russian notion presumes a capacity to live in a world whose conditions produce ambiguity with respect to security; the Western notion demands a final reckoning. Nevertheless, Western political culture has at its base a set of values concerning the worth and responsibility of the individual that sets the efficiency of "organizational man" in attaining this closure in contradiction to the very values he seeks to protect. The Soviets have no problem in this regard; as the collectivity goes, so goes the individual. If full security is not obtained, the individual sees himself as losing no more, gaining no more, than anyone else. Compared with the Eastern sense of security, the Western version is a formula for internal tension. Compared with the Western version, the Eastern is less demanding in one sense, and more confident in another.

How do Europe's historically grounded notions of security fit between these admittedly ideal types of "security"? Europeans have lived for centuries as if on a chessboard of international politics. Notions of absolute security that found a hospitable psychological environment in America were never able to set deep roots in Europe. Thus, Europeans are quite conversant with a relativistic attitude toward security. On the other hand, it was within European political culture that individual liberty was first enthroned as the highest of social values. To put it simply, Europe's "heart" is with America, but most of its experience is not.

DÉTENTE

As can be surmised from the foregoing discussion, détente is a concept that has different meanings in East and in West. As a consequence the term has occasionally been cause for more confusion than clarity. Its espousal or denunciation has, in the context of American and European politics, been an envelope for both broader and more parochial political argument. Thus, for example, President Ford sought to strike the use of the word from the White House vocabulary in 1976, lest the challenge on his right from Ronald Reagan overwhelm his chances of remaining in office.

In Western languages, especially in American English today, détente is used in many ways. For the more dovish, détente is something of a lost golden age from which we have been driven by Neanderthal cold warriors. For old hawks and prodigal hawks, détente signifies an era of blushing confusion and political deterioration from which we have passed. For analysts of many political stripes, the "decade of détente" is a convenient phrase that serves to bracket an era in U.S. foreign policy from the political dénouement of the Vietnam War in the late 1960s to the rise of the Republican right in the early 1980s.

Perhaps the ambivalence of the word itself is one reason for its enduring popularity. Coming from the French, *détente dans les relations internationales,* according to Larousse, means "relaxation of international tensions." On the other hand, the French phrase *presser sur la détente* means "to pull the trigger," and not only to increase tension. In certain respects, then, *détente* in its original language fits very nicely with the Soviet understanding of the term, wherein there is no contradiction between the gradual dispersing and the sudden discharging of tensions. Indeed, the Russian word most closely equivalent to détente, *razriadka,* also can mean both the dispersal and the discharging of tensions.

As distinct from the varying uses of the term "détente" in contemporary Western political culture, the Soviets have something rather more singular and definite in mind. Détente, as mentioned earlier, is viewed as a transitory stage of international politics signifying the attainment of effective global political parity of the socialist camp with the capitalist. In other words, the increase in Soviet strength has forced the capitalist world into a "more sober" attitude toward socialist countries and, as a result, has reduced the risk of war. It stands to reason, from a Russian point of view (and not only a Russian point of view), that an enemy's weakness discourages his resort to arms except in final desperation. Tensions can be dispersed, in other words, because the capitalist world can no longer afford the risks they bring.

It is important to understand, from the Soviet point of view, what this attitude means and what it does not mean. It does mean that "peaceful coexistence," the theoretical concept prior to détente in Soviet thinking, can be the effective, long-term political tool that Lenin had hoped it would be. The Western acquiesence to détente—that is how it is viewed in Moscow—allows the Soviet Union to chip away at Western interests in various ways without fear that it will be punished with war, at least not as an act of policy. Gone are the days of massive retaliation. It also means that the integrity of the socialist camp—via the Brezhnev Doctrine—similarly can be maintained without excessive risk. Thus, the suppression of uprisings in Eastern Europe is easier to contemplate the more détente is entrenched as a principle of East–West relations. The Soviets took very seriously the Sonnenfeldt Doctrine, which, as a part of détente, seemed to indicate that the United States would not let its bilateral relations with the Soviet Union be influenced by Soviet policies in Eastern Europe.

The Soviet understanding of détente, by its very definition, implies that, at some stage, détente will deteriorate. The dialectical structure of Marxist thinking mandates that tensions will reappear so long as the capitalist camp exists in some form. The question is: What will be the new balance of forces between East and West when tensions recur? The tireless efforts of the Soviet military during the entire decade of détente provide a vivid glimpse of what Moscow hoped for and, for the most part, achieved. The balance of military power has shifted; détente achieved its basic purpose.

If this is what détente means from the Soviet perspective, what does it not mean? It does not mean precisely what Western publics were led to believe would be the fruits of better U.S.–Soviet relations. It does not mean that each superpower will forego attempts to seek unilateral advantage at the expense of the other, thus reducing the chance of confrontation, war, and catastrophe. It does not mean a mutual acceptance that great power competition in the nuclear age is somehow qualitatively different from what it was in centuries past. It does not mean a liberalization of closed societies as the threat of war and tension diminishes, but a license for greater suppression. And, with respect to arms control, détente never meant, from the Soviet point of view, an effort to stabilize the arms race at parity, thereby quarantining nuclear weapons from international politics. There was never a moralist or pacifist strain to Soviet expectations of arms control, as there was to Western expectations. Instead, the Soviets saw SALT as a way to slow down Western arms programs while their own went forward—and, indeed, that is the most obvious legacy of the SALT experience.

It must be said, for the sake of fairness, that President Nixon and Dr. Kissinger understood at the outset that a military balance had to be maintained if the political advantages of détente were to be reaped. They insisted that military détente—arms control on strategic, theater, and conventional levels—not be separated from economic and political détente. They also saw the danger of allowing the Soviet cultivation of détente with the countries of Western Europe to progress in such a way as to drive a wedge into the Atlantic Alliance. Nevertheless, Soviet diplomacy and political weakness in the White House, as well as a recalcitrant U.S. Congress, led precisely to a double separation: the military aspects of détente both from each other and from the economic and political; and the European "version" of détente from the American. These divisions first announced themselves in the wake of the Yom Kippur War, and have been repeating themselves ever since. We are living today with the accumulated consequences. Indeed, we are faced today with the collision of these two problems.

How is this so? Despite the intention to move military and political/economic aspects of détente in parallel, American technology transfers and trade credits long preceded the resolution of SALT I in 1972—itself a disappointing achievement. So, too, did the quadripartite agreement on Berlin in 1971 and the beginning of the Conference on Security and Cooperation in Europe (CSCE) process, both of which had the effect of convincing West European publics that the Soviet Union had ceased to be a threat to them. It also convinced a great many that Communism could have a human face, and in the aftermath of these events, the curious phenomenon of Eurocommunism became headline news.

While détente between the Soviet Union and Western Europe began to take on concrete shape in human and economic terms, U.S.–Soviet détente remained somewhat diffuse and abstract. A great deal centered on the promise of SALT to reduce the danger of nuclear war and stabilize the arms race. Of course, when the SALT process showed that it could do no such thing by itself, the hopes that went with it merely contributed to the gulf that developed between U.S. and West European interests in détente as each understood it.

The United States also understood, early in the period of détente, that the military aspects of détente should be pursued together. SALT should not proceed without Mutual and Balanced Force Reductions (MBFR). Neither should be concluded without consideration being given to the theater nuclear balance. But the political pressure of SALT also led to a deterioration of this resolve. Moreover, the failure of SALT to constrain Soviet central strategic programs, and of MBFR to reduce the Soviet conventional preponderance, has made the theater balance all the more crucial. And here, too, as détente proceeded in Europe, the Soviets were augmenting their military strength and changing facts. In other words, the theater nuclear balance in Europe has reached maximum criticality just as European and American conceptions of détente have reached maximum divergence.

CONCLUSIONS

If anything is clear, it is that the renewal of America's military vitality and economic health is the key to what will become of Europe's security in the next few years. To the extent that America is strong and confident, it can lead. To the extent that it cannot lead, Moscow can interfere. American strength and leadership, however, do not preclude a new and more realistic détente relationship with the Soviet Union. Such a new strength need not imply a return to the "cold war"—as if such a thing were possible!—or an increased danger of war. But neither is holding out incentives to the Soviet Union for responsible international conduct appeasement, anymore than the traditional tools of diplomacy are ipso facto appeasement. Détente need not be a symbol of Western weakness any more than Western military modernization need be a symbol of cold war.

If the security of Europe is not to suffer again, however, the new détente must differ from the old in three ways. First, détente must not be sold to the American or European public in messianic garb, as if it could somehow negate the realities of superpower competition or transform a Marxist-Leninist empire into a status quo power. Détente must not be painted as an opposite to the era that preceded it, but as a modest method of removing a degree of acrimony and uncertainty from superpower relations in the interests of preserving peace.

Second, the United States and its allies should not allow the Soviet Union to make use of reduced tensions to unilaterally augment its military capabilities; the linkage between arms control negotiations on various levels and other aspects of U.S.- and West European–Soviet relations must be maintained consistently and predictably. This does not mean that every Soviet trespass or probe in the Third World should be justification for severing all communication between the sides, but it does mean that arms control cannot be sanctified as if it evolves in a political vacuum.

Third, it is high time that the Soviet Union be denied a free ride with respect to the "ideological struggle." We need to dedicate ourselves to competitive intellectual penetration of the Soviet Union and Eastern Europe, lest Western policy eventually become paralyzed by its habitual defensiveness. We sometimes act as if Communism was so obviously unappealing that combating it is not worth our time, but this is not so. Indeed, the target of such a penetration should be the Kremlin itself, the Soviet decision center. Using the facts of reality in the Soviet Union and applying the Communist analysis of society to the Soviet Union itself will have a greater impact on the Soviet leadership than anything else we might concoct. European governments and opinion makers have a special role to play in this competitive intellectual penetration because European culture stands to suffer first and foremost from a failure to stem Soviet expansionism.

Finally, Europe's taking a more active role as an advocate of liberty and democracy, as a center of intellectual gravity, may partially compensate for its unavoidably subsidiary role in military matters and the psychological consequences of such a role. Neutralist sentiment in Europe is partly a consequence of the frustrating helplessness of not being in control of one's own destiny. In some quarters a lack of real responsibility for one's fate has been translated into an equivocal attitude about one's values. It is, after all, a natural response to avoid valuing something that cannot be defended, lest the anticipated loss be too much to bear.

But the course of history is not determined solely by willful men, nor by sheer force alone. The resolve to influence political developments by influencing "the hearts and minds of people" is a more decisive historical factor than military force. The latter, of course, must be maintained to deter aggression. It must be credible and effective to signal to the Soviet Union that neither political pressure nor physical attack will succeed and result in its victory.

Against this background the intellectual struggle must be waged for our values. Values that democracies stand for are so much more appealing, especially to those who are shown the socialist reality. The West and especially Europe should concentrate on this evident superiority that it has rather than on attaining equality in the military sector so dear to any totalitarian state.

NOTES

1. Nikita Khrushchev, "Peaceful Coexistence," *Foreign Affairs*, vol. 38, no. 1 (October 1959), p. 3.

PART III:

Arms Control and Asian Security

5

Arms Control in East Asia

Hiroshi Kimura

INTRODUCTION

The subject of arms control most commonly calls to mind such historical events as the Strategic Arms Limitation Talks (SALT), the Strategical Arms Reduction Talks (START), the Mutual Balanced Force Reduction (MBFR), or Intermediate-Range Nuclear Forces (INF), which are mainly concerned with military controls in the European theater. If one delves into the subject of arms control in East Asia, it soon becomes clear that few writers have ventured to study the problem closely. Indeed, the would-be student is scarcely able to find even one article dealing with the topic of arms control in East Asia.[1]

Such benign neglect can be ascribed to the situation of relative calm that has prevailed in East Asia in recent years. However, as some have noted, the days of peaceful prosperity and coexistence among neighbors in the region may be numbered.[2] East Asia is the only area of the world where the interests of four of the major powers—the United States, the Soviet Union, the People's Republic of China (PRC), and Japan—converge, conflict, and sometimes clash. Such equilibrium as exists among the four powers is always very delicate. The presence of two "divided" nations—China and Korea—is a further complicating factor. Particularly noteworthy is the fact that the Soviet Union has been pursuing a policy of military buildup in the region. In contrast, the United States, which in the past has demonstrated much ambivalence and zigzagging in its defense policies and strategies for East Asia, is now showing signs of withdrawing its commitment to the defense of the region, as illustrated by the one-time decision of President Jimmy Carter to withdraw U.S. ground forces from Korea.

The issue of arms control in East Asia becomes a focal issue, then, if we also consider that in an age of globalization, what happens in one part of the world is closely linked to and may affect what happens in other parts. Thus, tension or relaxation of tension in one region immediately and easily affects the situation in another region as a result of the efficiency of modern developments in military technology and transportation. For these and other reasons, the question of arms control in Europe or any other part of the world cannot be separated from the situation in East Asia.

In order to discuss the question of arms control in any part of the globe, it is necessary to assess exactly the existing military situation in that area. Only after that are we able to judge which countries should reduce which forces to what extent. This is more easily said than done, for a variety of reasons. First of all, the "Communist" bloc countries have refused to release to the public needed data on their military affairs. Second, the assessment and comparison of military forces involves not only numbers of weapons but also their quality, and logistics. And, finally, the intentions and moral determinations of the country's leaders must be scrutinized.

Besides these general difficulties, in East Asia we must add one more reason, a very complicated power configuration that is far more inscrutable than that of Europe. In Europe there is a rather clear-cut division of two camps: the Warsaw Pact states, headed by the USSR, and the NATO states, led by the United States. This classification coincides with the ideological confrontation, which may be described in shorthand as Communism versus capitalism. In contrast, the picture in East Asia is neither as simple nor as clearly defined. In this region alliances among nations are not as historically and culturally bound, and thus may change more drastically over time. One of the major reasons for this complexity in power configuration in East Asia is the conflict between the two Communist giants, the USSR and the PRC. To complicate matters even further, the PRC has allied itself de facto with the capitalist countries, especially the United States and Japan, since the late 1970s. Even so, no one can say with certainty for how long and to what extent the United States and Japan will be able to rely on the PRC as their staunch ally.

Still, we can look at the power configuration in East Asia as a triangular one, whereas in Europe it is bipolar, between East and West. The picture becomes more complicated because of the de facto existence of two Chinas. Whereas both the United States and Japan have normalized diplomatic relations solely with the PRC in legal terms, both seem to trust the Republic of China (ROC) more than the PRC when it comes to strategic-military affairs, since the former is a capitalist country and the latter is a Communist one. The People's Republic of Korea (North Korea) is another complicating factor. It is without doubt a Communist state, but again, because of the Sino-Soviet conflict and the rapprochement of the PRC with the United States and Japan, the question arises as to which of the Communist giants North Korea is linked more closely ideologically, politically, diplomatically, strategically, and economically.

THE MILITARY SITUATION

As a result of this complicated power configuration in East Asia, a quantitative comparison of military forces demands some careful consideration. As for the ground forces, the Soviet Union has deployed about 51 divisions (460,000 men) on or near the Sino-Soviet border, out of which 39 divisions (360,000 men) are deployed in the Far East (roughly east of Lake Baikal).[3] Soviet ground forces around Japan include one division in Kamchatka, three divisions in Sakhalin, 16 divisions in the Maritime Provinces, and one division in what Japan claims as its Northern Islands. Along the Sino-Soviet border China currently fields 66 army divisions and 41 divisions of border guards with a total strength of some 1.5 million.[4] U.S. ground forces deployed in the Far East-Pacific region are about 28,000 troops stationed in the Republic of Korea, about 2,300 army personnel in Japan, and 30,800 in Hawaii.[5] The ground forces of the Japanese Self-Defense Forces (SDF) comprise 13 divisions (155,000 men).

As for operational combat aircraft, the Soviet Union has deployed about 2,210 aircraft in the Far East. The significant increase in combat aircraft is illustrated clearly by the 150 new-type aircraft that were added in the region in 1980–81, which equals almost a third of the number of aircraft deployed by the United States in the region. Furthermore, it is reported that more than ten Backfire bombers have been deployed at inland bases in Siberia.[6] In contrast, U.S. Air Force units deployed in East Asia and the Western Pacific possess a total of only 260 combat aircraft and 35,000 personnel.[7] The whole air force of the PRC consists of some 6,000 combat aircraft[8] and 490,000 personnel.[9]

When it comes to naval capability, the comparison of forces is somewhat simpler. The PRC and both Koreas have navies, but their capability is limited to their own offshore defense. Thus, as suggested by Naotoshi Sakonjo, former vice admiral of the Japanese maritime SDF, and presently a commentator on naval affairs, one need only estimate the naval strength and size of the USSR, on the one hand, and the United States and Japan, on the other.[10] The U.S. Seventh Fleet covers East Asia and the Western Pacific, and in a war or other state of emergency, the U.S. Third Fleet, covering the eastern Pacific, is expected to join and assist the Seventh Fleet. Thus we must add the U.S. Pacific Fleet, consisting mainly of the Third and Seventh fleets, to the Japanese maritime SDF as a navy force against the Soviet Pacific Fleet.

The Soviet Pacific Fleet possesses about 800 warships with a total displacement of 1.58 million tons and 121,000 personnel. The recent enhancement of this fleet is quite impressive. It has introduced to the region the aircraft carrier *Minsk*, the latest Kara-class missile cruiser, the assault landing ship *Ivan Rogov*, and nuclear-powered submarines.[11] In contrast, the U.S. Pacific Fleet has about 230 warships and 21,000 personnel. The Japanese maritime SDF has about 130 warships (207,000 tons) and 44,000 personnel.

In the field of nuclear forces, about 30 percent of the Soviet Union's strategic missiles—intercontinental ballistic missiles (ICBMs) and submarine-launched ballistic missiles (SLBMs)—are believed to be deployed in the Far East. As for theater nuclear forces, SS-20 missiles and TU-22M Backfire bombers are being introduced in this region following their deployment in Europe. About 50 Backfire bombers deployed in the Far East are now considered to have an enhanced capability to attack land targets in Japan, its sea-lanes, and U.S. forces deployed in the western Pacific, including the units of the Seventh Fleet.[12] The SS-20, numbering between about 75[13] and 100,[14] are believed to be able to cover the entire Japanese archipelago and almost all of East Asia with a range of 4,400 kilometers if fired from bases in the Soviet Far East. The American SLBM force deployed in the Pacific is defined by U.S. Secretary of Defense Caspar Weinberger as a nuclear deterrence to the Soviet SS-20.[15]

The above is a rough outline of the existing military arsenal situated in East Asia. Of course, this simple quantitative comparison of numbers of weapons does not tell the whole story. Qualitative aspects, such as the precision of weapons, must be compared as well. Moreover, politico-diplomatic and geographical factors, such as number and military capability of allies and accessibility of bases, ports, and straits, also greatly affect the military balance. However, it is very difficult to assess accurately these nonquantitative indexes, and different conclusions have been drawn by different analysts.[16]

THREE INTERPRETATIONS

Three views have been advanced concerning the military balance or imbalance in East Asia. The first view holds that the Soviet Union is still inferior in military strategy to the United States and its allies in East Asia. This view is held by many Western observers, and it is perhaps also believed by the Soviets. For example, B.N. Slavinskii, then academic secretary of the Far Eastern branch of the Soviet Academy of Sciences, has pointed out the contrast between a strong United States and a weak USSR, presenting a picture of a heavily handicapped USSR in the Pacific. He first underlines the advantageous position of the United States, which has at its disposal not only highly sophisticated military weapons but also a strong network of military bases and control of many strategic straits:

> As has been already pointed out above, the USA in this region [the Pacific] is equipped with a branch system of bases and maintains a huge unity of army–navy forces, including atomic aircraft carriers, submarines with atomic rockets and nuclear warheads. Having army–navy bases located close to the USSR territory . . . the USA has been concentrating its efforts in strategically important zones of the great ocean. By establishing control of these straits, the USA is intending to create all the conditions for security supremacy in this region in the case of outbreak of military action.[17]

Slavinskii then stresses another handicap of the Soviet Union, the lack of bases and free access to the Pacific Ocean: "The Soviet Pacific Fleet, without overseas bases, must overcome huge space-area in order to operate in the ocean and be able to pass by force those straits which are under the supervision of the USA and its allies."[18]

The second view concerning the state of military capability in East Asia holds that the balance of military-strategic power in the East Asia-Pacific Ocean region has been moving increasingly in favor of the USSR, mainly because of the remarkable buildup of the Soviet navy. The bases of the Soviet Pacific Fleet have been strengthened and their area of operation greatly enlarged. The principal Soviet base is Vladivostok, whose port is now being kept open by icebreakers even through the coldest months of the year, December to February. The second base is Sovetskaia Gavan, which has been the subject of much protest in Japan because of its radar installations on Sakhalin and the Kurile Islands. Petropavlovsk, the third base, has the great advantage of not being dependent on straits that are controlled, or partially controlled, by other countries.[19] The Sea of Okhotsk has almost become a sanctuary[20] for Soviet Delta submarines, which are capable of launching missiles (probably SS-N-18) having the precision and range to hit targets on the west coast of the United States.

The operation of the Soviet Pacific Fleet has extended to the Sea of Japan and the Pacific Ocean, and, as a result of Soviet victories, into several areas of crucial importance. Najin, a warm-water port linked to Vladivostok by rail, has been a Soviet base since a 1979 treaty with North Korea. Facilities at Cam Ranh Bay and Danang in Vietnam have been exploited by the Soviet Pacific Fleet since the 1978, and especially the 1980, cooperation treaties between the two countries. These developments have underscored the (somewhat exaggerated) words of Admiral James Holloway III, chief of naval operations, who declared in 1976: "In 1953, for example, the U.S. Navy operated task forces in the Sea of Japan. . . . We did so without fear of interference from the Soviets. . . . [However] I would have to say that today, any similar operations that we would want to conduct in the Sea of Japan would be with the sufferance of the Soviets."[21] With regard to the Pacific Ocean, Admiral Holloway stated: "Only a decade ago, the Pacific Ocean was called the 'American Lake.' Today, however, the naval supremacy of the United States in this vast area is being challenged by the Soviet Pacific Fleet."[22]

The third view concerning the current military status of East Asia claims that the Soviet Union has not yet reached the capability of the United States and its allies in East Asia, particularly when one takes into consideration both the quantitative aspects of weapons technology and the geographical, diplomatic-political disadvantages and handicaps that the USSR must overcome. At the same time, holders of this viewpoint have warned that the Americans and their allies may sooner or later be catapulted into the disastrous position of bowing to Soviet supremacy unless they make special efforts to prevent it.

The Soviet intention to obtain parity with, and then superiority over the United States and its allies is clear, and the facts show that this intention is being fervently put into practice. It is also clear that, despite its gestures of commitment, the United States is no longer able to undertake by itself the burden of coping with the buildup of the Soviet military forces in East Asia as it once did.

More realistically, the United States seems to have shifted to a strategy of sharing the military burden with Japan, the PRC, and other countries in the region. If this is the case, the chances are that if cooperation and an understanding of the mutual burden are not achieved between the United States and its East Asian allies, Washington may unilaterally limit the forward deployment of its military power, with the result that it may help the Soviets achieve military supremacy in the region.

ARMS CONTROL PROPOSALS: MOTIVES AND RESPONSES

Considering the facts and assessments of the military power balance in East Asia as described above, what kind of arms control proposals have been actually made? Unfortunately, no serious arms control proposals have been raised for the region. Some discussion of the reasons for this state of affairs will be offered following a brief examination of some of the "proposals" that have been brought forth.

Looking first at the Soviet Union, a proposal for arms control in Asia was introduced by Leonid Brezhnev in a speech addressed to the 26th CPSU Congress on February 23, 1981. In defining the term "confidence-building measures" used in the speech, Brezhnev explained:

> There is a region where we need to devise and apply confidence-building measures. . . . This is the Far East, where such powers as the Soviet Union, China and Japan are neighbors. . . . *The Soviet Union would be ready to hold specific talks with all interested countries on confidence-building measures in the Far East.* In submitting these far-reaching proposals on measures of confidence-building, we proceed from the fact that their implementation will also cause further progress in the cause of disarmament.[23]

The system of "confidence-building measures" initiated at Helsinki by the Conference on Security and Cooperation in Europe (CSCE) is the most recent expression of this traditional approach to the problem of disarmament. Its object is to reassure states about the political and military postures of their enemies and to demonstrate that their fears are groundless by undertaking various practical measures, such as prior notifications and observations of military maneuvers and movements. The implicit assumption is that once the uncertainties and misunderstandings are dispelled, the states of Europe will be willing to take more positive steps of arms control.[24] But no one has taken seriously the idea of constructing "confidence-building measures" for the Far East made by the general secretary of the Communist Party of the Soviet Union. Instead, the proposal is regarded simply as lip service, an appeal to the peace movement, or merely a gesture aimed at giving the impression that the Soviet Union is an advocate of peace. Particularly cool toward this proposal are the Japanese, who have long felt that the primary responsibility of the Soviets, as far as building up confidence with the Japanese is concerned, can be discharged by commencing a withdrawal of their military forces from the Japanese-claimed Northern Islands.

B. N. Slavinskii proposed measures for arms control between the USSR and the United States in the Pacific region. He contended:

> In the contemporary age one must refuse the old-fashioned idea of achieving "security" by means of unilateral military (and, particularly, army-military) superiority, as well as "supplement" these efforts by "coalition" of allies and vassals. Relaxation of the tension of the arms race between the Soviet Union and the USA has a decisive meaning for peace and security in the Pacific region. . . . Considering the accumulated experience of negotiations between these two countries on military problems, one can expect in the future the extension of this approach in the Pacific Ocean as well.[25]

This proposal also raises doubts about the seriousness of Soviet intentions, particularly because it came from the same Soviet spokesman who has recognized the weak position of the Soviet Union vis-à-vis the United States in the Far East. In general, Western Soviet watchers are convinced that so long as the Soviet Union has not achieved parity with the United States in this theater, the Soviets do not want a bona fide system of arms control.

Some Japanese opposition parties and intellectuals have proposed disarmament and arms control measures in East Asia and the Pacific with such slogans as "Let's Create a Non-nuclear Peace Zone in the Asia-Pacific" and "The Indian Ocean: A Peace Zone." However, almost all of these proposals remain simple political idioms, broad and abstract in meaning, and without much elaboration on the practical steps required to achieve stated goals.

The proposal to change the Sea of Japan into "the Lake of Peace" is a bit more concrete. It states, first, that the Sea of Japan must remain nonnuclear and that the deployment of nuclear aircraft carriers, warships, and submarines must be prohibited. It then specifies that aircraft and ground forces equipped with nuclear weapons are strictly banned from the sea. Second, it prohibits the conduct of naval exercises in the Sea of Japan. Third, it contends that, as a result of these measures, the Sea of Japan must be opened to all countries to serve as a route for trade and economic exchange. It is believed that these stringent guidelines, if followed faithfully, will be a valuable precedent or model for world peace that can be duplicated by other countries in other regions. But for all such proposals to materialize, a first necessary precondition is that Japan, the USSR, the United States, and North and South Korea come to the negotiating table to discuss the proposal. This is hardly likely at the present time.

The Japanese government under Prime Minister Zenko Suzuki has held the position that it is desirable for President Reagan's "zero-options" proposals for limiting medium-range and tactical nuclear weapons to be extended to Asia. Elaborating on this idea, Suzuki pointed out in his speech to the Japanese Diet on February 19, 1982:

> President Reagan has been proposing that the United States shall not deploy medium-range missiles if the USSR is willing to withdraw its own medium-range missiles from Europe. Japan wishes and supports that the same principle be applied in the Far East.[26]

Moreover, Shinichinro Asao, director-general of the U.S. Department of the Japanese Foreign Ministry, told a Diet committee that Japan had asked the United States to make Soviet weapons in the Far East a subject of the U.S.–Soviet negotiations on theater nuclear weapons reduction.[27] And, in the same session of the Diet, Foreign Minister Yoshio Sakurauchi mentioned that Japan had demanded of the Soviet Union, on the occasion of the Japan–USSR working-level talks held at Moscow in February 1982, that such theater nuclear missiles as SS-20s, SS-4s, and SS-5s be removed from the Far East.[28] Unfortunately, the Soviets do not seem to have any intention of taking these requests seriously. The statement made by Major General Viktor Strozuvokh, chief spokesman on the disarmament issue in the General Staff Headquarters of the Soviet Armies, is a good example. In an interview in February 1982 with the Kyodo News Service, Strozuvokh is quoted as having said bluntly that "in the Far East there are no superfluous weapons deployed by the USSR."[29] In an interview with *Asahi Shimbun* in February 1982, another official at the Soviet Ministry of Foreign Affairs clearly stated, "It is impossible for us to include the Far East in the theater nuclear weapon limitation talks, which have already been started."[30]

OBSTACLES TO ARMS CONTROL IN EAST ASIA

Let us now return to the question of why no serious proposals of arms control have been made in East Asia. Many factors may be addressed, but three are most significant.

The first lies in the prevailing "Europe first, Asia and the rest of the world second" line of thinking. No discussion on security-related affairs can be truly complete if it fails to take a global perspective. It is easy to recognize that security in the Atlantic, the Middle East, the Pacific, and other parts of the globe are inseparably linked. Nevertheless, world leaders have tended to look first at the situation of Europe and to consider any proposals and talks on arms control from the European point of view. Since the withdrawal of the French from Indochina, the Dutch from Indonesia, and the British from east of the Suez between the late 1940s and the early 1970s, it appears that Europeans have lost interest in the military developments in East Asia and the Pacific. The war fought by the

United States in Vietnam concerned them mainly because it drained U.S. military manpower and other resources from what they considered the more important task of defending NATO in Europe.[31]

Europe also occupies the first position in the list of geographical priorities for the Soviet Union. Malcolm Mackintosh, a British expert on Soviet external and military affairs writes: "Whatever aims and interests the Soviet Union may have are those of a European power and a global power in Asia, not those of an Asian power."[32] Soviet international behavior sometimes causes doubt that the Kremlin leaders have any definite policy designed exclusively for Asia. They seem almost automatically to apply in Asia those policies that have been successful in Europe. One good example is Brezhnev's proposal of Asian collective security, an idea that was revived after the European Security Conference had adopted the Helsinki Declaration. At that time Soviet commentator Vladmir Kudryavtsev wrote in *Izvestiia* that the principles adopted at Helsinki were "universally applicable to Asia."[33] Brezhnev's proposal of confidence-building measures in the Far East at the 26th Communist Party Congress (1981) is really nothing more than a simple, mechanical application of the confidence-building measures outlined in the Helsinki Declaration (1975).

The "Europe first, Asia next" way of thinking as it relates to arms control contains both positive and negative aspects. On the positive side, thanks to existence of precedents reached in Europe after prolonged, painstaking efforts, arms control in East Asia might be rather easily and promptly promoted when the issue is pushed to the forefront. But the negative side is that the concentration on Europe first has usually tended to delay arms control efforts in East Asia. Not only this, but agreements on arms control in Europe may be made at the sacrifice of security in Asia. More concretely, arms reduced in the European theater—such as the SS-20s, SS-4s, and SS-5s—may ultimately be transferred to the Asian theater.

This is exactly what Japanese politicians and intellectuals fear, as expressed by a senior Japanese Foreign Ministry official who told a Diet committee that "If Soviet medium-range missiles removed [from Europe] are transferred to the [East] area beyond the Urals, they will become a threat to Japan."[34] Tomohisa Sakanaka, commentator on defense affairs for *Asahi Shimbun*, writes that "Success in reaching an agreement on arms control in Europe does not make any sense if it simply means that arms will be transferred to the East beyond the Urals."[35] And the Soviet Union is reported by the AFP News Agency to be planning to demolish or to move any SS-20s that it will reduce from its European arsenal to the Far Eastern part of the USSR.[36] At any rate, because of this apprehension, one can say that Japanese attitudes toward theater nuclear weapons reduction talks in Europe are somewhat ambivalent.

The second reason that arms control efforts in East Asia have remained in an embryonic, primitive stage can be ascribed to the region's complicated power configuration. Unlike Europe, where there is bipolar opposition between the NATO and the Warsaw Pact member countries, in East Asia it is sometimes hard to tell which countries are friends and which are enemies. Taking the PRC as an example, it is hard to know to what extent the PRC can be relied upon as an ally for the Western powers. One cannot completely deny the possibility in the more distant future of a Sino–Soviet rapprochement. Furthermore, there are rivalries in the region between the PRC and the ROC, and between the two Koreas. It is thus hard to imagine that all of these countries will one day sit down together for discussions on arms control. No such conference has ever been held in Asia.

The last reason, but certainly not the least, for the poor progress in arms control in East Asia seems to lie in the ambivalent and unrealistic attitude of one of the major countries there: Japan. It is an undeniable fact that, unlike 15 or 20 years ago, what Japan does or does not do in its security policies has great importance to East Asian countries in both economic and noneconomic fields. Although its share of the gross national product is very small, about 0.9 percent, in quantitative terms, the percentage of the national budget given to defense expenditures ranks eighth in the world. It has recently become almost customary for U.S. politicians to pronounce that Japan is the cornerstone of U.S. defense policy in Asia.

It is quite understandable and desirable for Japan, being the sole country that has suffered atomic bombardments, to be active in movements toward nuclear disarmament. Japanese intellectuals engaged particularly in natural science, literature, art, and music have organized a movement to appeal for the annihilation of nuclear weapons. Writers who are supporters of the movement have received letters from Brezhnev that fully supported their cause,[37] and they are expected to receive a similar response from the heads of the United States, West Germany, and France.

There are, however, many problems in this Japanese approach to arms control. One is the extreme Japanese disdain for possessing nuclear weapons. They are so obsessed with their experience in the Hiroshima holocaust that they cannot recognize the deterrence capability of nuclear weapons. Dr. Masamichi Inoki, president of the Research Institute of Peace and Security, Tokyo, believes that without U.S. nuclear weapons, Japan is vulnerable to war in the future. Unfortunately, this sober view is not shared by the majority of Japanese.

Second, the Japanese seem to be very impatient to attain the goal of disarmament all at once. Although not infrequently used almost as synonyms, disarmament and arms control are really two different things. Disarmament means the elimination of weapons, while arms control means the management of them.[38] What the Japanese have been advocating is often not so much arms control as disarmament—and sometimes complete disarmament. Surely disarmament has long been an aspiration of human beings everywhere, yet it is one that is far from being realized. Even the most ambitious plan for disarmament does not envisage a world totally without arms. Such a world is almost impossible to imagine, let alone create.[39] A necessary, though not a sufficient, requirement for serious arms control in East Asia is therefore a more realistic and pragmatic attitude on the part of the Japanese people and their government.

NOTES

1. After completing this article, I became aware of the following literature on the subject of arms control in East Asia: John H. Barton and Ryukichi Imai, eds., *Arms Control II* (Cambridge, Mass.: Oelgeschlager, Gunn, and Hain, 1981); Reinhard Drifte, "Japan and Regional Arms Control in the Asia–Pacific Region," *Proceedings of the Annual Meeting of the British Association for Japanese Studies* 6, pt. 1 (1981): 202–08; Makoto Momoi, "From Disarmament to Arms Control," *Trialogue*, Summer/Fall 1982, pp. 14–17; Takahiro Yokomichi, "Security and Disarmament," ibid., pp. 40–45.

2. Hiroshi Kimura, "Soviet Strategy in Northeast Asia," *Problems of Communism* 30, no. 5 (September–October 1981): 71.

3. *The Military Balance 1981–1982* (London: International Institute for Soviet Studies, 1981), p. 12; *Asian Security 1980* (Tokyo: Research Institute for Peace and Security, 1980), p. 30; *Defense of Japan 1981* (Tokyo: The Japan Times, Ltd., 1981), p. 78.

4. *Defense of Japan 1981*, p. 96.

5. Ibid., pp. 87–88, 90.

6. Ibid.

7. Ibid., p. 87.

8. Ibid., p. 95.

9. *Military Balance 1981–82*, p. 75.

10. Naotoshi Sakonjo, *Kaijo-boei-ron* (Tokyo: Kojimachi-shobo, 1982), p. 41.

11. *Defense of Japan 1981*, pp. 80–81.

12. *Sankei Shimbun*, January 1, 1982.

13. *Soviet Military Power* (Washington, D.C.: U.S. Government Printing Office, 1981), pp. 2, 27.

14. *Asahi Shimbun* (evening edition), March 17, 1982.

15. *Soviet Military Power*, p. 26.

16. Makoto Momoi, "The Balance of Power in East Asia and the Western Pacific in the 1980s: A Japanese Perspective," in U. Alexis Johnson et al., *The Common Security Interests of Japan, the United States and NATO* (Cambridge, Mass: Ballinger, 1981), p. 47.

17. B. N. Slavinskii, in V. P. Lukin, I. B. Bulai and V. A. Kremenyuk, eds., *SSHAA i problemy Tikhogo okeana: Mezhdunarodno-politicheskie aspekty* (Moscow: Mezhdunapodnoe Otnosheniia, 1979), p. 269.

18. Ibid.

19. Terence Prittie, "Strategic Balance in the Pacific," *Soviet Analyst*, January 27, 1982, p. 3.

20. Dean W. Given, "The Sea of Okhotsk: USSR's Great Lake?" *U.S. Naval Institute Proceedings* 96 (September 1970): 47–50.

21. Quoted from Osamu Miyoshi, "The Growth of Soviet Military Power and the Security of Japan," in Richard B. Foster et al., eds., *Strategy and Security in Northeast Asia* (New York: Crane, Russak and Co., 1979), p. 55.

22. Ibid.

23. *Pravda*, February 24, 1981, p. 4.

24. John Garnett, "Disarmament and Arms Control Since 1945," in Laurence Martin, ed., *Strategic Thought in the Nuclear Age* (Baltimore: Johns Hopkins University Press, 1979), p. 207.

25. Lukin et al., op. cit., p. 271.

26. *Asahi Shimbun*, February 20, 1982.

27. *Japan Times*, February 20, 1982.

28. Ibid.

29. *Asahi Shimbun* (evening edition), February 19, 1982; *Hokkaido Shimbun* (evening edition), February 19, 1982.

30. *Asahi Shimbun*, February 26, 1982.

31. Johnson et al., eds., *The Common Security Interests*, p. 6.

32. Malcolm Mackintosh, "Soviet Interests and Policies in the Asian-Pacific Region," *Orbis* 19, no. 3 (Fall 1975): 764.

33. Quoted from Golam W. Choudhury, *Brezhnev's Collective Security Plan for Asia* (Washington, D.C.: Center for Strategic and International Studies), p. 1.

34. *Asahi Shimbun*, February 20, 1982.

35. Ibid., February 26, 1982.

36. Ibid., March 4, 1982.

37. *Izvestiia*, March 1, 1982; *Asahi Shimbun*, March 2, 1982.

38. Garnett, "Disarmament and Arms Control," p. 191.

39. Ibid., p. 195.

6

Nuclear Proliferation and the Balance of Power in South Asia

K. Subrahmanyam

REDEFINING PROLIFERATION

The term "nuclear proliferation" has acquired a particular connotation over the years, and in most of the literature it refers to the acquisition of nuclear weapon capability by new states. The *Oxford English Dictionary* meaning of "proliferate" is "to grow by multiplication of elementary parts; increase rapidly." The term should therefore cover the growth of nuclear arsenals in nuclear weapon countries as well. In fact, the most significant and continuous nuclear proliferation has been, and remains, that undertaken by the nuclear weapon states. Earlier "the spread of nuclear weapons" was the phrase used to refer to acquisition of nuclear weapon capability by new states. Even this term is somewhat misleading, since most of the spreading of nuclear arsenals to various areas of the world is again done by the nuclear weapon powers. Mobile platforms such as submarines and aircraft have spread nuclear weapons all over the globe, which has led to a sense of acute insecurity among nonnuclear nations.

The nuclear arms issue has to be viewed against the background of persistent attempts by the overwhelming majority of nations to delegitimize and ultimately prohibit the use of nuclear weapons, and the attempts by a smaller number of nations to legitimize the use and threat of use of the weapons. The United Nations, in its very first resolution in 1946, proclaimed that all categories of weapons of mass destruction—biological, chemical, radiological, and nuclear—should be banned. A biological weapons convention has been negotiated and come into force. Negotiations to ban chemical and radiological weapons are under way. Only in the case of nuclear weapons are there no negotiations designed to prohibit them. Indeed, such efforts that do exist, such as the Nonproliferation Treaty and nuclear weapon-free zone concepts, tend to legitimize the continuance of nuclear weapon arsenals in the hands of a few powers.

The U.S. guarantee on nuclear usage to nonnuclear weapon nations is phrased as follows: It will not

> . . . use nuclear weapons against any nonnuclear weapon state party to the nonproliferation treaty or any comparable internationally binding commitment not to acquire nuclear explosive devices, except in the case of an attack on the United States, its territories or armed forces or its allies by such a state allied to a nuclear weapon state or associated with a nuclear weapon state in carrying out or sustaining the attack.[1]

The British assurance is worded in a similar manner.[2] The above guarantee will permit the United States to use nuclear weapons when its own forces launch an offensive against another nation and the other nation, in its defense, rises to counter U.S. forces. Second, the phrase "associated with a nuclear weapon state in carrying out or sustaining the attack" is very vague and is subject to varying interpretations.

In these circumstances there is scope for genuine concern that references to limited nuclear war and the use of nuclear weapons below the central strategic level need not refer to East–West confrontations, but intervention operations undertaken by nuclear weapon countries against nonnuclear weapon states. According to a Brookings Institution study, there have been 215 incidents since the end of World War II in which U.S. forces were used as a political instrument.[3] The Soviet Union, according to the same computation, has demonstrated the use of force on 190 occasions. According to Hungarian historian Istvan Kende, between 1945 and 1976 there were 114 wars in the developing world, and in 70 of these wars the industrialized world intervened. Sixty-five of these interventions were by nuclear weapon powers.[4]

Certain pronouncements by people in authority in nuclear weapon countries have contributed to these grave uncertainties. In July 1975, U.S. Secretary of Defense James Schlesinger said:

> We will make use of nuclear weapons should we be faced with obvious aggression likely to result in defeat in an area of great importance to the U.S. in terms of foreign policy.[5]

In February 1980, after the Soviet intervention in Afghanistan and amid speculation on the future security of the Persian Gulf, a top Pentagon official said the United States was considering the possibility of using theater atomic weapons outside Western Europe, where they are now confined.[6] Secretary of Defense Caspar Weinberger, testifying before the Senate during his confirmation hearings on the issue of whether he would have used nuclear weapons in Vietnam, said:

> . . . if it is a serious enough situation to warrant a war and warrant the committal of United States forces, we owe it to them to be ready and not necessarily to do it but be ready to utilize the strengths that we have.[7]

There have also been pleas in the U.S. strategic literature on the need to have a tailored nuclear force capable of disarming incipient nuclear weapon powers.[8]

On a number of occasions—in the Korean War, the Quemoy-Matsu crisis, the Cuban missile crisis—nuclear threats had been held out and proved successful[9] when there was a clear asymmetry in nuclear capabilities between the threatener and the threatened. Therefore, while limited nuclear war and demonstration strike doctrines do not make much sense in situations of nuclear symmetry, they do in asymmetric situations. In such an overall strategic environment, the spread of nuclear weapons into the neighborhood of South Asia is a matter of grave strategic significance. Two nuclear weapon powers, the USSR and China, abut South Asia, and a third nuclear weapon power, the United States, stations a permanent carrier task force, presumably with nuclear weapons on board, in the Arabian Sea and prepares to operate B-52s, another type of nuclear weapon carrier, from Diego Garcia.[10] The United States is also reported to have an interest in developing a contingent capability to deploy ballistic missile submarines in the Indian Ocean.[11]

France, too, may be in a position to deploy nuclear missile submarines in the Indian Ocean when it completes development of the M-4 missile, since the Arabian Sea is an optimal area of deployment vis-à-vis Soviet cities. South Asia has thus become a crossroads of strategic interaction among three nuclear weapon powers—the United States, the USSR, and China. Consequently their nuclear proliferation and spreading of nuclear weapons are likely to have an impact on the security environment and balance of power in South Asia.

DEFINING SOUTH ASIA

It is difficult to define South Asia in strictly geographical terms. If Tibet were to be considered as South Asia, then nuclear weapons may already have been introduced into the area.[12] It is also difficult to exclude the waters around the Indian peninsula—taking into account the 200-mile extended economic zone, by South Asian definition—from nuclear weapon deployment. In that case one can only speculate about the presence or absence of superpower naval vessels with nuclear weapons on board within those waters.

China is reported to be constructing a Nuclear-Powered Ballistic Missile submarine (SSBN),[13] and is likely to follow this up with more submarines. If China is to deploy its missile submarines in a second-strike mode against the Soviet Union, the optimal area of deployment is the Arabian Sea and the northwest quadrant of the Indian Ocean. This is yet another factor that will influence the strategic balance in South Asia.

Israel and South Africa are believed to be clandestine nuclear weapon powers. The CIA reported in a special national intelligence estimate as long ago as October 1974 that, according to its belief, Israel had already produced nuclear weapons.[14] Preparations for a South African nuclear test in the Kalahari Desert in August 1977 were detected, and at that stage international pressure stopped the test.[15] A bright flash over the Indian Ocean, detected by a VELA satellite on September 22, 1979, has not been satisfactorily explained despite a White House panel report that concluded: "Although we cannot rule out the possibility that this signal was of nuclear origin, the panel considers it more likely that the signal was one of the 'zoo events.' "[16] A number of statements made by South African authorities have hinted at a nuclear capability.[17]

In light of these developments, former Pakistani Prime Minister Zulfikar Ali Bhutto wrote in his death cell testament in 1978: "We know that Israel and South Africa have full nuclear capability. The Christian, Jewish and Hindu civilization [sic] have this capability. The Communist powers also possess it. Only the Islamic civilization was without it, but that position was about to change."[18] It has now been established that Bhutto initiated his nuclear weapons program in a meeting at Multan in January 1972,[19] many months before India decided to develop a peaceful nuclear explosive device (PNE). From the evidence published in the West, it would appear that the Israeli nuclear capability triggered the Pakistani efforts with financial support from Libya and other Islamic states.[20]

The Indian underground nuclear test was part of a comprehensive and broad-based nuclear energy development program for peaceful purposes. India from the beginning has maintained the right to conduct peaceful nuclear explosions along the lines that the United States and the Soviet Union were pursuing in the 1960s and early 1970s. Reservations about PNEs is a comparatively recent phenomenon, and the two superpowers have not yet been able to reach an agreement on banning them. Therefore, it would appear that at least one superpower still sees useful applications for PNEs.

In any case, it is now common knowledge that India has not built up a nuclear arsenal. The Indian nuclear energy program is based on a three-phase plan drafted by the late Dr. Homi Bhabha. The first phase was to consist of natural uranium–heavy water reactors, the second phase of a fast breeder reactor using plutonium extracted from natural uranium–heavy water reactors, and the third phase would use uranium 233 for reactors, U-233 being obtained by irradiating thorium in the fast breeder reactors. The development of reprocessing technology, fast breeders, and heavy water technology all fit in with this overall program. These programs have been published and discussed in consultative committees of Parliament, appropriations for them have been made in budgets available to the public, and annual reports of the Indian Nuclear Energy Department have been issued every spring.

On the other hand, all evidence points to Pakistan's primary interest in a nuclear weapons program.[21] Pakistan had taken the position in the conference of the Committee on Disarmament in 1970 that there is no distinction between the technologies of PNE and those of nuclear weapons and that, therefore, no non-weapon country should undertake any PNE. Until 1981 Pakistani leaders maintained this position. Since then, however, there has been some hedging of this

stand. In the mid-1970s Pakistan published a very ambitious program of constructing nuclear power reactors. The former chairman of the Pakistan Atomic
Energy Commission, Dr. Usmani, has expressed serious reservations, however,
about the program and about whether Pakistan can sustain it on the basis of its
uranium resources. Moreover, he has questioned whether Pakistan's industrial
development alone warrants setting up a number of reactors, each with several
hundred megawatts of generating capacity.[22] Extensively documented accounts
of Pakistan's clandestine purchases of plant and equipment for its enrichment
and reprocessing technologies rule out the possibility of extensive nonweapons-
related research and development programs. They point instead to the use of
industrial programs designed to obtain weapons-grade fissile material at the earli-
est possible time.

Pakistan has as much right to nuclear weapons as nuclear weapon powers
and, for reasons earlier stated, the behavior of nuclear weapon powers is not
confidence-inspiring for nonnuclear weapon states. The nuclear weapon states
have been attempting to derive political advantage from their possession of nuclear weapons, and the trend has been to convert nuclear weapons into a cur-
rency of power. Two garrison states, Israel and South Africa, have led the way in
reinforcing their isolated positions with nuclear weapons. Pakistan has its share
of difficulties in developing a national identity and in adjusting to its environment, and presumably looks upon nuclear capability as a means of ensuring its
survival in a hostile environment. Whatever the rationale of Pakistan's nuclear
weapons program, it is bound to have repercussions on its neighborhood.

The majority of informed military opinion in India is of the view that the
asymmetric possession of a nuclear arsenal by Pakistan could not be effectively
deterred by any conventional superiority of Indian armed forces. Nuclear weapons can be deterred only by other nuclear weapons.[23] There are also fears that,
just as has happened with the Israeli and South African nuclear arsenals, over a
period of time the United States and some West European nations may come to
accept a Pakistani nuclear arsenal as well. During the 1982 debate in the U.S.
Congress on arms transfers to Pakistan, the Reagan administration pressed for
an unlimited waiver of the Symington Amendment, freeing Washington from
having to impose an automatic cutoff of conventional arms transfers consequent
to any nuclear test by Pakistan. The Indian strategic community therefore has to
take into account the possibility of a Pakistan armed with nuclear weapons continuing to receive U.S. arms. U.S. relaxation of trade and other interactions
with South Africa does not reassure India.

Professor Stephen Cohen of the University of Illinois, an acknowledged expert on the subcontinent, has summed up Pakistan's position in the following
words:

> Pakistan belongs to that class of states whose very survival is uncertain, whose
> legitimacy is doubted and whose security-related resources are inadequate. Yet

these states will not go away, nor can they be ignored. Pakistan (like Taiwan, South Korea, Israel and South Africa) has the capacity to fight, to go nuclear, to influence the global strategic balance (if only by collapsing) and, lastly, is in a strategic geographical location surrounded by the three largest states in the world and adjacent to the mouth of the Persian Gulf.[24]

Presumably many Pakistanis believe that a Pakistani nuclear force would neutralize an assumed Indian nuclear force. As Cohen notes:

> Others point out however, it would provide the umbrella under which Pakistan could reopen the Kashmir issue; a Pakistani nuclear capability paralyses not only the Indian nuclear decision but also Indian conventional forces and a brash, bold, Pakistani strike to liberate Kashmir might go unchallenged if the Indian leadership was weak or indecisive.[25]

Given these perceptions in the subcontinent, it is not surprising that there are demands in India that Pakistani nuclear capability should be matched, and if possible overtaken, by Indian nuclear efforts. No one disputes that India has the necessary capability to overtake Pakistan in a short time if it decides to do so.

One aspect of the Chinese nuclear program—the possible deployment of SSBNs in a second-strike mode in the Indian Ocean—was referred to earlier. Another aspect is the obsolescence of Chinese conventional arms even as its nuclear weapons program advances in sophistication and numbers. This combination of obsolete conventional arms and sophisticated nuclear arms is an unusual one not applicable to other nuclear weapon powers. Will this unusual combination mean a lowering of nuclear threshold in any major conflict in which China may become involved? No doubt China has given an assurance that it will not use nuclear weapons first, but the credibility of such assurances may be doubted in circumstances in which Chinese conventional forces face major defeat. In the 1960s Chinese forces were equipped with armaments that were reasonably current by international standards. This is no longer so, and the effect of this obsolescence became evident in the Sino–Vietnamese border war. As China builds up its nuclear arsenal both in quantity and in quality, its nonnuclear neighbors cannot remain unconcerned.

There have been suggestions that a nuclear weapon-free zone in South Asia could take care of some of these problems. India does not share this view and has pointed out that the acceptance of a nuclear weapon-free zone amounts to legitimization of nuclear weapons in the hands of nuclear weapon powers, and therefore runs counter to the objective of the total prohibition of nuclear weapons.[26] Moreover, an acceptance of guarantees from nuclear weapon states in effect constitutes a protectorate status for nonnuclear weapon powers, and this is totally unacceptable. Many West European nations talk of "Finlandization" while that concept has no historical basis. For the former colonies, however, protectorate status and the loss of sovereignty are genuine historical memories. The Nonproliferation Treaty and nuclear weapon-free zones appear to be analogous to Lord Wellesley's subsidiary alliance system.

With Chinese nuclear weapons stationed in areas adjoining India and nuclear weapon-bearing naval vessels of the superpowers in adjacent seas, South Asia appears to be an artificially demarcated zone quite unlike the Latin American continental area. Even there, with Brazil and Argentina not acceding to the Tlatelelco Treaty in full measure, the effectiveness of that nuclear weapon-free zone is not entirely free from doubt. There have been reports that nuclear weapons of a country to be included in the South Asian nuclear weapon-free zone may be tested in some adjoining nuclear weapon states.[27] It is also not clear whether all nuclear activities of the states are easily monitorable; certain activities can be kept apart from the purview of national atomic energy commissions, and hence outside the purview of any mutually agreed inspection system. For these reasons India does not consider nuclear weapon-free zones to be realistic solutions to regional security problems.

THE REGIONAL BALANCE OF POWER

It is against this nuclear background that the balance of power in South Asia must be evaluated. In attempting this, one encounters the problem of defining the balance of power both in conceptual terms and in its application to the area. One may consider the balance of power in various ways: within the region (the Indian subcontinent) and between the region and its neighbors. The Sino–Indian balance of power on the Himalayan front and in Burma, the balance of power on the Afghan–Pakistani and Iranian–Pakistani borders, and between the region and superpower intervention may also be relevant within a comprehensive analysis. Before proceeding to an analysis of various balances of power in and around the region, it is useful to examine the role of war in the current international context.

Between the end of World War II and 1976, there were only 6 instances of international violence in the developed world, but 114 such instances in the developing world.[28] In the developed world it is clearly recognized that Clausewitz's maxim that war is a continuation of politics by other means can no longer be applied so simply in the nuclear age. Even in the developing world it is no longer possible to envisage high intensity conventional wars for prolonged periods except in those cases when a superpower becomes involved. Keeping an area under occupation is very costly.

While mini and micro nations, of which there are several dozen as a result of the fragmented decolonization of the late 1960s and 1970s, continue to suffer risks of occupation, most medium-size and large nations cannot be easily overrun and occupied. In their cases the risk is one of partial occupation of territory. If there are sparsely populated areas in such nations, they can be more easily occupied. Nations with significant populations and even modest defense capabilities can be invaded only at significant political and economic costs to the aggressor, and even then it is difficult to dictate terms to the victims in the current international political milieu.

However, there are various other kinds of threats to the security of nations besides invasion and territorial occupation: external support for various secessionist and insurgent movements; intervention in the internal affairs of a nation, including the manipulation of its economic policies and economic exploitation; transgression in territorial waters and extended economic zones; denial and withholding of resources—food, oil, technology, various raw materials—the non-military threats to the security and well-being of nations; and manipulation of one's neighbors and their policies against the interests of a particular nation. There is also the possibility of partial occupation of territory to be combined with some or all of the above kinds of security challenges.

In light of the above, the balance of power concept must be evaluated not according to the absolute strengths of nations but in terms of the risks and gains inherent in a nation's actions vis-à-vis its adversary. Since the occupation of a nation is difficult and costly, even smaller nations with fewer resources to wage war can pose various kinds of threats to bigger neighbors. Success in such confrontations depends upon the ability to pose various categories of threats short of a full-scale military attack. They could be asylum, arms, and trade for insurgents and secessionists, or financial and other material support to dissidents. In the current international environment the fear of punishment for such actions is absent in many cases, especially if the smaller nation has a superpower protector or patron. Ideologies and religious affiliations become convenient instruments in such campaigns to destabilize a neighbor. Some states having an identity crisis resort to such confrontations in pursuit of their own national consolidation through nurturing hostile postures against neighbors. For nations that have been carved out of a larger polity, there are compulsions to differentiate themselves from their neighbors in order to promote their separate identities.

For large federal polities in the developing world that have yet to cohere and consolidate into common nationhood, secessionism poses a significant threat. Even small setbacks in across-the-border conflicts or the inability to prevent insurgents from getting support and assistance across borders creates a sense of insecurity and political destabilization wholly disproportionate to the magnitude of the threat. In these circumstances the image of the nation with respect to its military capability to protect itself against threats below full-scale aggression is very important among developing nations. Any balance of power analysis within South Asia, and between the region and its neighbors, must take these aspects into consideration.

In South Asia, India and Sri Lanka are liberal democracies. Pakistan and Bangladesh are under military rule. Nepal and Bhutan are monarchies. Burma is a military-supported, one-party state. Afghanistan is under Marxist rule, and

China and the Soviet Union, adjoining South Asia, are Communist states. The whole of South Asia is subject to turbulence consequent on the transition from colonialism to nation-statehood, and from traditionalism to modernity. This turbulence is an integral part of the process of moving from retarded development to modernity. Among these states India and Sri Lanka are relatively more stable polities. The more stable polities have to protect themselves from the turbulence in neighboring states spilling over their borders. In 1971, 10 million refugees were displaced from East Pakistan into India. In the 1980s refugees have spilled over from Afghanistan into Pakistan. The continuous infiltration of people from East Pakistan into the Indian state of Assam during the 1950s and 1960s has resulted in the current agitation by native Assamese to deport aliens who have entered over the last few decades. Therefore, prevention of turbulence in the neighboring states spreading into one's own territory requires preparedness. So does the protection of offshore oil assets and the living and nonliving resources of the extended economic zone.

Within the sub-continent today there is a balance of ground forces between India and Pakistan, as is indicated in the following table.

	India	Pakistan
Army		
Infantry divisions	18 (some earmarked for northeast)	16 (2 more corps are being raised; when completed, up to 4 divisions may be deployed on Afghan border)
Armed divisions	2	2
Ind. armed brigades	6	4
Ind. infantry brigades	1	4
Parabrigades	2	—
Tanks	2,120	1,285
Antitank missiles	SS-11-B1	TOW
India's ten mountain divisions are being deployed on the northern borders		
Air Force		
Light bomber squadrons	3	1
Interceptor squadrons (Gnats, MiG 21s)	19	—
Fighter-bomber squadrons (Hunters, Maruts, Su-7s, Jaguars, MiG 23s)	10	—
Multirole squadrons	—	11 (3 Mirages, 8 MiG-19s)
Air defense missiles	SAM 2s, 3s, 6s	Crotale

Source: International Institute for Strategic Studies, *Military Balance 1981-82* (London: IISS, 1981). Raising of additional divisions is from Shirin Tahir-Kheli "Defense Planning," given at Columbia University Seminar on Defense Planning in Less Developed Countries.

Indian air superiority exists but is not decisive enough. While Pakistan is likely to add 40 F-16s from the United States, 100 M-48 A5 tanks, additional TOW missiles, 64 self-propelled 155-mm howitzers and 40 8-inch self-propelled howitzers, 75 towed 155-mm guns, and 10 attack helicopters,[29] India is likely to replace its Hunters, Maruts, and Sukhois with MiG 23s and Mirage 2000s, and its Gnats with MiG-21s. Besides its domestic production of Vijayanta tanks, India may also acquire limited numbers of T-72 tanks.

Most Pakistanis, according to an assessment made by staff consultants of the Committee on Foreign Affairs of the U.S. House of Representatives, perceive India to be their chief threat.[30] Fifteen of Pakistan's divisions are deployed along the border with India, though Pakistan emphasizes its sense of threat arising out of Soviet presence in Afghanistan. While Pakistan has nearly all its forces on the Indian border, a significant portion of Indian forces earmarked for deployment on the Pakistani border are stationed in cantonments in central and south India, and it would take up to two weeks to bring those forces to full strength to be deployed against Pakistan.[31] In both 1965 and 1971 Pakistan's forces had setbacks in the wars with India, and on both of those occasions, even though it had a less favorable force ratio, Pakistan started the war or initiated actions that escalated into war. Consequently, with the ratios improving for Pakistan, the risks of miscalculations may further increase.

India is a status quo power, while Pakistan lays claims to territory in Kashmir that is now part of India. Pakistan continues to maintain the validity of the "two nations" thesis (according to which Hindus and Muslims, because of their different religions, constitute two different nations) and claims Kashmir on that basis. Pakistan also claims a right to intervene on behalf of Muslims in India. While such a two-nation theory has no relevance to Pakistan, which is 97 percent Muslim, India cannot accept the validity of the doctrine in view of the fact that 12 percent of its population—over 80 million persons—are Muslims. Acceptance of such a thesis would rend the fabric of Indian society and negate the concept of secularism that forms the fundamental basis of the Indian nation. This is one of the instances where an ideology espoused by a smaller state, based in this case on denominational loyalty, poses a threat to the security of a larger, composite state.

While Indian national identity is based on centuries-old civilizational factors and the prolonged national liberation struggle, Pakistan has problems with its identity. Consequently, the Indian national identity is well developed and Pakistan needs to project India as an adversary to build up its identity. Therefore, the balance of power between the two states has to be related to respective interests of the two states in maintaining and changing status quo and in espousing an expansionist ideology.

Looking at the balance of power on the Pakistan–Afghanistan border, it has been estimated that there are 85,000 Soviet troops in Afghanistan, including about 9 motorized rifle divisions, air force personnel, and support units.[32] The Soviets are reported to have more than 300 helicopters and aircraft, in addition to 100 Afghan air force planes, in Afghanistan. An estimated 15,000 to 30,000 troops are believed to be stationed on the Soviet side of the Afghan border. It has been assessed that there are 9 divisions in the Turkestan military district, 13 in the Transcaucasus military district, and 10 in the Central Asia military district. This deployment of Soviet forces does not appear to lead the Pakistani authorities to fear any full-scale attack on Pakistan. Five of the six army corps face India, as does much of the armor. The army corps in Peshawar, which was held as reserve against India, is now oriented as a frontline force against a Soviet threat. Another Pakistani reserve division is deployed against the Soviet threat in Baluchistan, and a new army corps is being raised in Quetta. The ultimate goal appears to be to deploy only 4 divisions facing the Afghan frontier, and the balance of 17 divisions against India.[33] Most Pakistani scenarios of a Soviet threat visualize less than full-scale attacks. The Pakistani foreign minister, in his address to a seminar in LaHore on June 30, 1981, stated:

> The Soviet Union has assured us that we pose no danger to you. We have to take the Soviet Union at her word. Again here, if I were speaking to you off the record, I could tell you something more. But I shall have to confine myself on this issue by saying that an attack by a superpower on another country in the region will not remain confined to the aggressor and the victim. The interest of the world community will become involved, particularly in the situation and there is every likelihood of that becoming a main superpower confrontation. Not because the other superpower wants to champion the integrity of Pakistan for altruistic reasons but because the whole regional balance in the Gulf region and the future of the flow of oil which is vital to Europe, Japan and all other countries of the world may come under danger, and, therefore, this fear in your mind about the danger of an attack by the Soviet Union should be allayed. And the Soviets have categorically assured us, and this has been stated by President Brezhnev a number of times that we should not take into account this possibility. Any other attack, well this is precisely the reason why we want to get the arms quickly. We should be able to defend ourselves against an attack from any quarter. As long as our military defence capability is strengthened, the would-be aggressor knows that it will not be a walkover, that it will suffer a crippling damage if Pakistan is attacked.
>
> · · ·
>
> Well I think now about the other question: will not [the] Soviet Union become even more threatening? Will the Soviet Union commit aggression against Pakistan just because we want to buy some military equipment from the United States? It will appear ridiculous. There must be a more substantive reason for any such aggression and I am sure that we accept the word of President Brezhnev that this is fantastic and a slander against the Soviet Union. So these are unfounded fears. I could say more, but, as I have said, this is an open forum and it would not be appropriate for me to do so.[34]

It is quite obvious from the above that Pakistan does not visualize much of a threat from the Soviet Union and is conscious of the presence of the U.S. fleet in the Arabian Sea to provide countervailing power. Most of Pakistan's efforts to acquire armaments are directed toward countering a perceived Indian threat or pursuing its policy of confronting India, with its "two nations" theory and dispute on Kashmir as the basis for that thesis.

Pakistan claims that it does not pose a threat to the regime in Afghanistan and will not become a channel for the flow of arms there.[35] However, President Sadat of Egypt disclosed that after the Soviet intervention in Afghanistan, the arms supplied by the Soviet Union to Egypt in the period before 1974 were transported by the United States, to be passed on to Afghan rebels.[36] This could be done only via Pakistan. According to Carl Bernstein, General Zia ul-Haq felt that passing on up to two planeloads of arms per week to Afghan rebels was within the limits of Soviet tolerance.[37] The Soviet Union and Afghan authorities have repeatedly accused Pakistan of training insurgents, providing them with asylum and arms, and the former maintains that its troops can withdraw from Afghanistan if external intervention ceases. This appears to be a case of controlled, low-intensity, but sustained confrontation on both sides, and neither side seems to expect an escalation to higher levels of direct conflict.

How will these balances of power be affected if Pakistan succeeds in its attempts to go nuclear? There would be an enormous pressure on India to go nuclear and to overtake Pakistan, in view of its more advanced state of technology and industrial infrastructure. Once that happens, there is no reason to believe that a state of stable mutual deterrence would not set in among the two nations, as has happened among other hostile pairings or blocs of nations. One tends to agree with Kenneth Waltz's observation:

> New nuclear states will confront the possibilities and feel the constraints that present nuclear states have experienced. New nuclear states will be more concerned for their safety and more mindful of dangers than some of the old ones have been. Until recently, only the great and some of the major powers have had nuclear weapons. While nuclear weapon powers have spread, conventional weapons have proliferated. Under these circumstances, wars have been fought not at the centre but at the periphery of international politics. The likelihood of war decreases as deterrent and defensive capabilities increase. Nuclear weapons, responsibly used, make wars hard to start. Nations that have nuclear weapons have strong incentives to use them responsibly. These statements hold for small as for big nuclear powers. Because they do, the measured spread of nuclear weapons is more to be welcomed than feared.[38]

Since India is the status quo power, such stability of deterrence will not be unfavorable to India. It might at the same time help to assuage the sense of insecurity among the Pakistani elite vis-à-vis both India and the Soviet presence in Afghanistan. Development of an increased sense of security among the Pakistani elite may have domestic repercussions. While on the one hand it might in the short run increase the popularity of the military regime, over the longer run the increased sense of security may lead to the feeling that there is no justification for the perpetuation of military rule.

It is difficult to predict the effects of a Pakistani nuclear arsenal on Arab–Israeli confrontation. So far nations have not passed on nuclear weapons to others. However, as nuclear arsenals grow larger and weapons spread, it may become difficult to identify the exact source of a particular nuclear weapon and to assert that weapons could not be stolen from the arsenals of superpowers just as large-scale diversion of nuclear fissile materials and the hijacking of uranium have taken place.[39]

Pakistan's relations with Iran are not what they were during the time of the shah. Khomeini's Iran has called on the people of Pakistan to overthrow the Zia regime. There is a view that Pakistan shares some mutuality of interests with the United States in regard to Iran. There are apprehensions about the likely instability in Iran when Khomeini dies, the future shape of events in that country in its aftermath, and their impact on the other Persian Gulf states. Any secessionism in Iranian Baluchistan will have its impact on the Pakistani side of the border. One observer traces Pakistan's motivation to reach a "no war" pact with India to its shared concern with the United States about the Iranian front and the future course of developments in that country.[40]

Regarding the balance of forces on the Himalayan front, the long border between India and China has been quiet since the late 1960s. India deploys ten mountain divisions on this border to face Chinese troops in Tibet. Since the Chinese attack on India in 1962, significant improvements in China's military infrastructure in the Tibetan region have taken place. All-weather airfields have been constructed in Tibet and aircraft are deployed year round. The oil pipeline into Tibet has been operational since 1977. The railway line into Tibet is progressing, though more slowly than anticipated. According to *Military Balance 1981–82*, China deploys nine infantry divisions and six local force divisions in its Southwest military region, which comprises the Tibet and Sichuan military districts. Besides these, there are also two to three divisions of border troops in this region. China is in a position to strengthen its forces in the region with troops from its South and West military regions. While China is able to field a larger force, Indian troops are now fully acclimated to high altitudes and have better equipment. There is perhaps an overall balance on this frontier. Very often when Indian and Pakistani forces are compared and the larger size of the Indian force is highlighted, this vigil on the long Himalayan frontier is overlooked.

Since Mao Zedong's death China has significantly reduced its interventionism in the affairs of the subcontinent. Armed support for Naga and Mizo insurgents has not been renewed of late, and support to the Naxalite movement (Maoist Communists in India) has been discontinued. China has displayed an increasing interest in peace and stability among the nations of the Indian subcontinent. However, four developments relating to China have a bearing on the security perspectives of its neighbors. Its nuclear weapon development program and deployment will be watched with concern. The issue of deployment of Chinese SSBNs has already been discussed. Given the global perspective, in which nations see threat in deployment of SS-20s and Pershing IIs, it is only natural that Chinese missiles in western and southwestern China should cause a sense of unease among the nations within range of those missiles, especially in India, with which China has fought a war and still has unresolved disputes. These are more genuine grounds for concern than those between nations that have no active disputes and that have never fought a war, or at least not in the last century.

A second cause for concern is the likely program of modernization of Chinese military forces with technological assistance from the West. Third is the construction of the Karakoram highway, which has no conceivable commercial significance. This highway provides a capability for Chinese forces to enter the subcontinent rapidly. Last, Chinese policy toward Southeast Asia is likely to influence Indian perceptions. The attempt to impose the infamous Pol Pot regime on Kampuchea has not inspired confidence about Chinese intentions toward the area, nor has the "punishing" military campaign against Vietnam.

Chinese assurances about keeping party-to-party relationships separated from state-to-state relationships have not convinced the Malaysians and Indonesians. The Chinese maintain their relationship with the major insurgent group of north Burma—the Communist Party of Burma—and there is no sign of their decreasing the arms supplies to them and other insurgent groups allied with them. In view of these factors, India has to deploy a part of its forces in the northeast part of the country. This aspect is also generally ignored by those who compare the entire Indian force with the Pakistani force and conclude that India has a vast superiority.

With two nearby nations—Israel and South Africa—believed to have clandestine nuclear arsenals, it is unrealistic to expect the Indian Ocean to be converted into a nuclear weapon-free zone in addition to becoming a zone of peace. The latter concept envisages only that extraregional powers should not deploy forces in the Indian Ocean with missions in that area. The former proposal signifies all nearby nations giving up their nuclear weapon option. With the evidence already available on Israeli and South African nuclear capabilities, it is not realistic to have them included in a nuclear weapon-free zone without adequate and credible international verification, which would include a strict accounting of all fissile materials that have been available to these two countries. Excluding them from nuclear weapon-free zone proposals would only legitimize their clandestine arsenals and would not be acceptable to their regional neighbors.

The South African nuclear arsenal appears to be designed to deter the frontline black African nations from supporting the struggle of black and colored people within South Africa. Already South Africa has attacked Mozambique, ostensibly to destroy the bases of the African National Congress. This has led to Soviet assurances to Mozambique.[41] There was an unsuccessful coup attempt in Seychelles directed from South Africa. Such attempts are likely to increase the sense of insecurity of nations vis-à-vis a nuclear-armed South Africa. Such developments may lead to the involvement of the countervailing influence of a superpower in the region.

CONCLUSIONS

Nuclear proliferation is taking place at an accelerated pace around South Asia, on the Indian Ocean littoral, and on the Indian Ocean itself. Pakistan is perhaps next on the list of nations that is likely to become a nuclear weapon power, and India may be compelled to follow suit. There are no reasons to conclude that the behavior pattern of these nations, once they become nuclear weapon powers, will be any different or less responsible than that of the existing nuclear weapon powers. Fifteen NATO nations, five Warsaw Pact nations, China, Japan, Australia, New Zealand, Ireland, Israel, and South Africa—27 nations in all—rely on nuclear weapons and nuclear war doctrines for their security. Since this list includes most of the militarily advanced nations, they influence security thinking all over the world.

Nuclear weapons on both sides of an unfriendly border may stabilize the situations in South Asia, as they have done elsewhere, and at the same time they continue to carry a nonnegligible risk of some weapons being used, as the existing arsenals have done all these years of the nuclear era. In the light of this situation, nuclear proliferation may help stabilize the existing balance of power in South Asia. The United States alone is to produce 10,500 additional nuclear weapons between 1982 and 1992. It is to be logically presumed that other nuclear weapon powers will add to their arsenals in similar proportions. Such galloping proliferation can hardly fail to have an impact in South Asia, where the interests of three major nuclear weapon powers interacts. Any marginal proliferation by a local power or two is not likely to affect the balance of power in the region significantly.

NOTES

1. Quoted in United Nations, *Study on Nuclear Weapons*, A/35/392 (New York: United Nations, Sept. 12, 1980), app. II.

2. Ibid.

3. Quoted in Guy Parker, "Military Implications of Possible World Order Crisis in 1980s," Rand Memorandum R (2003 AF) (1977).

4. Istvan Kende, "Wars of Ten Years (1967–1976)," *Journal of Peace Research* 15, no. 3 (1978): 227–41.

5. Quoted in Inder Khosla, "Use of Nuclear Weapons," *IDSA Journal* 13, no. 4 (Apr.–June 1981): 14–15.

6. *International Herald Tribune*, Feb. 4, 1980.

7. Testimony before Senate Armed Services Committee, Jan. 6, 1981.

8. Lewis Dunn, "U.S. Strategic Force Requirements in a Nuclear Proliferated World," *Air University Review*, July– Aug. 1980: 26–33.

9. Kenneth Waltz, "The Spread of Nuclear Weapons: More May Be Better," Adelphi Paper 171 (London: International Institute for Strategic Studies, 1981).

10. *National Herald* (Delhi), 18 Apr. 1980.

11. "United States Foreign Policy Objectives and Overseas Military Installations," prepared by Congressional Research Service for the U.S. Senate Committee on Foreign Relations, 1979.

12. *Jane's Weapon Systems, 1972–73* (New York: Jane's, 1972).

13. *Jane's Fighting Ships, 1981–82* (New York: Jane's, 1981).

14. The Special National Intelligence Estimate of Oct. 1974, quoted in Gen. D. K. Palit and P. K. S. Namboodiri, "Pakistan's Islamic Bomb." Testimony of Carl Duckett quoted in *New York Times,* 2 Mar. 1978.

15. *SIPRI Year Book, 1978* (Stockholm: Swedish International Peace Research Institute, 1978).

16. U.N. document General Assembly A/35/358, Aug. 19, 1980. Editor's Note: The term "zoo event" is used for signals whose cause is not understood. The VELA has produced about 70 such oddities in the last decade.

17. *Economic Times* (Delhi), 8 June 1976; *International Herald Tribune,* 17 Feb. 1977; and *Newsweek,* Sept. 29, 1980.

18. Zulfikar Ali Bhutto, *If I Am Assassinated. . .* (New Delhi: Vikas Publishing House, 1979), p. 138.

19. BBC Panorama Programme, 16 June 1980.

20. Ibid.

21. P.K.S. Namboodiri, "Pakistan's Nuclear Posture," in K. Subrahmanyam, ed., *Nuclear Myths and Realities* (New Delhi: ABC Publishers, 1981).

22. Dr. Usmani in *MAG* (Karachi), Mar. 26, 1981.

23. See Combat Paper no. 1, "Effects of Nuclear Asymmetry on Conventional Deterrence," and no. 2, "Nuclear Weapons in Third World Context" (Mhow: College of Combat, 1981).

24. Stephen Philip Cohen, "Identity, Survival, Security: Pakistan's Defense Policy," in Edward A. Kolodziej and Robert Harkavy, eds., *Security Policies of Emerging States: A Comparative Approach* (Lexington, Mass.: D.C. Heath, 1982).

25. Ibid.

26. Indian prime minister's address to the U.N. Special Session on Disarmament (1978); text reproduced in *Strategic Digest* (New Delhi) 8, nos. 7 and 8 (July–Aug. 1978).

27. *New Scientist* 23 (July 1981); Edgar O'Balance, "Islamic Bomb," *National Defence,* Dec. 1980.

28. Kende, "Wars of Ten Years."

29. International Institute for Strategic Studies, *Military Balance 1981–82* (London: IISS, 1981).

30. "Proposed U.S. Assistance and Arms Transfer to Pakistan," report of Staff Study Mission to Pakistan and India for the Committee on Foreign Affairs of the U.S. House of Representatives, Nov. 20, 1981.

31. Ibid.

32. Ibid.

33. Shirin Tahir-Kheli, "Defense Planning," given at Columbia University Seminar on Defense Planning in Less Developed Countries.

34. Foreign Minister Agha Shahi, speech at Seminar on Renewal of Pakistan's American Connection, Lahore, 30 June 1981; reported in *Public Opinion Trends and Analyses and News Service* (New Delhi), July 2 and 30, 1981.

35. General Zia ul-Haq, interview in *SUNDAY,* 6 June 1981 and in *Morning News,* 8 June 1981; Pakistani official spokesman's comment on Sadat's disclosure on 28 Sept. 1981; Agha Shahi, op. cit.

36. President Sadat's statement at the first meeting of the Constituent Assembly of the League of Muslim and Arab Peoples on 9 Nov. 1980, quoted in *Muslim* (Islamabad), 11 Nov. 1980; President Sadat's interview on Cairo TV on 28 Dec. 1980, quoted in *Hindu* (Madras), 27 Dec. 1980; President Sadat's interview with NBC, quoted in *Tribune,* (Chandigarh), 25 Sept. 1981.

37. Carl Bernstein, in *The New Republic,* repr. in *Guardian Weekly* 125, no. 6 (9 Aug. 1981).

38. Waltz, "The Spread of Nuclear Weapons."

39. David Burnham, "The Case of the Missing Uranium," *Atlantic Monthly,* Apr. 1969.

40. Nikhil Chakravarty, "Meaning of West Asian Connection," *Times of India* (New Delhi), 15 Jan. 1982.

41. *Hindustan Times* (New Delhi), 27 Feb. 1981.

PART IV:

Strategic Threats of the Future

7

Subnational Proliferation, Technology Transfers, and Terrorism

Fabienne Luchaire

INTRODUCTION

Terrorism is a method of open conflict, and in its widest sense can be defined as a form of violence and coercion aimed at generating fear and creating a climate of insecurity that can be used for political or criminal purposes.

History shows that it is not a new phenomenon—we have only to refer to the writings of Sun Tzu, which describe the role of terrorism in a strategy of conquests—and that it is of considerable complexity. Indeed, whether they are the result of planning by a single person or an organization, whether they are carried out by an individual in isolation or by a group of well-trained people, terrorist activities are either revolutionary or reactionary in character, and are the work of both left-wing and right-wing movements.

An examination of events that have occurred throughout the centuries brings out three distinct levels of terrorism, whose volume and degree of gravity are of increasing intensity: "primary" terrorism, revolutionary or nationalistic terrorism, and subversive terrorism.

At the first level we have the most classical form of terrorism, that of contestation and refusal in the face of a given economic or political situation. It is the consequence of an unequal struggle between its originator and the Establishment, usually takes the form of independent action against a specific target, and seems to have individual motivation. The wave of attacks perpetrated by French anarchists between 1892 and 1894 are an example of this. Léauthier's random stabbing of the Serbian minister in Paris (13 November 1893), Auguste Vaillant's assassination attempt on members of Parliament in the Palais Bourbon (9 December 1893), Emile Henry's destruction of the police station in the Rue des Bons-Enfants with a bomb (8 November 1892), and the assassination of President Sadi Carnot by Jeronimo Caserio (24 June 1894) all express the same determination: to wreak vengeance on the wealthy business class and do harm to its interests. Together with this vengeance goes indictment of society: Ravachol[1] and Vaillant had both lived in great poverty. However, none of these famous anarchists belonged to a really structured organization. In such cases criminal acts are improvised from day to day, following the inspiration of each individual, and are carried out with whatever means are available. Their effects are limited in time and space, and their repercussions on political affairs do not threaten the state machinery.

At the second level are revolutionary terrorism and nationalistic terrorism. These are much more dangerous for the authority of the states concerned, and aim at discrediting the government in power by fostering a process of violence or riots, followed by a cycle of provocation and repression that will help to develop collective psychological trauma and lead to the fall of the system.

Revolutionary terrorism appeared in Russia in 1879, and continued in the early years of the twentieth century. Narodnaia Volia[2] (The People's Will) and the Fighting Organization adopted terror as the strategy of a movement directed against Tsar Alexander II, and subsequently against the members of successive governments and administrations. Acts of terrorism, exaggerated by propaganda, were aimed at arousing hostility to the tsar among the masses. In more recent times the period since 1960 has been marked by an increasing number of left-wing extremist revolutionary movements (such as the Japanese Red Army, the Baader-Meinhof gang, Direct Action, the Turkish People's Liberation Army, and the Red Brigades) that challenge the political, economic, and social foundations of democratic government, and have as their primary objective complete destabilization of society.

Nationalistic terrorism, employed by secessionists who are unwilling to continue accepting subjection to foreign powers, is a very ancient method, as shown by the activities of the Zealots[3] as early as the first century of the Christian era. History is full of further examples: in Macedonia, the Macedonian Interior Revolutionary Organization (MIRO) started the struggle against Turkish supremacy, then against Yugoslavia. In Ireland, against a background of extreme poverty, the Irish Republic Brotherhood (IRB) and Irish Republican Army (IRA) attempted to disorganize Great Britain's government machinery. In 1939 the Israeli Irgun and the Stern group attacked the Arabs, then the British, in order to lessen their prestige and their unity. Finally, the Organisation Spéciale (OS), created in 1946, and the Front de Libération National Algérien (FLN) struck at the pro-French Muslim population of Algiers. During the 1970s there was a tremendous increase in violence by nationalist terrorist movements: Black September, founded by Arafat's Al-Fatah organization, the Palestine People's Liberation Front, the Moluccan Movement (which claims independence from Indonesia), the Grey Wolves in Turkey, and the Provisional IRA, to cite but a few, committed an impressive number of criminal deeds ranging from piracy in the air and the taking of hostages—particularly in embassies—to summary executions.

At the third and last level, and under a less easily recognizable appearance, slumbers subversive terrorism. Its context is a prelude to civil or international war, and it is a redoubtable means of action, for there is hardly any way of thwarting it. In a related field it is worth recalling the attempts made by the Germans in 1916 to supply the Irish rebels with arms and equipment in order to weaken England on the French front by forcing it to withdraw troops and send them to Ireland.

At each of these three levels there is a corresponding threat gradually facing the existing political system, as well as a wide range of material resources of an increasingly high degree of sophistication. The more rational and careful the planning of terrorist activities, the more inflexible the will of their originators, and the more ambitious the plan, the more highly developed the types of weapons and explosives used. This development, which has been greatly facilitated by the scientific and technological progress of the twentieth century, is a cause for the greatest concern. The daggers and rudimentary pistols of the nineteenth century have been replaced by automatic weapons whose increased firepower and smaller size make them infinitely more suitable for use in urban areas. The Soviet Kalashnikov rifle used to equip the Palestine Liberation Organization (PLO) and Black September, the VZ 58 assault rifle used in the massacre at Lod Airport in Jerusalem, the MP5, Sten, and Thomson machine guns of the Baader-Meinhof gang and the IRA, the M60 submachine guns, and the M26 fragmentation grenades that threatened the OPEC ministers in Vienna during the attack by Carlos on 21 December 1975, have led up to the Sam 7 Strela infrared guidance missile launchers that destroyed a Rhodesian Viscount in flight on 12 February 1979, and to the RPG7 rocket launchers used by Carlos on 13 and 19 January 1975, in attempts to destroy an El Al plane at Orly Airport, near Paris.

There have also been considerable improvements in the quality of bombs and explosives. The first "infernal machines" used by the Russian revolutionaries were extremely inaccurate, and often dangerous to handle. They could not be relied upon to work properly; for example, the mine that was placed under the Kharkhov railway line on 18 November 1879 and was intended to derail the train to Crimea in which Alexander II was traveling, did not explode. Furthermore, most of the explosive machines of that time required the person handling them to get too close to the intended victim, thus causing the handler's death. Ryssakov, a member of Narodnaia Volia, threw a bomb on the tsar's coach and was captured immediately; Grinieivetzky, also a member of Narodnaia Volia, was blown to pieces by the bomb that killed Alexander II. The Belgian anarchist Pauwels was riddled with shrapnel from his own weapon in the Madeleine Church in Paris on 15 March 1892, and the bomb thrown by Cabrinovic (armed by the Black Hand) missed Archduke Ferdinand of Austria on 28 June 1914.

Improved techniques have been developed. The engineer Kilbatchin invented a bomb, capable of exploding in any position, that was used by the Russian revolutionaries. Sticks of dynamite bound together, containing a load of nails, and set off by a fuse, are still used by the IRA. But plastic, which is easy to mold, has come to be the explosive favored by all terrorist groups. The firing mechanisms have a high level of performance and are safer: whether the mechanism responds to pressure (a booby trap fixed in a car that explodes when the driver sits down was the method used by the Israelis in Paris, on 28 June 1973, to liquidate Mohammed Boudia, the well-known Arab terrorist) or to the transmission of electric or electronic signals (the system used to murder Lord Mountbatten in Mullagmore Bay on 27 August 1979, by long-distance detonation of a bomb hidden in his fishing boat), terrorists are able to strike with greater ease and discretion.

One of the most serious consequences of terrorists possessing such highly perfected weapons is that these groups sometimes appear to be better armed than the police forces that are called upon to fight them. What hope is there for the future if we remember that the collapse of Egypt, of Greece, and of Rome was preceded by dissemination of new technologies concerned with weapons and the processing of metals, and by easier access to raw materials, thus enabling the barbarians to acquire an arsenal of weapons qualitatively and quantitatively at least equal, if not superior, to that of the civilizations in question?

Will further improvements in the terrorists' weaponry, combined with the will to destroy an increasing number of human lives, one day lead these terrorists to decide on the use of nuclear weapons? Is it possible that the development of civilian nuclear industries, the transport of strategic materials, and wide dissemination of technical know-how may encourage a group of particularly motivated people to acquire a nuclear weapon, or to steal the raw materials required for its production (the phenomenon of subnational proliferation)? Might such attempts prove successful in spite of the security measures surrounding the installations concerned? Is it conceivable that governments should find themselves reduced to the status of hostages? On another level, might a state acquire nuclear capability as a result of transfers of technology, and in violation of the principle of nonproliferation, and in so doing act as a terrorist? Or might it give a nuclear bomb into the hands of terrorist organizations under its control? Finally, might such a weapon, or the fissile materials required for its production, be stolen on its territory? These questions are facing governments, scientists, and the mass media with increasing intensity.

PSYCHOLOGICAL FACTORS OF TERRORISM AND THE USE OF NUCLEAR WEAPONS

Terrorism is a tactical method that is influenced by a series of psychological factors that it is important to identify when considering the hypothesis of a decision to use nuclear weapons.

Factors Conducive to Escalation

As far as the public has been informed, subnational proliferation—that is, acquisition by private individuals or groups of a nuclear weapon or of raw materials from which it could be made—luckily appears to be a subject of pure speculation. Until now no terrorist organization seems to have succeeded in seizing an atomic bomb, and none of the thefts of uranium committed in the past has led to the production of a nuclear device subsequently used for a criminal purpose. However, many incidents that have occurred in the past few years prove not only that the possibility of this type of terrorism cannot be ignored, but also that such an eventuality already looms on the horizon.

The Beginning of a Trend

A considerable number of nuclear threats (feigned), directed against American towns, were recorded during the 1970s, the first of them in Orlando, Florida, on 21 October 1970, which turned out to be a hoax thought up by a young student who demanded $1 million and a safe-conduct to leave the United States. All subsequent blackmail attempts that imitated this one proved to be without foundation, but this of course does not mean that it will always be the case in the future. In the second place, a large number of thefts of nuclear material have been recorded. Although most of them concerned "nonsensitive" material not usable for military purposes—as at the Bradwell power plant in Great Britain in 1966, and in Bihar, India, in 1974—there was a much more serious theft of 200 kilos of highly enriched uranium from a plant belonging to Nuclear Materials and Equipment Corporation in Apollo, Pennsylvania, in the 1960s, for which Israeli secret agents were widely thought to be responsible.

Finally, several armed attacks against nuclear power plants have taken place in different parts of the world. Most of them seem to have been connected more with a wish to be malicious than with the precise intent of stealing fissile materials: for example, the occupation of the Atucha power plant in Argentina on 25 March 1973 by the People's Revolutionary Army,[4] at a time when the building was not yet completed; the bomb attack at Fessenheim, France, by the Meinhof-Puig Antich[5] group in 1975; and the missile aimed at Creys-Malville, France, in 1981. In the last two cases the power plants did not house reactors containing sensitive materials.

Nevertheless, these events lead us to consider seriously the threat of nuclear terrorism. The fact that this has not so far occurred only goes to prove that there are a certain number of factors standing in the way, but we must be careful not to draw the conclusion that the will to resort to nuclear terror does not exist. A number of contradictory psychological factors may in fact come into play.

Two types of arguments are likely to encourage terrorists to brandish nuclear blackmail: the "shockingness," in the traumatic sense of the term, of an atomic threat, and its power to overcome the "devaluation" of the tactics employed by terrorists at the present time.

The Shock of the Threat

Terrorism is the weapon of weak minorities, and its primary objective is to strike people's minds and create an intense psychological shock, in order to assert power over the population. The repercussions of the event and mobilization of public opinion are the two pillars upon which the success of terrorist activities rests. Any movement that does not succeed in involving the mass of the people is doomed to failure, a principle that is well illustrated by the past. At the time of the Russian revolutionaries, terror already appeared to be the only effective method of bringing the population around to the idea of a revolution. The IRA, FLN, and OAS (Organisation de l'Armée Secrète, Secret Army Organization) all chose the same procedure: to commit a number of murderous attacks in the center of a large town that were at once reported in the international press. The IRA executed the pro-British members of the population, the FLN liquidated the pro-French Muslim elite in Algiers, and the OAS subjected the part of the population that remained hostile to it to bloody reprisals.

The lower prestige of a terrorist group, the higher must be the degree of violence required to impose fear. Thus the FLN was able to acquire an international hearing in only a few months. This almost "chemical" process of actions and reactions, of provocation and repression, must be emphasized in the phenomenon of terrorism, for in the long run it causes the government in power to be discredited as a result of its brutal and hasty measures against the terrorists. The wave of bomb explosions in Algiers between September 1956 and July 1957 led to intervention by French paratroopers who took the place of the police in order to maintain law and order in the city, and resorted to increasingly strong action—arrests, house searches, and torture—to break the ranks of the terrorists, whose extreme cruelty became continually worse. Movements to counter their action were organized, and the gulf between the Muslim and European communities grew wider day by day. International currents of opinion were roused, and these in fact enabled the FLN to be victorious.

The mesh of circumstances was the same in Great Britain when the army took increasingly severe reprisals against the IRA. The execution of 13 British secret agents by Irish terrorists in Dublin, on 21 November 1920, caused a violent reaction by British soldiers, who opened fire on a crowd massed around Croke Park football ground on the same day, killing 17 people and seriously wounding more than 60 others. The indignation among both the British and the Irish gave rise to further acts of violence; sudden house searches and arrests made the population angry and turned their sympathies to the side of the rebels, which resulted in the resignation of many English magistrates who refused to apply the sanctions required by law (more than 150 resignations were recorded during August 1920 alone).

In general, terrorism makes every effort to create this feeling of hostility resulting from a psychological effect, and thus banks on the logical condemnation of the government in power, particularly when the latter seems to be incapable of stemming the tide of violence and danger. In this context the existence of authorities powerless to meet the threat of elimination of a whole city would probably be very short-lived.

The Devaluation of the Usual Tactics

The second argument that might encourage escalation of the level of terrorism and recourse to nuclear weapons by a terrorist organization lies in the simple fact that there is a "devaluation" of the tactics used at present. Bomb explosions—like those that ravaged the Bologna railway station in Italy on 2 August 1980, causing 85 deaths and more than 180 wounded, and plunged the Munich beer festival (26 September 1980) into mourning with the massacre of 12 people and the mutilation of more than 300 others—the spectacular hijacking of planes, sometimes accompanied by their destruction before the lenses of cameras—we all recall the impressive hijacking of four airliners on 6 September 1970 and the destruction of a Pan Am jet in Cairo—and finally the assassinations of famous people—Anwar Sadat (at Cairo, 6 October 1981, by al-Takfir wal-Higra), Lord Mountbatten (at Sligo, 27 August 1979, by the Provisional IRA), Aldo Moro (at Rome, 10 May 1978, by the Red Brigades), and M. H. Schleyer (at Mulhouse, France, 19 October 1977, by the Red Army Faction)—and the taking of hostages in embassies all result in the event becoming a commonplace because it is too frequently described by the mass media for its horrific value to be kept up indefinitely. To some extent the interest of the public flags, and this means that the blackmail loses its effectiveness. The authorities no longer yield, and do not hesitate to make an assault thanks to the creation of special anti-terrorist units. The Israelis have given an example in this connection on many occasions, especially during the attack on the Sabena plane in Tel-Aviv on 8 May 1972, and the raid at Entebbe on 27 June 1976.

It might therefore be necessary to find a new form of coercion in order to keep up the effectiveness of terrorism. In this context, nuclear weapons stand out as an extraordinary instrument of mass intimidation. Of course, the use of explosive devices has always been chief among terrorist tactics, but the terrifying coercive effect of the atom, which is several thousand times more powerful than the bombs used at present, would give a fantastic dimension to the shock imposed on the population. The threat would no longer be limited to a few individuals, but would hang over a whole community and would be all the weightier because of the "myth" and the obsessive, almost religious, terror connected with nuclear power, particularly in the Christian democracies since Hiroshima and Nagasaki.

Although other methods of mass destruction—such as the poisoning of a city's drinking water sources—are undoubtedly easier to put into operation, they would appear not to have the same psychological impact. An atomic weapon would mean a change in dimension, both in the formulation of the demands and in the nature of the threat. It would be an ideal means of destabilizing a society, overthrowing a government, and producing the worst possible psychological conditions by exaggerating the terrorist action out of all proportion and establishing a supreme level of insecurity. Luckily, in spite of these potential advantages, it would seem that various dissuasive arguments have prevailed so far.

Dissuasive Factors

Two essential psychological factors may be mentioned: first, the risk of repression beyond any practiced so far, and of general repudiation; second, the lack of a theory of mass destruction of victims.

The Risk of Isolation and Repression

Terrorism is a two-edged weapon. While selective terror can indeed draw attention to a cause, blind fanaticism arouses waves of disapproval on all sides and tends to compromise the interests of the terrorists. Yet the mobilization of public opinion and its support are constant elements that are essential to the existence of a movement. The Irgun, the OAS, the IRB, the IRA, the MIRO, and more recently the PLO could not have stood up to their adversaries for so long if they had not had the help of sympathizers.

Furthermore, when a certain amount of dissension begins to appear within a group over methods to be used and their degree of violence, internal rivalries will very soon destroy the cohesion of the organization. To mention only one example connected with the war in Algeria, the pitiless torture, the irrational crimes, and the indiscriminate killings of the OAS Delta Commandos were very largely responsible for their final defeat. It is also worthwhile to mention the split in the Popular Front for the Liberation of Palestine (PFLP), from which some of its militants who were in favor of extreme terrorism were excluded, then regrouped on the initiative of Khaddafi and mixed with members of Black September to form the National Arab Youth for the Liberation of Palestine (NAYLP) in 1972. Only dangerously fanatical nihilist groups, comparatively unconcerned with their popularity, would probably not be dissuaded from committing odious crimes. The cruelty shown by the Japanese Red Army indicates that its militants are probably among the most fearsome archetypes of terrorists, and it can only be hoped that nuclear blackmail will always remain beyond their means.

Finally, the threat to use a nuclear weapon, implying the potential death of thousands, if not millions, of victims, carries with it the tremendous risk of unprecedented repression. No government concerned would hesitate to mobilize all its resources, or to exterminate the originators of such a crime. The Soviets have already adopted the principle of having any terrorist who harms the interests of the USSR eliminated by the KGB.

Absence of a Theory of Mass Destruction

The historical record of terrorism is full of bloody acts that caused large numbers of deaths from explosions, from the attack on the cathedral in Sofia in 1925 to that on the King David Hotel in Jerusalem, committed by the Irgun against British headquarters in Palestine in July 1946, and to the destruction of airliners in flight. The first caused more than 130 deaths and 330 wounded; the second, 91 deaths and 45 wounded. The explosion of a Swiss plane in flight on 21 February 1970, for which the PFLP claimed responsibility, killed 47 victims. That of a TWA plane between Israel and Greece on 8 October 1974 killed 88, and the SAM 7 fired by the Zimbabwe African People's Union (ZAPU) on a Rhodesian Viscount flying over Rhodesia on 12 February 1979 caused the death of more than 60 persons. Such cases are, however, comparatively rare. With a few exceptions—the massacre at Lod Airport on 31 May 1972 (28 dead and 76 wounded), and that in Rome on 17 December 1973—the aim of terrorist activities connected with civil aviation is to take hostages and press political claims. The elimination of millions of people is not yet a terrorist ambition, and neither chemical nor bacteriological weapons have so far been used, at least not on a large scale.

Perhaps the explanation of this phenomenon lies in the fact that a terrorist act has only a limited aim, intended mainly to draw attention, and thus is part of an overall strategy, enabling the fight to continue by other means. The Palestinian case is one of many examples. Moreover, only very rarely does terrorist blackmail succeed in obtaining satisfaction on specific demands, such as freeing of political prisoners or accomplices, provision of weapons, or the payment of money. It is not certain that the position would be different if the threat reached nuclear level, since most governments have established the principle of not yielding to criminals.

Only the determination to jeopardize directly the sovereignty of a state might justify recourse to nuclear weapons. However, at the present time few terrorist organizations have expressed a political ambition of this kind—with the exception of the Palestinian-Libyan NAYLP movement and the PLO, but neither of these possesses the means of achieving such a purpose.

To these elements must be added the fact that various "classical" methods exist that involve infinitely less risk yet have a power of persuasion.

"Classical" Methods

The destruction of passenger planes during flight, particularly with the help of antiaircraft missiles, which are easy to handle, would seem to be a "classical" method, to the extent that systematic protection of all airports is impossible to achieve. We have mentioned some of the precedents (Paris in 1975 and in Rhodesia in 1979).

Action of this kind, perpetrated several times against planes of big Western airlines, would have worldwide repercussions, and would without any doubt cause definite fear among the population.

This being the case, why should terrorists resort to nuclear bombs, which are weapons out of all proportion to their objectives? Above all, what proof would they have that the risks incurred in attempting to get hold of such devices would give any further weight to their blackmail or would increase their chances of success? The basic problem is concerned with quantifying the value of human lives, and the question "At what point must a government yield?" cannot be answered. Is it when the potential number of victims reaches 100, 1,000, or 10,000? Any estimate is subjective, and there is no reason to believe that classical blackmail aimed at hundreds or thousands of people would be less effective. Nuclear weapons are no more a panacea for the terrorists than they have proved to be in the hands of the great powers, and holding back from violence through fear of uncontrollable consequences remains an overriding necessity.

In conclusion, it is essential to remember that use of the atom is not in keeping with the avowed objectives of most of the terrorist groups known at the present time. Its use would entail reconsideration of the limited aims of contemporary terrorism, in the same way it forced the great powers to reconsider the relationships among politics, strategy, and technology after 1945, with a view to harmonizing the end with the means.

Apart from these considerations of a moral nature, many technical factors stand in the way of a risk of subnational proliferation.

TECHNICAL FACTORS AND THE RISK OF SUBNATIONAL PROLIFERATION

Subnational proliferation could result from two types of action: theft of a nuclear weapon from a military store or in transport, and construction of an explosive device with fissile materials stolen or diverted for this purpose.

However, the technical difficulties that the originators of such plans would find in their way limit considerably the risk of such things happening, though they do not rule them out altogether. Terrorist organizations have never yet dared attack targets of this kind, because both plants and convoys are extremely well protected.

Safety Measures for Nuclear Weapons

At first sight it may appear easier to seize a ready-made weapon than to steal fissile materials. The degree of protection varies from country to country, but there is undoubtedly a higher degree of security when a country's strategic and tactical nuclear weapons are all located within its frontiers instead of being disseminated elsewhere, as is the case with NATO forces, which are widely scattered, particularly in the German Federal Republic, where for a time terrorism was rife.

Protection of the Components of Weapons

The first difficulty to be overcome is the dissemination of the various components of the bombs, and their storage in separate buildings, located in the middle of clearly defined security areas within which any intruder may be arrested or shot. Such areas are, in addition, equipped with infrared detectors, ultrasonic systems, and cameras, and are under the close supervision of armed guards who are sufficiently numerous and well prepared to withstand an attack, theoretically, until reinforcements arrive. The transport of such material is carried out as secretly as possible, with the assistance of police and military security forces.

In addition to these precautions, a series of codes and combinations exists with the object of preventing an unplanned explosion.

The Buildup of "Locks and Bolts"

Several special codes have to be put into operation, in a strict order of sequence and by carefully selected persons, none of whom holds the whole combination. In the United States this device is called Permissive Action Link (PAL). We shall not go into details of it here.

It should be noted that a number of accidents involving planes carrying atomic weapons have been recorded; they have aroused considerable anxiety as to the possibility of thefts in such circumstances. One such accident was the collision of a B-52 and a KC-135 on 17 January 1966, which occurred during refueling in flight over Spain and caused the bomber to crash near Palomares. On that occasion it took more than two months for American experts to locate two of the four nuclear weapons, which had not exploded.

The other alternative is to attempt to obtain sensitive materials in order to produce the device required.

Difficulties in Manufacturing a Nuclear Weapon

First of all, it is important to emphasize that although a sensation-loving press has often announced the possibility of producing a homemade bomb "in the kitchen," the hazards of such an undertaking should not be underestimated. Although the basic principles of nuclear physics and the working of a weapon of this type are known, this is not the case for the principles underlying the construction itself, which is an extremely complex operation, beyond the capacity of the ordinary terrorist.

However, a theft of uranium or plutonium, together with large technical resources, could result in the manufacture of a bomb, if certain conditions were present.

The Possession of Raw Materials

The first of these conditions is of course the possession of a "significant" quantity of materials—that is, enough to produce a weapon: at least 8 kilos of plutonium or 25 kilos of highly enriched uranium. More may be required if the terrorists are not highly skilled in production techniques.

The Dangers of Handling Nuclear Material

In the second place, the terrorists would have to be able to move the radioactive materials without jeopardizing their own lives, and then to store them. With regard to plutonium, the difficulties are not insurmountable insofar as it comes in the form of oxide (for accelerators in civilian industry, for instance) made up into bars of 1 or 2 kilos that can be placed in special containers.

The whole operation would require a tremendous effort, and certainly could not be carried out successfully without assistance from a team of scientists and technicians particularly skilled not only in the field of physics but also in the production of nuclear arms.

Finally, supposing that all these conditions are met, there is still the possibility that the weapon produced may be of unusual shape and of doubtful quality, and that there may be a very great risk of its exploding unexpectedly (provided that it is capable of doing so). It is not enough to create the critical mass essential to set off the chain reaction; it is also necessary to know how to prevent the device that has been produced from exploding before it is supposed to.

The undertaking is therefore a hazardous though not impossible one, but remains the prerogative of specialists. However, the increase in the number of industries connected with nuclear energy, and the consequent increase in the amount of transport of uranium and plutonium (intensified by the practice of reprocessing radioactive wastes), unfortunately help to make the danger even greater in spite of the protective measures taken.

Measures for the Physical Protection of Sensitive Materials

The International Atomic Energy Agency (IAEA) has made a series of recommendations on protective measures aimed at foiling attempted theft or diversion. These directives are respected at the present time in most of the countries that have developed their nuclear industry, but there is nevertheless a consensus that they are insufficient. France, which has a command of all stages in the fuel's cycle, including enrichment and reprocessing, has always considered itself particularly concerned with security problems. Some of its regulations will help to illustrate the kinds of precautions taken to stave off any criminal action.

The basic consideration is the strict maintenance of absolute secrecy on these questions. Contrary to the practice in the United States, French experts consider that total discretion must be the basic principle in safeguarding security.

The only people allowed to have information connected with security are rigorously selected on the basis of professional criteria. Neither the range of emergencies envisaged, nor the level of damage that can be tolerated, nor the choice and placement of facilities for surveillance, must ever be divulged.

These rules apply to the storage as well as the transport of sensitive materials, and thus help to make the terrorists' task more complicated.

Protection of Materials in Storage

The civilian nuclear industry is being developed all over the world. In 1981 there were more than 250 power reactors in service, including 30 in France. This does not mean that all such installations are targets that attract terrorists; for instance, plants producing or processing low-enriched materials are not.

It is a very different matter, however, for plants that use highly enriched uranium (93 percent) to produce fuels or plutonium, and for reactors that work with these materials (if such reactors were to be used as a source of supply, they would have to be attacked before the fuels were introduced into their heart).

Let us look at some of the measures taken at the reprocessing plant at La Hague, France, where the premises are divided into three security areas. The first, which covers all the buildings, is surrounded by several miles of electrified fences; entrance is authorized after an identity check. The second is more difficult to enter because this is possible only with an electronic badge linked to a computer and impossible to imitate. Parking of vehicles is strictly regulated. Times of visits and the reasons for them are recorded. The third area contains the buildings in which the materials are stored. The bars of plutonium are stored in a strong room with concrete walls made to resist explosives. Persons authorized to go in regularly are carefully selected. Several systems of keys are needed to enter this storeroom, and these are under the responsibility of different departments (custodial department, store management department). No member of the staff may stay there alone. The stores are permanently watched by cameras connected to a guardroom that is in direct touch with the police and the département (county) authorities.

A complex system of detection has been installed, in particular radiation-sensitive devices placed near the doors. Even if intruders were able to get into the storeroom and procure bars of plutonium, these devices would record the radiation and at once give the alarm.

In order to be able to repel a possible attack, the guards at the Compagnie Générale des Matières Nucléaires (COGEMA), which specializes in reprocessing, and Commissariat à l'Energie Atomique (CEA) are armed, which is not the case in private firms or in Electricité de France (EDF, the supplier of electricity). They can be assembled in any part of the plant in a matter of seconds, and would probably delay the terrorists long enough for reinforcements to be able to reach them in time.

In general, as in any highly specialized organization, the greatest danger is from complicity within the house and collusion, either voluntarily or under force, between members of the staff and outside agents. Nevertheless, with such an abundance of security systems it would doubtless take too many converging circumstances for any such attempt to result in a theft.

Protection of Materials in Transit

The intensive protection of the buildings, and thus of the materials stored in them, might incite terrorists to attack a transport convoy. In France sensitive materials are transported chiefly by road, in special trucks. These vehicles are armor-plated, and several keys have to be used together to open the doors. There are always two drivers, each of whom holds only one of these keys. Transit takes place in daylight and on highways, and the journeys are quick, in contrast with what happens in the German Federal Republic, where the trucks involved are very heavy, have an armored outside covering, and are driven slowly (at about 35 miles an hour). During the journey the trucks remain in constant radio contact with the CEA. A call is sent out once an hour. The location and the speed of the vehicles are recorded every three minutes. The police escort accompanying them has its own radio network linking it to its headquarters. The frequencies are changed each time a new *département* is entered.

Even if the terrorists were to succeed in shooting down all the members of the escort and stealing the truck, an alarm would be set off instantaneously. Furthermore, the vehicles are fitted with additional ultrasecret security systems that are designed to add considerably to the time needed to get hold of their contents. The police therefore would probably have the time to locate the stolen transport. Training exercises are held frequently, and it takes only a few hours to find the truck. Timetables are always changed. Stops are allowed at CEA centers or police barracks or police stations. In the United States problems of road transport are very much greater because of the long distances to be covered.

International transport sometimes takes place by air, particularly of plutonium from Great Britain being sent to Super Phoenix, the French supergenerator at Creys-Malville, France. Here again there is very strict protection; selection of the pilots is very closely scrutinized, and the cargo is accompanied. The planes land at civilian airports, in a specially prepared area where police escorts await them.

"Normal" materials—natural uranium or slightly enriched uranium (3 percent)—which are in no immediate danger as far as terrorism is concerned, and present no danger to the population, are carried by train or ship. They are of no use to terrorists, since at least 20 percent enriched uranium is needed to make a bomb, and are therefore given no special protection.

No security system can be considered completely reliable, and the possibility of highly enriched uranium, plutonium, or uranium 233 being stolen cannot be excluded.

There is less risk in France because, in contrast with the United States, it has no private plutonium industry, and this reduces considerably the dangers of misappropriation for purposes of terrorism. The precautions to be taken are decided upon at the highest level and are scrupulously applied. Also, the fact that there are very few places where such materials are held further reduces opportunities for terrorism. The chief places are COGEMA, the CEA, and EDF, all three of which are in close touch with the government. Small quantities of uranium, carefully recorded but not enough to make an explosive device, are in the hands of various bodies, such as universities with reactors for research, and firms with chemical needs, such as those that make paint. Large quantities are also controlled by COGEMA, CEA, and EDF.

The exporters of sensitive materials are mainly CEA, Compagnie pour L'Etudes et la Réalisation de Combustibles Atomiques (CERCA), and COGEMA. The London Agreements state that the levels of physical protection of sensitive materials must be worked out in agreement between the providing country and the receiving country, and there must be no interference with the latter's sovereignty: application of these measures within its territory is under its authority alone. Neither the seller nor IAEA has any supervisory power. This comparative powerlessness is also evident with regard to transfers of technology, since the IAEA, in Vienna, does not possess sufficiently extensive prerogatives to ensure that no beneficiary state can make use of its civilian industry for military purposes. This situation leads us to a number of questions on the risk of terrorism that could originate in those countries that acquire nuclear technology.

DANGERS INHERENT IN TRANSFERS OF TECHNOLOGY

Until now we have linked nuclear terrorism with the supposed action of individuals or groups, but it must also be considered in the context of transfers of technology. The latter expression covers concepts of know-how, secrets of production, technical data, procedures for reprocessing, descriptions of chemical reactions, and advice on the maintenance of the apparatus.

Transposition of the Problem to the State Level

The basic question arises at the state level, and brings us back to the subject of proliferation: should plants be sold and technology transferred to third countries that might one day expel the international supervisors and use their civilian nuclear industry for military or terrorist purposes?

This risk is increased by three factors: the weakness of international guarantees, the training of foreign staff, and the delivery of patents.

The Weakness of International Guarantees

There is a consensus among those who deal with security on a nuclear level that the safety measures now in force are totally insufficient. The Nonproliferation Treaty, which was signed by some 100 states, could not gain the support of a number of important holders of nuclear technology: France, the People's Republic of China, Israel, Pakistan, South Africa, India, Argentina, and Brazil.

The London Agreements establish a number of regulations covering arrangements dealing with transfers of technology related to the reprocessing and enrichment of uranium or production of heavy water. The exporting countries are obliged to limit such transfers and to ensure that the guarantees of the IAEA are strictly applied, the agency being kept informed of, and the exporting country having to approve, the construction of any plant producing uranium enriched more than 20 percent.

There are several types of installations that involve a danger with regard to proliferation. Light water reactors, which involve the use of low enriched uranium, are not considered to be "proliferating" because it is not possible to obtain from them materials that can be diverted for the construction of a nuclear bomb, and because they are not particularly easy to use for this purpose. The position is quite different with regard to heavy water reactors, reprocessing plants—which in any case are not within the reach of ordinary individual terrorists because of the sophisticated manipulators and robot systems required—and enrichment plants. The production of heavy water can be controlled only by restrictions on the transfers of the appropriate technology that put obstacles in the way of making reactors capable of producing plutonium of military quality. The example of India, which possesses the technology for reactors moderated with heavy water received from Canada, shows how ineffective the restrictions on "sensitive" transfers can be.

Training of Staff

The sale of nuclear installations is usually accompanied by a specialized foreign staff. To a certain extent, dissemination of technical knowledge may be equivalent to a transfer of technology.

Certain technicians, after receiving special training, would be in a position to help their country equip itself with nuclear arms or, either voluntarily or under constraint, to serve a terrorist network. A fear of this kind was probably at the root of the Israeli decision to attack the Tamuz base in Iraq on 7 June 1981, because Osirak, which was a pool-type research reactor placed under the dual control of IAEA inspectors and French technicians working on the spot, could not, according to CEA headquarters, have been used to produce a bomb. Furthermore, the French experts were supposed to work in Iraq for several years and would not have turned the installations over to the Iraqis until enough time had elapsed for the fuels to become highly radioactive, thus preventing any diversion of the uranium. As for the production of plutonium, this would have required modifications in the equipment that would have been difficult to carry out discreetly. On the other hand, this reactor would undoubtedly have helped familiarize scientists with the techniques of nuclear physics.

Every year France receives some 1,500 trainees—most of them students in physical metallurgy or chemistry—and takes a great many precautions. First, candidates coming to the CEA are presented by their government, which constitutes a preliminary selection and to a certain extent eliminates the possibility of opponents to the regime of the beneficiary state later undertaking terrorist activities against it (though it cannot provide the same assurances with regard to operations carried out in a foreign country). Furthermore, no training is provided in the sensitive techniques of enrichment or reprocessing. Finally, the CEA does not accept trainees from countries that give anxiety as far as proliferation is concerned, such as South Africa, Pakistan, and Israel. None of these measures, however, really ensure security, since there is no escaping the fact that services can be hired in all fields or can be obtained by force, but they do ensure a certain measure of control.

Delivery of Patents

In France the most sensitive technologies, connected with the conception and working of enrichment or reprocessing plants, are transferred from state to state, and are covered by government restrictions. On the other hand, certain types of transfers escape government supervision through lack of a legal basis. The French authorities manage to exercise an unofficial right of veto, since the large firms that would be in a position to sell very sensitive technologies are very few in number and keep in close touch with the ministries concerned and with the CEA.

Scenarios

As soon as a state is in possession of a nuclear industry or an atomic weapon, several scenarios are foreseeable in connection with terrorism. Three types of possibilities need to be considered: "direct" state terrorism, state terrorism through an intermediary, and individual terrorism resulting from a lack of precautions by the beneficiary state.

"Direct" State Terrorism

The term "terrorism" should not be applied only to individuals or nonstate organizations; a sovereign state, its secret service, or its agents abroad may commit or finance acts of violence. Recent occurrences in France have once more proved the existence of such a phenomenon, including the expulsion of two Syrian diplomats from France in April 1982 for breach of the national interest and involvement in a bomb attack against the premises of the Lebanese newspaper Al-Watan al Arabi in Paris.

The theme of nuclear blackmail exerted by a state appears in many novels of political fiction, and sometimes seems doubtful. As far as motivation is concerned, it must be admitted that any country that took the risk of acquiring a nuclear weapon and using it for terrorist purposes, thereby coming into direct collision with the world of politics as a whole, would be putting its very existence at stake. But it would have very considerable means at its disposal, far more than any ordinary individual or group of individuals. It must therefore be admitted that if nuclear terrorism should one day occur, it would be more likely to originate from a state than from an isolated and less powerful organization—unless, of course, it were controlled from outside.

At this stage in the discussion, the question arises as to whether a state that threatens to resort to a nuclear weapon in order to obtain a political advantage should be considered a "terrorist." Is there a fundamental difference in principle between a threat of war and a surprise atomic attack, and that of the explosion of a nuclear device hidden in some large city? Is the underhand nature of the second situation enough to remove the stamp of "terrorism" from the first? The language of doctrines of strategy tends to reply in the negative, using expressions such as "balance of terror," "mutual assured destruction," and "hostage populations or cities." It would seem that the words "terror" and "terrorism" cover the same concept of exploitation of fear to political ends, even if the aims and methods are entirely different. In substance, the two practices are identical.

However, an act of nuclear blackmail would constitute an act of open hostility carrying the risk of dangerous reprisals. For this reason it may be that a state planning terrorist activities prefers to work behind the scenes, in order not to compromise itself before the rest of the world.

Terrorism Through an Intermediary

To some extent, terrorism is a solution of substitution. The declared use of a nuclear weapon would constitute a casus belli, and would have much too serious consequences for its originator. Nuclear parity, which has so far prevented a world conflict from breaking out, has allowed large numbers of limited wars to take place, in which terrorism is one of the methods of fighting. Such terrorism is a kind of indirect strategy aimed at destabilizing Western society to the greatest possible extent, and gives rise to support from numerous movements backed or manipulated by foreign governments. The attempt on the life of Pope John Paul II in Rome on 13 May 1980, by Mehmet Ali Agca, confirms this interventionist trend, and without going so far as to claim, as some people do, that a terrorist international exists, nobody can deny that active help in both funds and arms comes from Iron Curtain countries. The great majority of weapons found as a result of house searches or captures comes from the Soviet Union (Kalashnikov, Makarov, Tokarev, Sam 7) or Czechoslovakia (VZ 58, VZ 61). Terrorist organizations have established links with one another, including Baader-Meinhof, the PLO, and the Japanese Red Army.

It is not possible to give precise examples of states whose interests may be linked to the use of "indirect" nuclear terrorism; they could only be based on theory. However, everyone is aware of the antagonisms that might well bring about such an attitude. The growing number of countries coming into possession of modern technologies adds further to the dangers.

Thus we find, halfway between individual terrorism and state terrorism, a third kind of terrorism of undefinable origin, whose organization is still a matter of guesswork and that is perceived rather than analyzed rationally.

Individual Terrorism Resulting from Theft in a Beneficiary State

Here we are once more faced with the problem of subnational proliferation. Transfers of sensitive technology to a third country that on its own is unable to ensure effective protection of its civilian installations, its materials, or its nuclear arms (if it has any) might jeopardize international security.

Several states in the Middle East are striving to develop their nuclear industry and might be tempted to make use of their technical experience for military purposes. The climate of political insecurity that characterizes this area is far from excluding many changes of government in the future. The appropriation of atomic weapons by uncontrolled groups would represent a grave threat to the international community. Iran is an edifying example. Four nuclear power plants were to have been built between 1980 and 1984, and 14 projects were under study. If Iran had become a member of the nuclear powers' "club" before the revolution, what would have happened to the arms, in view of the political anarchy, the summary executions of leading figures, and the internal rivalries? Also, if Iran had developed only a civilian nuclear industry, the further problem would have arisen of physical protection of the materials stored within the country.

It is thus clear that the only way to avoid creating risks would be to stop passing on valuable knowledge to countries that are not in possession of nuclear technologies; but such an extreme and utopian solution is actually in glaring opposition to the principles of the Nonproliferation Treaty (NPT) and comes up against the exasperation of the developing countries, which accuse the major powers of wishing to keep the Third World in its present position of technical inferiority.

To stop the supply of special materials in order to lessen the risks of proliferation in case of violation of the NPT can be only a short-term solution. Furthermore, such an attitude could lead to the development of a black market in uranium or plutonium; this would certainly be sufficiently lucrative to attract organizations like the Mafia, which undoubtedly has an international network extensive enough to make such trading possible.

CONCLUSIONS

Of all the forms of terrorism foreseeable at the present time, nuclear terrorism would seem to be the least credible, since it does not correspond to the avowed aims of the organizations that we know. Recourse to this type of fighting would mean a profound change in the terrorist methods used until now, and would carry with it the risk of total elimination of the group responsible for such an act.

However, this eventuality cannot be overlooked in the future, and the first incidents that occurred during the 1970s give an indication of a possible move toward this kind of terrorism, which, it would seem, must be the work of a state, either openly or through remote control of movements from outside, rather than the work of isolated individuals.

The fear, not to say the psychosis, surrounding nuclear power in the minds of the population would increase disproportionately the psychological shock to which it was subjected, and the mere possession of nuclear materials by terrorists, without their holding an atomic weapon, would undoubtedly be enough to dramatize the impact of the situation.

In spite of the "devaluation" of contemporary terrorist tactics and the need to find new forms of coercion, dissuasive factors have prevailed until now and have prevented the threat of nuclear blackmail from becoming a reality; this phenomenon is due to the vast number of technical difficulties that, beyond moral constraints, prevent access to nuclear weapons or materials. But this is only a question of technological resources, since no arrangements for protection are infallible. The growing sophistication of modern technology is as useful to terrorists who rebel against established order as to the societies that have secreted it, thus bringing about a paradoxical weakening of Western countries. The strengthening of security measures regarding sensitive materials, development of international cooperation in fields related to transfers of technology, and intensification of the fight against terrorism are all vital for our countries, but are not really given all the attention they deserve, since there is no escaping the fact that private interests clash with state interests, and commercial profit with security requirements, both nationally and internationally.

NOTES

1. François-Claudius Koenigstein (1859–92), alias Ravachol, was executed on 11 July 1894 for the bombing of several magistrates' homes and of barracks.

2. Founded in 1879, its main leaders were Jeliabov, Vera Fignier, and Sophie Perovskaia. The Fighting Organization, founded by Guerchouni, assassinated ministers, governors, officials, and the tsar.

3. A sect of Jewish patriots that sought independence and murdered officials suspected of compromising with Rome. They launched a revolt in A.D. 66 that led to the taking of Jerusalem in A.D. 70 by Titus.

4. Marxist-Leninist group, founded in 1969 and fighting against capitalism in South America.

5. Unknown group; Salvador Puig Antich was a Catalan anarchist executed on 2 March 1974.

8

U.S. Military Space Policy

Colin S. Gray

IN SEARCH OF COHERENCE

Given the growing U.S. dependence on the military uses of space,[1] and the great immaturity of weapons and tactics to be employed in space, confident prediction of specific future capabilities and bold advocacy of particular military postures, tactics, and strategies would be premature. Nonetheless, the United States does need, urgently, to clarify its thinking concerning its military policy in, and bearing upon, space—while leaving many of the technical details to be determined as and when. . . .

The U.S. Secretary of the Air Force Verne Orr wrote in 1982 that

> Just as transcontinental and intercontinental air transportation in the 1930s and 1940s revolutionized the way we conduct commerce and the way wars were fought, space transportation today holds the same potential.[2]

Assertions such as this have been made so often and for so long that there is some danger that the important, indeed vital, truth that they contain may be overwhelmed by the contempt and disinterest that attends the overly familiar. It seems unlikely, looking forward from the early 1980s, that the way wars are fought will be revolutionized by space transportation before the year 2000. However, given the great maturity of ground, sea, and air instruments of combat, and the scarcely less great immaturity of space weaponry, this claim is very likely to be true one day. On the negative side for Western national security, the most radical near-term impact of the military uses of space upon armed conflict may prove to be its contribution to policy-decision paralysis.

If the United States fails to look adequately to the survivability of its space-based or space-deployed assets for Command, Control, Communications and

Intelligence (C³I) and surveillance/reconnaissance, or if more mundane terrestrial backup systems are not sustained, then the space age could spell military catastrophe for the West. For example, one need not be addicted to "worst case" analysis in order to be disturbed by the fact that many senior U.S. officials appear to view the enduring survivability of satellites in geosynchronous orbit as constituting a near-canonical truth. There is both major risk and major benefit attending the military use of space. A well-informed debate in the early 1980s should help to encourage the U.S. government to endeavor to identify and minimize the risks. The principal danger, which is already evident to a noteworthy degree, is that considerations of peacetime efficiency and convenience will be allowed to close out serious preparations for war.

Military space activity, in common with much other defense endeavor, provides ample evidence of the victory of suboptimization. In other words, individual military problems have tended to be resolved on their own narrow, individual terms, while the whole dynamic mosaic of military space activity has not enjoyed any very noteworthy measure of genuinely central direction or forward thinking from the overall perspective of U.S. national security. There is evidence that this anarchic condition may be changing for the better, but the evidence of greatly improved integrated policy performance has yet to be provided.

Notwithstanding a quarter century of space experience, the United States remains confused as to what its space policy should be, how it should think about the military uses of space, and how military space activity may impact upon national military policy as a whole. It may be unfair, or perhaps premature, to include the Reagan administration in this general indictment, since a new policy has been announced only very recently, and major bureaucratic innovations have been registered. It is far too early to pass judgment on the quality of these developments—the evidence is not in.

It is helpful to review very briefly why confusion has characterized official U.S. thought and action in the military space policy arena. The principal reasons are the following:

1. Outer space adds a new dimension to war, and new dimensions to war are inherently very difficult to comprehend (their meaning is unambiguous only in retrospect), while the vast majority of those who have to attempt the comprehending tend to have very strong, and other unhelpful, strategic preconceptions that flow from their career experience and from the culture and doctrine of the organizations within which they serve.

2. Military space activity has grown piecemeal in response both to "technology push" and to "operational pull" from military users who have sought improved ways of fulfilling generally existing mission requirements. To date there has not been any "operational pull" upon potential military space technology exercised by an organization concerned primarily with military space activity and, in extremis, with preparation for the conduct of conflict in space.

3. Space-weapon technology is so immature that there has been, and remains, great difficulty in achieving and sustaining discipline in debate over military space

questions. The layman interested in military space matters (a description that includes many very senior, responsible government officials) may perhaps be excused some confusion in his understanding when proponents of space-based ballistic missile defense (BMD) weapons promise strategic superiority through an operationally workable system early in the 1990s,[3] while no less well-informed skeptics advise that "[i]n general, it is difficult to conceive of even a conceptual space-based weapon system which could be strategically significant prior to the turn of the century."[4]

4. To date, U.S. governments have not felt the need to concentrate much intellectual energy upon questions of national military space policy, qua national policy, because policy and program issues have tended to be presented within a narrow frame of reference.

5. The potential importance of space as a field of conflict, and possibly even as the most important field of conflict, has long been recognized by busy senior officials who are not in the habit of anticipating problems and opportunities. Minimal policy making is the rule in government. That is, one tends to decide as little as one can as late as one can. This perennial phenomenon does not always reflect confusion of thought—and hence protracted indecision—absence of forward vision, and the like. As often as not, minimal policy making is a prudent, sensible modus operandi that helps officials to cope with irreducible uncertainties (irreducible, that is, save through the passage of time). In short, one copes with the uncertain needs and opportunities of the future by maximizing one's future options—by maintaining policy flexibility. However, there is a critical difference between tactical and strategic flexibility. All too often strategic flexibility attempts to conceal uncertainty of long-term purpose. While there are dangers in doctrine, scarcely less impressive are the lost opportunities that the absence of doctrine tends to produce.

The final point above is relevant to the contemporary state of U.S. military space policy. The Reagan administration has chosen to commit itself to a space policy that is strong in declaratory generalities. Given the profound technical uncertainties that pertain to projections of space combat potential, a policy bereft of any very specific national security vision is certainly prudent. What appears to be lacking in U.S. military space policy is recognition of the possibility that the full military exploitation of space might enable U.S. policy makers to effect a genuine revolution in strategy. Even in the absence of strategic vision, the United States might one day discover that as a consequence of many minimal policy decisions in incremental steps, a revolution in warfare had been implemented. However, as a general rule, progress is more likely to be achieved if one knows where one would like to go.

ASAT AND ARMS CONTROL

U.S. military space policy today specifies the goal of achieving an operational anti-satellite ASAT capability (reportedly by fiscal 1987), both in order to deter attacks on U.S. spacecraft and to deny an enemy the use of its space-based assets. In addition, the United States has adopted an approach to ASAT arms control that is reminiscent of the official position on the "launch under attack" option for intercontinental ballistic missiles (ICBMs)—"we do not rule it out." As an example of prose that commits the government to nothing in particular, the Reagan administration's statement on ASAT arms control is a minor master-piece and may well become a collector's item:

> The United States will continue to study space arms control options. The United States will consider verifiable and equitable arms control measures that would ban or otherwise limit testing and deployment of specific weapons sys-tems, should those measures be compatible with United States national security.[5]

This statement usefully holds the door to arms control slightly ajar, but—less usefully—it may reflect an absence of genuine policy on the subject of ASAT arms control that flows in part from an absence of real policy objectives in the military space arena. The Reagan administration, if it is guilty with respect to military space policy, is guilty of sins of omission rather than sins of commission. The policy, as outlined on July 4, 1982, does not envisage, either specifically or even by distant implication, the pursuit, or defense of pursuit, of any national security activities in space beyond those currently conducted or scheduled to be conducted. Strategic vision can be dangerously blinkering in its effect upon its proponents, but its cautious and contingent delineation should help policy makers decide wisely on policy questions today that must have a major legacy value for the future—even the long-term future.

BALLISTIC MISSILE DEFENSE AND STRATEGIC DOGMA

For example, the U.S. government cannot make a responsible decision on its attitude toward ASAT arms control unless it has first decided what attitude it prefers toward a strategic context characterized, indeed dominated, by the pres-ence of a multilayered architecture of active and passive strategic defenses. Space-based BMD weapons are not plausibly in sight today, given both the prim-itive character of the key technologies and the wide range of countermeasures to both conventional and "exotic" systems that should be available. However, there is no very persuasive reason why space-based conventional and directed-energy weapons will not, one day, be as capable as endoatmospheric BMDs of the Sentry generation give the appearance of being in the 1980s. The U.S. gov-ernment need not, indeed cannot, make predictions today as to the technical prospects for, say, space-based high-energy laser HEL weapons in the year 2000 and beyond. But the government can and should develop an attitude toward a hypothetical strategic context wherein strategic offensive forces should be able to inflict but a small fraction of the damage that they could wreak today.

The dynamic relationship between the offense and the defense may not render such a context technically possible for many decades to come, but if the possibility is to be kept alive, let alone advanced, the technological development of new active defense concepts should not be constrained by treaty. One need not sign on for General Graham's "High Frontier"[6] in order to believe that it is responsible for the superpowers to endeavor to extricate mankind from the threat of holocaust that is implicit in contemporary strategic nuclear capabilities (if not in contemporary nuclear strategy, at least by purposeful design).

Contrary to much of popular belief, the proximate danger in the increasing military exploitation of outer space has far less to do with the (alleged) evils of an unconstrained arms race in that arena than it has to do with the very real possibility that the United States, through an unwise measure of dependence upon military space assets and an unduly dilatory approach to defense of satellite DSAT and ASAT missions, may offer the Soviet Union a strategic Achilles heel for attack. Furthermore, there is the distinct possibility that, probably for the best of reasons, a U.S. administration may be so ill-advised as to seek to constrain, through arms control, military innovation that bears upon conflict in space. Aside from the consideration that technological innovation really cannot be frozen by arms control, though it can be delayed and redirected, proposals to prevent or severely constrain the weaponization of space tend to neglect the baseline from which they begin. The nuclear protest movements of the early 1980s are misguided in much of their analysis and their prescriptions,[7] but they do rest upon one unarguable fact—that the current system of nuclear deterrence, wherein the offense is unquestionably dominant, is fraught with major peril for the human race. The true solution to the dilemmas of the nuclear deterrence system lies in politics, not in weapon technologies or in arms control "Band-Aids."

Nonetheless, so long as a political solution to East–West competition is beyond reach, it is the duty of policy makers to explore the technical feasibility of a new deterrent system that would be benignly bereft of the "fail deadly" character of the extant nuclear relationship. Vigorous pursuit of new space weaponry may affront some long-standing shibboleths concerning arms race stability and its purported perils, but history, prudent strategic logic, and arms control theory would all support such pursuit. We should not want to "stabilize" a strategic environment wherein the nuclear warhead "will always get through." Laurence Martin has offered the following pertinent judgment:

> It may be that the mere fact that the technological context of deterrence is continually changing creates an element of international tension. But it may equally be argued, on the principle that qualitative arms competition is less dangerous than quantitative, that a process of continual innovation postpones indefinitely the appropriate occasion for war.[8]

The operational mandate of the U.S. Air Force Space Command and its responsibility to "develop space defense doctrine and strategy"[9] could, and should, do much to strengthen the trend in official U.S. thinking toward considering military space activity in a potential conflict environment. However, Space Command will be hampered in its mission of developing operational requirements so long as the government as a whole declines to confront the fundamental strategic question of the desirable balance, for the long term, between strategic offense and defense. Given the short-term focus that seems endemic to nearly all in-house official policy reviews, it is more likely than not that the official studies conducted in 1982 in connection with the second quinquennial review of the ABM Treaty of 1972 will be judged in the future to have neglected to consider adequately possible connections between policy decisions taken today for very near-term reasons, and issues of the offense–defense balance in the long term. A major in-house official study, titled "National Security Implications of Ballistic Missile Defense," was launched in the summer of 1982—a study that has been characterized as required to examine "the long-range aspects of ballistic missile defense, not just on defense related to MX."[10] However, even though this study exercise may well explore the technological story concerning, and prospects for, directed-energy weapons and "high frontier," what is likely to be missing is a sense of desired strategic direction. The resources price and the technical risks that the United States would be willing to pay and assume in connection with technologically ambitious BMD research and development programs, cannot be unrelated to the strength of the official motivation to succeed. In other words, "technology push" could well foredoom the admittedly distant prospect of the United States achieving a robust homeland defense.

SPACE POLICY AND NATIONAL SECURITY

What is needed—and this is a major challenge for Space Command, is not so much a military strategy for outer space as a proper appreciation of the strategic roles that are, and might be, played by military space assets within the framework of an overall national security policy that properly accommodates military space realities. Since Space Command could no more wage a conflict on its own than could the parent Air Force, the Navy, or the Army, the need is for inclusivity rather than exclusivity. In the context of U.S. national security policy as a whole, space defense doctrine and strategy probably should stress the strong desirability of the United States doing the following:

1. Achieving and sustaining the potential for asserting clear strategic superiority in space in the event of war. Given the degree of its military dependence upon space, the United States could not afford to lose a space campaign: the stakes would be too high.

2. Developing its near- and medium-term space assets with long-term goals in mind. Those goals probably should include the deployment of a robust space-

based BMD system that, functioning as one layer of a multilayer, damage-limiting defense posture, would vastly reduce the potential liability of American society in the event of a breakdown in the deterrence system.

3. Adopting an attitude toward all arms control issues bearing upon military space capability, extant and potential, that would be supportive of the agreed contributions that space capabilities could and should make to the achievement of U.S. national security goals.

4. Evolving a space force structure appropriate to implement national military strategy.

It must be recognized that U.S. military space policy will be no more immune to the shifting sands of fashion in national security ideas than will any other region of military activity. Unfortunately, it is not even the case that a major policy shift is always, at most, possibly four years away. The Carter administration registered a noteworthy shift in declaratory strategy over the course of four years,[11] and the Reagan administration may yet fail to stay the four-years course for the robust "classical strategy" theory of deterrence that it endorsed during its first year of office. Notwithstanding the apparent fact that U.S. operational nuclear strategy, as reflected in actual plans, has evolved incrementally with a quite remarkable continuity in the presence of shifting emphases in declaratory policy, the development of U.S. military space policy should anticipate many policy shifts that will have the potential to disrupt programs between the early 1980s and the end of the century.

Directed-energy weapons for possible space deployment are long lead-time items. So long as they are many years of needed technological maturity away from an actual deployment decision, doctrinal issues may be evaded very substantially. Space weapon research and development programs will be adequately defensible on the grounds of the U.S. hedging against technological surprise. Also, programs tend not to consume very large quantities of scarce defense dollars through most of their research and development phases. Few things so spur a doctrinal debate as sharp competition for finite resources. However, as space weaponry of all kinds matures, decision dates for acquisition must loom. When that happens, the apparently perennial indeterminacy of U.S. strategic doctrine—the absence of a robust and enduring political consensus on "directing concepts"—likely will assert itself to throw into question the basic rationale for the military technology. Since it is improbable that there will be a truly serious HEL weapon candidate for deployment much before the year 2000, little imagination is required to appreciate just how rocky the road may be for the practice of any space defense doctrine or strategy developed by Space Command early in the 1980s.[12]

In developing strategy for conflict in space, Space Command will not, of course, be making national policy. Strategy is the practical art, or applied science, of translating military power into achieved political purpose. U.S. space defense doctrine can be developed only with guidance from higher echelons of government as to the U.S. theory of war and deterrence and as to U.S. war aims. To repeat a most important refrain, the strategic challenge of the military uses of space confronted by the U.S. government today should not be thought of as a need to design doctrine for conflict in space—rather, the challenge should be defined as a need to design doctrine for conflict in space, in the context of limited and general war campaigns that will be conducted by all arms of the U.S. military establishment. To this end it is entirely appropriate that General Hartinger of Space Command should specify the need to "push for understanding and awareness of the Soviet space threat" as the first task of his organization.[13]

U.S. military space policy today, as outlined by the government on July 4, 1982, begs as many questions as it answers. For example, it holds that:

> —Survivability and endurance of space systems, including all system elements, will be pursued commensurate with the planned use in crisis and conflict, with the threat, and with the availability of other assets to perform the mission. Deficiencies will be identified and eliminated, and an aggressive, long-term program will be undertaken to provide more-assured survivability and endurance.[14]

But what is "the planned use in crisis and conflict" of U.S. space assets? Moreover, "the availability of other [nonspace] assets to perform the mission" will not be solely a matter of luck and the character of Soviet targeting policy. It will also be a matter very substantially predetermined by U.S. defense planning in peacetime. The growing U.S. dependence upon military space systems is not an unfolding act of God; it is U.S. policy choice. If truly essential war-waging, war-supporting assets are deployed in space, then they must be defended, actively or passively.

The U.S. government has committed itself to full engineering development of ASAT capability, looking to early deployment. This is sensible, but nonetheless it is a policy theme that requires the most careful net assessment of probable U.S. advantages and disadvantages. To date, very few people indeed in the U.S. defense community, in or out of government, have a tolerably firm grasp of the structure of the problem/opportunity offered by maturing ASAT capabilities. U.S. interest in ASAT capability must be a function of the official U.S. theory of deterrence and the closely associated structure of forces (and their supporting systems) evolved to wage conflict, the promise in DSAT capability of all kinds, and the prospective operational performance of ASAT weapon systems in a severe countermeasures environment.

Furthermore, as yet there has been little consideration of the respective realms of freedom and necessity with regard to ASAT development. The public agitation for ASAT arms control clearly rests upon the belief that ASAT capabilities of important kinds can be precluded or severely controlled and that the United States does have some freedom of policy choice as to whether it should seek to pursue ASAT arms control. While issues of ASAT arms control should be explored and examined rigorously, so many and diverse are the actual and potential threats to military space systems that ASAT arms control is very unlikely to achieve results beneficial to U.S. national security.

ASKING THE RIGHT QUESTIONS

Military space policy questions that need careful, and in some cases urgent, attention at the present time include the following:

1. How important a contribution to U.S. national security do, or could, space assets make in times of peace, crisis, and wars of different kinds?

2. In the light of answers to the preceding questions, how can minimum essential U.S. space assets best be protected, in light of the fact that the United States has a strong incentive to develop the capability to deny free access to, and exploitation of, outer space?

3. Might space-based weapons, conventional and/or "exotic," effect a revolution in the relationship between strategic offense and defense?

4. Given the very strong Soviet incentive to threaten U.S. space systems, and the somewhat lesser, though still strong, U.S. incentive to threaten Soviet space systems, does the United States have any prudent alternative other than to strive to achieve the potential for military superiority in space?

5. Does the military exploitation of space offer a plausible path for both superpowers to escape some of the worst dilemmas of a nuclear deterrence system?

6. What is the military utility of permanent manned assets in space?

7. What are the likely implications of possible developments in space technology for the range of strategy choices open to U.S. policy makers?

The relative novelty of U.S. military space policy as a subject for intensive debate, and the great uncertainties that pertain to the timing of operational readiness and prospective performance of technologies that today are only concepts or laboratory devices (designed to provide proof of principle), explain why I choose to pose such questions. Debate over military space policy is at a stage where there is disagreement even as to the identity of the correct questions to ask. This particular policy area is usefully uncluttered with many entrenched military-doctrinal beliefs, though should U.S. military space preparations begin to threaten budgets for more traditional military missions, doctrinal opposition certainly will make itself felt. There is still time for very basic questions to be identified and explored. For example, in this arena at least, one can still ask whether "ASAT capability should be constrained by arms control," whereas, with respect to strategic nuclear arms, one is virtually compelled to ask *how* arms competition can be constrained.

This article does not advocate U.S. acquisition of particular military technologies for employment in space, but it takes note of the logical policy implications of evident trends. The following conclusions are appropriate:

1. The commitment to the use of outer space for vital military purposes is irreversible. This fact guarantees provision of very large incentives to the USSR to develop and deploy a major space-warfare capability.

2. The United States has no practical choice other than to be prepared to fight in space—an enterprise that must involve both active and passive defense measures.

3. Notwithstanding its asymmetrical dependence upon space-deployed assets, the United States has a truly major interest in deploying a reliable ASAT capability. Deterrence will not work in space, but even if it would, the U.S. interest in denying the USSR ocean surveillance and other reconnaissance capabilities probably outweighs any hypothetical benefits that might be obtained from an ASAT arms control regime. Such a regime would have to exclude many ASAT capabilities, and even with specific reference to capabilities unambiguously regulated by treaty, could not be verified with high confidence.

4. Space-based HEL weapons, although fraught with very challenging engineering difficulties, are likely to be technically feasible for ASAT missions in the 1990s. However, many technical approaches to ASAT and DSAT tasks are possible, and it seems more likely than not that space-based HEL will be judged to be a high-cost and very high-risk solution.

5. Space-based HEL weapons for the boost-phase destruction of ballistic missiles are not on the horizon. HEL development will have to move short-wavelength devices from the drawing board and the laboratory into "the field" before even a modestly plausible case for HELs in a BMD role can be advanced. Even if a laser technology with adequate power output can be developed (to effect a heat transfer sufficient to overcome the nominal hardness of Soviet missile boosters), and even if the essential auxiliary technologies can be demonstrated to function precisely and reliably, the system—to function well as an operational weapon—must be robust in a highly stressful countermeasure environment. Given the doctrinal centrality of ICBMs in contemporary Soviet strategic culture, it is only prudent to assume that the Soviet defense establishment would respond massively and redundantly to an anticipated HEL threat.

6. Research on neutral particle beam weapon technology must proceed, both as a hedge against the distant possibility of a devastating technological surprise and as a long-term investment in a class of technologies that might, one day, contribute very substantially to the removal of the nuclear missile threat. With reference to the time horizon of most concern here (to the year 2000), I would agree with Patrick Friel's judgment that ". . . it can be predicted with reasonable confidence that the neutral particle beam research in progress will not lead to a space-based weapon in this century."[15]

7. No satellite system, no matter how high its orbit or sophisticated its survival aids, enjoys assured survivability. Space is not a sanctuary.

Two final thoughts merit renewed emphasis. First, it is critically important that U.S. policy makers and policy commentators disabuse themselves of the notion that outer space will be, or can be, a "sanctuary." In the event of a general war, the superpowers will fight in and for the control of space as they will fight everywhere else. However, this judgment may not apply in the event of more limited superpower conflict. Second, highly speculative technically though it is, the idea that there may be a long-term trend favoring the defense over the offense, and resting critically upon space-based assets, is not at all absurd. The weaponized "high frontier" may be science fiction today, but its prophets may well have a clearer and more intelligent strategic vision than it is "responsible" or fashionable to admit.

NOTES

1. Details of this growing dependence are provided in the full study from which this article is drawn, Colin S. Gray, *U.S. Military Space Policy to the Year 2000* (Cambridge, Mass.: Abt Associates, 1983).
2. Verne Orr, "Thoughts at Thirty-Five: The Air Force's Future Is Now," *Air Force Magazine* 65, no. 9 (September 1982): 94.
3. Daniel O. Graham, *High Frontier: A New National Strategy* (Washington, D.C.: High Frontier, 1982).
4. Patrick J. Friel, "Status of U.S. Ballistic Missile Defense Technology," paper presented at the annual meeting of the American Association for the Advancement of Science, Washington, D.C., January 6, 1982, p. 28.
5. White House Fact Sheet on National Space Policy, July 4, 1982.
6. Graham, *High Frontier.*
7. See Edward N. Luttwak, "How to Think About Nuclear War," *Commentary* 74, no. 2 (August 1982): 21–28; Theodore Draper, "How not to Think About Nuclear War," *The New York Review of Books* 29, no. 12 (July 15, 1982): 35–43; and Colin S. Gray, " 'Dangerous to Your Health': The Debate over Nuclear Strategy and War," *Orbis* 26, no. 2 (Summer 1982): 327–49.
8. Laurence Martin, "The Determinants of Change: Deterrence and Technology," in *The Future of Strategic Deterrence, Part II*, Adelphi Paper no. 161 (London: IISS, 1980), p. 16.
9. General James Hartinger, commander of U.S. Air Force Space Command, speaking at the Command activation ceremony, Colorado Springs, Colorado, September 1, 1982.
10. Clarence A. Robinson, Jr., "Study Aimed at Missile Defense Policy," *Aviation Week and Space Technology* 117, no. 7 (August 16, 1982): 25.
11. See Jay Kelley and Desmond Ball, "Strategic Nuclear Targeting," Unpublished paper, August 1981, pp. 41–55; and Desmond Ball, *Developments in U.S. Strategic Nuclear Policy Under the Carter Administration*, ACIS Working Paper no. 21 (Los Angeles: Center for International and Strategic Affairs, University of California, Los Angeles, February 1980).
12. On doctrine for space application, see Dino A. Lorenzini, "Space Power Doctrine," *Air University Review* 33, no. 5 (July–August 1982): 16–21. For more general commentaries on doctrine, see Perry M. Smith, *The Air Force Plans for Peace: 1943–1945* (Baltimore: Johns Hopkins University Press, 1976), pp. 27–38; and Harry G. Summers, Jr., *On Strategy: A Critical Analysis of the Vietnam War* (Novato, Cal.: Presidio, 1982), ch. 6.

13. Hartinger, speech at Colorado Springs, September 1, 1982.
14. See the White House Fact Sheet on National Space Policy, July 4, 1982.
15. Friel, "Status of U.S. Ballistic Missile Defense Technology," p. 16.

Appendixes

APPENDIX I

Symposium Plenary and Working Group Organization

Thursday, May 6

9:00 a.m.–9:15 a.m.

Welcome and Opening Remarks
Alan Ned Sabrosky, President, Foreign Policy
    Research Institute
(South Cameo Room)

9:15 a.m.–11:45 a.m.

**Plenary 1: Arms Control, Strategic
    Instability, and International Security**
Chair: Wolfgang Pordzik, Konrad Adenauer
    Foundation
(South Cameo Room)

"Challenges to Global Stability in the 1980s:
    Contrasting Views"
William R. Van Cleave, Defense and Strategic
    Studies Center, University of Southern
    California
Genrikh Trofimenko, Institute of the USA &
    Canada

"Arms Control and the Strategic Balance"
Yves Boyer, Consultant

Discussant: Nils H. Wessell, Foreign Policy
    Research Institute

12:00 noon–1:45 p.m.

Luncheon
(Rose Garden Room)

2:00 p.m.–3:00 p.m.

Working Groups I

A. Rethinking SALT: Comprehensive vs. Limited Accords
Chair: Martin Edmonds, University of Lancaster
(Panorama Room)

B. Soviet-American Strategic Doctrines for the Eighties
Chair: Robert Legvold, Council on Foreign Relations
(South Cameo Room)

C. The Role of Strategic Arms Control in Soviet-American Relations
Chair: W. Scott Thompson, Center for Strategic & International Studies
(Skyline Room)

D. The Impact of U.S.-Soviet Arms Control on Regional Security
Chair: Derek Leebaert, John F. Kennedy School of Government, Harvard University
(Terrace Room)

3:15 p.m.–4:15 p.m.

Working Groups 2

A. The Vulnerability of Strategic Weapons: Arms Control Implications
Chair: Walter C. Clemens, Jr., Boston University
(South Cameo Room)

B. Verification of Strategic Arms Control Agreements
Chair: Richard K. Betts, The Brookings Institution
(Panorama Room)

C. Testing, Qualitative Limits, and the Strategic Balance
Chair: Pierre Dabezies, Centre d'Études Politiques de Défense
(Skyline Room)

D. Moral Aspects of Deterrence

Chair: The Honorable A. K. Damodaran,
Institute for Defence Studies and Analyses
(Terrace Room)

8:00 p.m. **Keynote Address at Independence Hall**

**The Honorable Eugene V. Rostow
Director, U.S. Arms Control and
Disarmament Agency**

IMPORTANT NOTE: All Working Group meeting rooms, except the
Bellevue Suite and the Ambassador Suite, are
located on the 19th floor. The Bellevue
and Ambassador suites are located on the
10th floor.

Friday, May 7
9:00 a.m.–11:00 a.m. **Plenary II: Arms Control and European
Security**
Chair: Alan Ned Sabrosky, Foreign Policy
Research Institute
(North Cameo Room)

"Implications of Strategic, Eurostrategic, and
Conventional Arms Control in Europe"
Philip Williams, University of Southampton

"Superpower Competition, Detente, and
European Security"
Wolfgang Schreiber, Social Science Research
Institute, Konrad Adenauer Foundation

Discussant: Catherine Kelleher, National
Defense University

11:15 a.m.–12:15 p.m. **Working Groups 3**
A. Theater-Nuclear Forces and the Regional
Balance
Chair: Jean Klein, Institut Francais des
Relations Internationales
(Panorama Room)

B. Conventional Force Reductions: MBFR
Chair: Steven L. Canby, C & L Associates,
Inc.
(Ambassador Suite)

C. Contrasting Perspectives on European
    Security: Equal Security vs. Equality
Chair: Arthur Cyr, Chicago Council on
    Foreign Relations
(Terrace Room)

D. The Domestic Political Context of
    European Security
Chair: Michael Dillon, Centre for the Study of
    Arms Control and International Security,
    University of Lancaster
(Bellevue Suite)

12:30 p.m.–2:00p.m. **Luncheon Address**
(Rose Garden Room)

Introductory Remarks: Buntzie Ellis Churchill,
    World Affairs Council of Philadelphia

**Speaker: The Honorable Richard R. Burt
Director, Bureau of Politico-Military
Affairs, U.S. Department of State
"Deterrence, Arms Control, and Public
Opinion"**

2:15 p.m.–4:00 p.m. **Plenary III: Arms Control and Asian
Security**
Chair: The Honorable William H. Sullivan,
    The American Assembly
(North Cameo Room)

"Arms Control in East Asia"
Hiroshi Kimura, Slavic Research Center,
    Hokkaido University

"Nuclear Proliferation and the Balance of
    Power in South Asia"
K. Subrahmanyam, Institute for Defence
    Studies and Analyses

Discussant: Gerald Segal, University of
    Leicester

4:15 p.m.–5:15 p.m. **Working Groups 4**
A. Triangular Strategic Relations and Arms
    Control

Chair: Allen S. Whiting, Center for Chinese Studies, University of Michigan
(Panorama Room)

B. Japanese Security Policy: Arms Control and Rearmament
Chair: Masashi Nishihara, Visiting Research Fellow, Rockefeller Foundation
(Ambassador Suite)

C. Nuclear and Conventional Capabilities of the PRC and Asian Security
Chair: George H. Quester, University of Maryland
(Terrace Room)

D. Proliferation in South Asia: The Indo-Pakistani Arms Competition
Chair: The Honorable T. N. Kaul, Executive Council, UNESCO
(Bellevue Suite)

Saturday, May 8
9:00 a.m.–11:00 a.m.

Plenary IV: Strategic Threats of the Future
Chair: Makoto Momoi, National Defense College (Japan)
(South Cameo Room)

"Subnational Nuclear Proliferation, Technology Transfer, and Terrorism"
Fabienne Luchaire, Centre d'Études Politiques de Défense

"Military Uses of Space to the Year 2000"
Colin S. Gray, National Institute for Public Policy

Discussant: Major General D. K. Palit, Institute for Defence Studies and Analyses

11:15 a.m.–12:15 p.m.

Working Groups 5
A. Nuclear Terrorism and Political Blackmail
Chair: Richard E. Bissell, Foreign Policy Research Institute
(Ambassador Suite)

B. Exotic Weapon Systems
Chair: Donald M. Snow, University of
   Alabama
(Panorama Room)

C. Nuclear Technology Transfer and
   Proliferation
Chair: Manfred Hamm, Foreign Policy
   Research Institute
(Terrace Room)

D. Chemical-Biological and Radiological
   Warfare
Chair: Philip Towle, University of Cambridge
(Skyline Room)

12:30 p.m.–2:00 p.m.   **Luncheon**
(North Cameo Room)

Concluding Remarks: Alan Ned Sabrosky,
   President,
Foreign Policy Research Institute

APPENDIX II

List of Participants

Dr. Benson D. Adams
Nuclear Policy Adviser
Office of the Assistant to the
    Secretary of Defense (Atomic
    Energy)

Colonel Robert L. Albertson
Chief, Secretary's Staff Group
Office of the Secretary of the Air
    Force

Mr. Yuriy A. Arkharov
Counselor
Embassy of the USSR
Washington, DC

Dr. Shaheen Ayubi
Research Associate
Foreign Policy Research Institute
Philadelphia, PA

Mr. Nimrod Barkan
Vice-Consul of Israel
Philadelphia, PA

Mr. William Beecher
Diplomatic Correspondent
Boston Globe
Washington, DC

Dr. Valentin M. Berezhkov
Institute of the USA & Canada
Embassy of the USSR
Washington, DC

Major Gilbert A. Bernabe
National Security Affairs Committee
U.S. Army Command and General
    Staff College
Fort Leavenworth, KS

Dr. Richard K. Betts
Senior Fellow
The Brookings Institution
Washington, DC

Dr. Richard E. Bissell
Coordinator
Economic Security Studies
Foreign Policy Research Institute
Philadelphia, PA

Mr. Leonard Boasberg
Philadelphia Inquirer
Philadelphia, PA

Mr. Derek Boothby
Centre for Disarmament
United Nations
New York

Dr. Yves Boyer
Centre d'Etudes Politiques de
    Défense
Paris, FRANCE

Matthew Boyse
Intern
Foreign Policy Research Institute
Philadelphia, PA

Dr. R. Jean Brownlee
Dean Emeritus, College for Women
University of Pennsylvania
Philadelphia, PA

Mr. Ronald Burton
Research Assistant
Foreign Policy Research Institute
Philadelphia, PA

Mr. W. W. Keen Butcher
Butcher & Singer
Philadelphia, PA

Mr. Gunning Butler, Jr.
Director, START and Arms Control
Office of Undersecretary of
    Defense/Research and
    Engineering
Washington, DC

Mr. Bruce K. Byers
Information Officer/Media
U.S. International Communication
    Agency
Washington, DC

Dr. Steve L. Canby
C & L Associates
Potomac, MD

Mr. Rodney Carlisle
Senior Associate
History Associates, Inc.
Gaithersburg, MD

The Honorable Giuseppe Cassini
Consul General of Italy
Philadelphia, PA

Mrs. Buntzie Ellis Churchill
Executive Director
World Affairs Council of Philadelphia
Philadelphia, PA

Dr. Stephen Cimbala
Assistant Professor of Political
    Science
Penn State University
Media, PA

Dr. Walter C. Clemens, Jr.
Professor of Political Science
Boston University

Dr. J. I. Coffey
Distinguished Service Professor of
    Public and International Affairs
University of Pittsburgh

Mr. J. Foster Collins
Special Assistant to the Secretary
    (National Security)
Department of the Treasury
Washington, DC

Mr. Bert H. Cooper
Specialist in National Defense
Congressional Research Service
Library of Congress
Washington, DC

Dr. Arthur Cyr
Vice-President and Program Director
Chicago Council on Foreign
    Relations

Dr. Pierre Dabezies
Centre d'Etudes Politiques de
    Défense
Paris, FRANCE

The Honorable A. K. Damodaran
Institute for Defence Studies and
    Analyses
New Delhi, INDIA

Mr. Robert Dean
Deputy Director, Office of Strategic
    and Theater Nuclear Affairs
Bureau of Politico-Military Affairs
Department of State
Washington, DC

Dr. Michael Dillon
Centre for the Study of Arms
    Control and International
    Security
Lancaster, UNITED KINGDOM

Ms. Paula Dobriansky
National Security Council
Washington, DC

Mr. George J. Donovan
Vice-President, Marketing
Thiokol Corporation
Newtown, PA

Mr. Michael Dorfman
Research Assistant
Foreign Policy Research Institute
Philadelphia, PA

Dr. Keith A. Dunn
Strategic Studies Institute
U.S. Army War College
Carlisle Barracks
Carlisle, PA

Dr. Martin Edmonds
Senior Lecturer
Department of Politics
Fylde College
Lancaster, UNITED KINGDOM

Mr. Harold Finnigan
Staff Assistant
Congressman Robert W. Edgar
Upper Darby, PA

Dr. Robert Foelber
The Heritage Foundation
Washington, DC

Ms. Adrienne Fontanella
Research Assistant
Foreign Policy Research Institute
Philadelphia, PA

Mr. Gregory D. Foster
Associate Director for Research
Foreign Policy Research Institute
Philadelphia, PA

Dr. Adam M. Garfinkle
Coordinator
Strategic Security Studies
Foreign Policy Research Institute
Philadelphia, PA

Mr. William Garner
Doctoral Candidate
Georgetown University
Washington, DC

Mr. Charles R. Gellner
Congressional Research Service
Library of Congress
Washington, DC

Dr. Victor Gilinsky
Commissioner
Nuclear Regulatory Commission
Washington, DC

Dr. Robert G. Gilpin, Jr.
Eisenhower Professor of International
  Affairs
Woodrow Wilson School
Princeton University

Major Thomas A. Gladstone, USAF
Defense Nuclear Agency
Washington, DC

Mr. Michael Gordon
National Journal
Washington, DC

Dr. Rose E. Gottemoeller
Research Associate
The Rand Corporation
Washington, DC

Dr. Daniel Goure
Senior Associate
Jeffrey Cooper Associates
Arlington, VA

Dr. Colin S. Gray
President
National Institute for Public Policy
Fairfax, VA

Dr. William C. Green
Editor, National Security Record
The Heritage Foundation
Washington, DC

Mr. Robert Grey
Deputy Director-Designate
U.S. Arms Control and
  Disarmament Agency
Washington, DC

Dr. William E. Griffith
Department of Political Science
Massachusetts Institute of
  Technology
Cambridge, MA

Mr. Brad Hahn
Visiting Fellow
Foreign Policy Research Institute
Philadelphia, PA

Mr. Manfred Hamm
Research Fellow
Foreign Policy Research Institute
Philadelphia, PA

Commander Robert Hawthorne,
  USN
Office of Program Appraisal
Office of the Secretary of the Navy
Washington, DC

Dr. J. L. Husbands
Senior Research Associate
CACI, Inc.
Arlington, VA

Mr. Wolfgang Ischinger
First Secretary
Embassy of the Federal Republic of
  Germany
Washington, DC

Colonel Frank W. Jenkins, USAF
Chief, Nuclear Negotiations Division
Office of the Joint Chiefs of Staff
Washington, DC

Dr. Lloyd Jensen
Professor of Political Science
Temple University
Philadelphia, PA

Ms. Susan Joyce
Intern
Foreign Policy Research Institute
Philadelphia, PA

Professor Jiang Kai
Visiting Fellow
Center of International Studies
Princeton University

Dr. Francis X. Kane
Director, Aerospace Concepts
Corporate Engineering
Rockwell International Corporation
El Segundo, CA

Dr. Herschel Kanter
Institute for Defense Analyses
Alexandria, VA

Dr. Sergei Karaganov
Institute of the USA & Canada
USSR Academy of Sciences
Moscow, USSR

The Honorable T. N. Kaul
Institute for Defense Studies and
    Analyses
New Delhi, INDIA

Colonel John G. Keliher, USA
National Defense University
Fort Leslie J. McNair
Washington, DC

Dr. Catherine M. Kelleher
Faculty, Naval War College
National Defense University
Fort Leslie J. McNair
Washington, DC

Dr. Robert Kennedy
Strategic Studies Institute
U.S. Army War College
Carlisle Barracks
Carlisle, PA

Dr. Roy Kim
Research Fellow
Foreign Policy Research Institute
Philadelphia, PA

Dr. Hiroshi Kimura
Professor of Political Science
Slavic Research Center
Hokkaido University
Sapporo, JAPAN

Dr. William R. Kintner
Professor
Political Science Department
University of Pennsylvania

Dr. Jean Klein
Institut Francais des Relations
    Internationales
Paris, FRANCE

Mr. Brad Knickerbocker
Christian Science Monitor
Washington, DC

Dr. Stanley Kober
Managing Editor
Comparative Strategy
SRI International
Arlington, VA

Mr. Yoshihisa Komori
Mainichi Newspapers
Washington, DC

Major Carl C. Krehbiel
International Relations Support
    Division
Defense Intelligence Agency
Washington, DC

Ms. Mary L. Kuhn
Program Associate
Glenmede Trust Company
Philadelphia, PA

Captain Ned K. Kulp, USCGR
Chelfont, PA

Dr. Franz G. Lassner
Senior Vice-President
Freedoms Foundation
Valley Forge, PA

Dr. Chong-sik Lee
Chairman
Graduate Program in International
    Relations
University of Pennsylvania

Dr. Derek Leebaert
JFK School of Government
Harvard University
Cambridge, MA

Dr. Robert Legvold
Senior Fellow
Council on Foreign Relations
New York, NY

Ms. Marian Leighton
Analyst
Central Intelligence Agency
Washington, DC

Ms. Fabienne Luchaire
Centre d'Etudes Politiques de
    Défense
Paris, FRANCE

Mr. Alan H. Luxenberg
Assistant Director for Fund Raising
    and Operations
Foreign Policy Research Institute
Philadelphia, PA

Mr. Kishore Mahbubani
Minister-Counselor
Embassy of Singapore
Washington, DC

Mr. Christopher J. Makins
Science Applications, Inc.
McLean, VA

Dr. Gerhard Mally
Foreign Affairs Officer
Arms Control & Disarmament
    Agency
Department of State
Washington, DC

Professor Gale A. Mattox
Department of Political Science
U.S. Naval Academy
Annapolis, MD

Mr. John Maurer
Research Fellow
Foreign Policy Research Institute
Philadelphia, PA

Mr. Sean N. McCauley
Chairman, Young Republican
    International Affairs
Philadelphia, PA

Dr. James M. McConnell
Professional Staff Member
Center for Naval Analyses
Arlington, VA

Mr. Gordon H. McCormick
Coordinator
Theater Security Studies
Foreign Policy Research Institute
Philadelphia, PA

Dr. Patrick P. McDermott
Principal Scientist
B-K Dynamics, Inc.
Arlington, VA

Colonel Joel McKean
Senior Military Adviser
Arms Control & Disarmament
    Agency
Washington, DC

Dr. Karen McPherson
Foreign Policy Research Institute
Philadelphia, PA

Mr. Donald E. Meads
Chairman
Carver Associates, Inc.
Plymouth Meeting, PA

Mr. E. Victor Milione
President
Intercollegiate Studies Institute
Bryn Mawr, PA

Dr. Mark E. Miller
Senior Analyst
Advanced International Studies
    Institute
Bethesda, MD

Mr. Michael H. Mobbs
Representative to START
Office of the Assistant Secretary of
    Defense, International Security
    Policy
Washington, DC

Dr. Makoto Momoi
Dean, Faculty of Defense Studies
National Defense College
Tokyo, JAPAN

Mr. Joseph Murray
Group Director, International
    Division
U.S. General Accounting Office
Washington, DC

Dr. Masashi Nishihara
Visiting Research Fellow
International Relations
The Rockefeller Foundation
New York, NY

Dr. Joseph L. Nogee
Professor of Political Science
University of Houston
Houston, TX

Dr. Eugenia Osgood
Research Analyst
Library of Congress
Washington, DC

Mr. Paul T. O'Sullivan
First Secretary
Embassy of Australia
Washington, DC

Maj. General D. K. Palit
Institute for Defence Studies and
    Analyses
New Delhi, INDIA

Dr. Norman D. Palmer
Political Science Department
University of Pennsylvania
Philadelphia, PA

Mr. Frank N. Piasecki
President
Piasecki Aircraft Corporation
Philadelphia, PA

Mr. Albert C. Pierce
Deputy Director
Strategic Concepts Development
    Center
National Defense University
Fort Leslie J. McNair
Washington, DC

Dr. Wolfgang Pordzik
Director
Washington Research Office
Konrad-Adenauer-Stiftung
Washington, DC

Mr. Richard H. Porth
Conference Coordinator
Foreign Policy Research Institute
Philadelphia, PA

Major Gary Potter, USAF
Intelligence Estimates
Bolling Air Force Base
Washington, DC

Dr. George H. Quester
Chairman
Department of Government and
    Politics
University of Maryland
College Park, MD

Mr. Vladimir Reshetilou
TASS News Agency
Washington, DC

Mr. David B. Rivkin, Jr.
Washington, DC

Mr. David Rose
Counselor, Political Division
Embassy of Canada
Washington, DC

Dr. Karl Ryavec
Professor of Political Science
University of Massachusetts
Amherst, MA

Dr. Alan Ned Sabrosky
President
Foreign Policy Research Institute
Philadelphia, PA

Mr. John C. Scharfen
ATAC
Arlington, VA

Dr. Mark B. Schneider
Policy Planning Staff
Department of State
Washington, DC

Colonel Wolfgang Schreiber (Ret.)
Konrad-Adenauer-Stiftung
Bonn, FRG

Dr. William F. Scott
Adjunct Professor
Georgetown University
Washington, DC

Lt. Col. Michael B. Seaton, USAF
Office of the Director for Plans
Washington, DC

Dr. Gerald Segal
Lecturer in Politics
University of Leicester
UNITED KINGDOM

His Excellency Mohammed Shakir
Ministry of Foreign Affairs
Embassy of Egypt
Washington, DC

Mr. Siddharth Singh
Counselor
Embassy of India
Washington, DC

Mrs. Lynne H. Smith
Assistant Director for Business
    Administration
Foreign Policy Research Institute
Philadelphia, PA

Mr. Richard N. Smith
Research Assistant
Foreign Policy Research Institute
Philadelphia, PA

Dr. Donald M. Snow
Director of International Studies
University of Alabama
University, AL

Dr. Henry Sokolski
Public Affairs Fellow
Hoover Institution
Washington, DC

Mr. Bruce Stanley
Doctoral Candidate
Department of International
    Relations
University of Pennsylvania
Philadelphia, PA

Dr. Helen Schevill Starobin
Elkins Park, PA

Dr. Leonard Starobin
Elkins Park, PA

Mr. Fred Stein
Coordinator
Century IV Celebration Committee
Philadelphia, PA

Shri K. Subrahmanyam
Director
Institute for Defence Studies and
    Analyses
New Delhi, INDIA

The Honorable William H. Sullivan
President
The American Assembly
Columbia University
New York, NY

Dr. W. Scott Thompson
Senior Fellow
Georgetown Center for Strategic and
    International Studies
Washington, DC

Mr. Ferdinand K. Thun
Wyomissing, PA

Mrs. Ferdinand K. Thun
Wyomissing, PA

Dr. Philip Towle
Defence Lecturer, Queen's College
University of Cambridge
Cambridge, UNITED KINGDOM

Dr. Marc Trachtenberg
Associate Professor of History
University of Pennsylvania
Philadelphia, PA

Dr. Frank N. Trager
Research Professor
Naval Postgraduate School
Department of the Navy
Monterey, CA

Dr. Genrikh Trofimenko
Head, U.S. Foreign Policy
   Department
Institute of the USA & Canada
USSR Academy of Sciences
Moscow, USSR

Mr. Jonathan Tucker
Intern
Foreign Policy Research Institute
Philadelphia, PA

Dr. Victor A. Utgoff
Institute of Defense Analyses
Alexandria, VA

Dr. William R. Van Cleave
Director
Defense and Strategic Studies Center
University of Southern California
Los Angeles, CA

Mr. Richard A. Ware
President
Earhart Foundation
Ann Arbor, MI

Mr. Kenneth Warner
Foreign Policy Research Institute
Philadelphia, PA

Mr. Greg Weaver
Foreign Policy Research Institute
Philadelphia, PA

Dr. Robert G. Weinland
Center for Naval Analyses
Alexandria, VA

Mr. John Weinstein
Visiting Research Professor
Strategic Studies Institute
U.S. Army War College
Carlisle Barracks
Carlisle, PA

Dr. Henry Wells
Chairman
Department of Political Science
University of Pennsylvania
Philadelphia, PA

Dr. Samuel F. Wells, Jr.
Secretary
Woodrow Wilson International
   Center for Scholars
Washington, DC

Dr. Nils H. Wessell
Associate Director for Publications
Foreign Policy Research Institute
Philadelphia, PA

Dr. Allen S. Whiting
Center for Chinese Studies
University of Michigan
Ann Arbor, MI

Dr. Philip Williams
Lecturer
Department of Politics
University of Southampton
UNITED KINGDOM

Mr. Brian Wynne
Fulbright Scholar
FEDERAL REPUBLIC OF
   GERMANY

Dr. Dov Zakheim
Special Assistant
Office of the Assistant Secretary of
    Defense, International Security
    Policy
Washington, DC

Professor Jiang Zejun
Luce Foundation Visiting Scholar
Fletcher School of Law and
    Diplomacy
Tufts University
Medford, MA

Professor Hu Zhengqing
Visiting Fellow
Center of International Studies
Princeton University

Dr. Paul E. Zinner
Department of Political Science
University of California-Davis
Davis, CA

Afghanistan, 16, 23, 25, 26, 37–38, 96, 102; Soviet force levels in, 104–05
Africa, 16, 19, 25, 26, 37
Allison, Graham, xi
Anti-Ballistic Missile (ABM) treaty, 42, 138
Arab countries, 37, 70
Arab-Israeli conflict, 15
Argentina, 15
arms control (*see also* INF, MBFR, SALT, START), 1–2, 4, 6, 10, 23, 24, 25, 29, 49, 52–53, 57–58; detente and, 53–54; disarmament and, 56–57; East Asia and, 83–84, 88–93; failings of, 51–52; "linkage" and, 25–26, 45; Soviet objectives in, 25, 26, 76; substantive value of, 54–56; uncertainties of, 49–50; U.S. objectives in, 1, 2, 5–7, 11, 25
arms race, 2–3, 35, 42, 43, 70; economic consequences of, 38–39, 43
Asia, xiii, 36–37
Association of South-East Asian Nations (ASEAN), 37

B-1 bomber, 22
B-52 bomber, 22
Backfire bomber, 10, 22, 85, 86
ballistic missile defense (BMD), 8, 138; space and, 136–37, 138
Bangladesh, 102
Betts, Richard, xii
Bhutan, 102
Bhutto, Zulfikar Ali, 98
bombers, 22
Bowie, Robert, x
Boyer, Yves, xii

Brazil, 70
Brezhnev, Leonid, 7, 59, 64, 72, 88, 91
Brezhnev Doctrine, 76
Brown, Harold, 20
Brzezinski, Zbigniew, 18, 36
Bundy, McGeorge, 4, 8, 62
Burma, 102, 108
Burt, Richard, xi, 51

Camp David accords, 37
Caribbean region, 3, 16, 25
Carter, Jimmy, 83
Carter Administration, 41, 139
Carter Doctrine, 36
Central America, 16, 36–37
Central Intelligence Agency (CIA), xi
Centre d'Etudes Politiques de Defense, vii, xi, xiii
Centre for the Study of Arms Control and International Security, vii
chemical warfare, 42
China, Peoples Republic of (PRC), 70, 71, 83, 84–85, 87–88, 92, 103; India and, 107–08; military forces of, 85; nuclear weapons of, 100–01
China, Republic of (ROC), 83, 84, 92
Chinese International Strategic Studies Institute, viii
Clausewitz, Carl von, 69, 71
cold war, 2, 44, 45
collective security, 1
Conference on Security and Cooperation in Europe (CCSE), 60, 77, 88, 91
confidence-building measures (CMBs), 60, 88
conventional war and weapons, 2, 58–60

cruise missile, 22, 61–63, 64–66;
ground-launched (GLCM), 61;
submarine-launched (SLCM), 22
Cuban missile crisis, 2, 97

"Decoupling," 62
detente, x, xii, xiii, 4, 21, 23, 24–25, 34,
37, 43, 54, 59, 62, 65, 69, 72, 75, 77–78;
breakdown of, 40–41; effect on strategic
balance, 24, 25; failure of, 25; future of,
24, 25; importance of, 41; stability and,
40; Soviet definition of, 75–76; U.S.
definition of, 75, 77
deterrence, 2–3, 4, 6, 8, 11, 20, 52, 57, 62
Diego Garcia, 97
disarmament, 1, 44, 56–57, 60, 92
Dougherty, James E., x, xi
Dulles, John Foster, 36

East Asia, 83–93; arms control and,
83–84, 88–93; geopolitical view of,
90–91; political situation in, 84, 92;
military situation in, 85–88
El Salvador, 37
escalation, 2, 23, 61, 63
Europe, 3, 5, 8–9, 10, 19, 37, 69, 71; arms
control and, 50–51, 52, 54, 58–59;
detente and, 77–78; **disarmament** and,
57, 66–67; ideological conflict and,
78–79; superpowers and, 70
European Community, 70

Falkland Islands, 15
"firebridge," 63
first-strike capability, Soviet, 6, 8, 21
first-strike weapons, Soviet, 5
first-use vs. no-first-use, 3–4, 8, 11, 44
flexible response, 61, 64
Foreign Policy Research Institute, vii–viii
France, vii, viii, xi; protection of nuclear
materials by, 125–27

Garfinkle, Adam M., vii-viii
Germany, Federal Republic of, vii, viii,
xi, 64
global stability and instability, 15–16, 23,
34, 35; sources of instability (according

to USSR), 35, 36–40, 44; sources of
instability (according to U.S.), 15–16,
19, 23; Soviet definition of, 33, 34; U.S.
definition of (according to USSR), 34
grain embargo, 26, 41
Great Britain, vii, viii, xi
Guatemala, 37

Haig, Alexander, 11, 15, 26, 29
Honduras, 36–37
Horn of Africa, 37

Iklé, Fred I., xi
imperialism, 39
India, viii, ix, xi, xiii, 70, 103; China and,
107–08; military forces of, 103–04;
nuclear program of, 98; Pakistani threat
to, 100–06
Indochina, 37, 91
Indonesia, 91
Institute for Defence Studies and
Analyses, viii, xiii
intercontinental (ground-based) ballistic
missiles (ICBM), 5, 6–7, 9, 22, 85
Intermediate-range Nuclear Forces (INF)
negotiations, 2, 6, 9, 26, 43, 58, 61, 64,
65, 66, 83, 91; Soviet reaction to U.S.
proposal for, 6; U.S. proposal for, 6, 64;
intermediate-range (theater) nuclear
forces (*see also* cruise missile; Pershing
II), xi, 2, 5, 6, 9, 22, 58, 64, 77; strategic
purpose of, 61–62
international trade and economic
competition, 38
Iraq, 37
Iran, 37; Pakistan and, 107
isolationism, 4, 5, 8
Israel, 15, 36–37; nuclear weapons and,
98, 99, 108

Jackson, Sen. Henry M., 9
Japan, 3, 5, 8, 9, 10, 19, 70, 71, 83, 84–85,
87–88, 91; arms control and, 89–90,
91–93; disarmament and, 92; military
forces of, 85
Jones, Gen. David, 20

Kampuchea, 108
Konrad Adenauer Foundation, vii, xii
Korea, 83, 84, 85, 92
Korean War, 97
Kennan, George, 4
Khrushchev, Nikita, 11, 70-71
Kirkpatrick, Jeane, 36
Kissinger, Henry, 5, 16, 24, 66, 77

Lebanon, 37
Lehman, John F., x
Lenin, Vladimir I., 71, 76
Libya, 98
limited nuclear war, 66, 96

Mao Zedong, 107
McNamara, Robert, 4, 9
Middle East, 3, 15, 19, 25, 36-37, 40
military balance and imbalance, 2, 4, 5,
    19-23, 25, 33, 34-35; military
    consequences of, 23; political
    consequences of, 5, 19; Soviet
    superiority, 20-23
military forces as political tool, 38-40
Minuteman missile, 61
multipolarity, 72
Muskie, Sen. Edmund, 2
Mutual Balanced Forced Reduction
    (MBFR) negotiations, 58-60, 67, 77, 83;
    purpose of, 58-59
MX missile, 22

Namibia, 38
National Security Council, xi
Nepal, 102
Nigeria, 70
Nixon, Richard M., 24, 59, 77
Nonproliferation Treaty, 95, 101, 127
North Atlantic Treaty Organization
    (NATO), 6, 8, 37, 52, 60; Euromissile
    deployment decision by, 61-62, 64-65,
    66-67
nuclear blackmail and coercion, 2-3, 5,
    6, 20
nuclear "freeze," xi, 7, 9, 44
nuclear "overkill," 7
nuclear proliferation, x, xiii, xiv, 38, 95,

127-29; in South Asia, 97-101, 108-09;
    subnational, 117, 122-27, 131;
    prevention of, 124-27; technical
    difficulties of, 122-24; terrorism and,
    15, 116-18
Nuclear Regulatory Commission, xi
nuclear terrorism, xiii-xiv, 116-19,
    119-22, 129-32
nuclear war, possible results of, 39-40
nuclear weapon free zone in South Asia,
    100-01, 108
Nunn, Sen. Sam, 29

Pakistan, 37, 103; Afghan rebels and,
    106; India and, 104; Iran and, 107;
    military forces of, 103-04, 105; nuclear
    weapons and, xiii, 98, 99-100, 106, 109;
    Soviet threat to, 104-05
Pershing II missile, 6, 61-62, 63, 64-66
Persian Gulf, 3, 16, 96
Poland, 11, 16, 25
public opinion and nuclear arms, 3-4

Quemoy-Matsu crisis, 97

Rapid Deployment Force, 36
Reagan, Ronald, 1, 4, 5, 10, 11, 20, 22,
    26, 34, 41, 42, 65, 66
Reagan Administration, 22, 26, 28, 29,
    36, 38, 41, 42, 64, 66, 134, 135-36, 139
Research Institute for Peace and Security,
    vii
role of nuclear weapons, for Soviet
    Union, 4, 8, 20; for U.S., 4, 8, 20
Rostow, Eugene V., ix, xi, 16, 20, 26
Rostow, Walt W., x

Schell, Jonathan, 39
Schlesinger, James, 34, 96
Schmidt, Helmut, 5, 64
second-strike capacity, 3
security, 8; European perception of, xii,
    75; Soviet perception of, xiii, 18, 73,
    74-75; U.S. perception of, xiii, 1, 73-75
Seventh International Arms Control
    Symposium, vii, ix, xi, xiv
Sino-Soviet dispute, x, 84-85

Smith, Gerard, 4

sociopolitical change, 35-37; Soviet attitudes toward (according to USSR), 34, 35; U.S. attitude toward (according to USSR), 34, 35-36

South Africa, 38, 70, 99, 108; nuclear weapons and, 99, 108-09

South Asia, 97; balance of power in, 101, 103-09; nuclear weapons in, 97-101, 106, 108-09

Southeast Asia, 19, 37

Soviet Institute of the USA and Canada, viii, xi

Soviet Union, ix, xi, 2, 103; aggression and expansion by, 3-4, 6, 11, 16, 18-19, 20, 78; domestic problems for, 11, 17, 18-23; East Asia and, 83, 84-86, 87, 88-89, 90-91; military growth and spending, 3, 16, 21, 23-24, 25; military superiority, 17, 20-22; (conventional, 8, 20, 23; nuclear, 5-6, 9-10, 19, 20-22, 24); nature of system (according to U.S.), 17-18, 23; space weaponry and, 141, 142; threat to global stability by, 15-16

space weaponry, 42, 133-35, 137, 139, 141; anti-satellite (ASAT) capability, 135-36, 140, 142; arms control and, 137, 139, 141, 142; ballistic missile defense (BMD), 136, 138, 142; defense-satellite (DSAT) capability, 137, 140, 142; deterrence and, 137, 139, 140, 142; high-energy laser (HEL) weapons, 136, 139, 142; offense-defense balance and, 138, 141; particle beam weapons, 142; U.S. strategy for, 138-39, 140-41

Sri Lanka, 103

SS-4, 6, 64, 90, 91

SS-5, 6, 64, 90, 91

SS-20, xiii, 5, 6, 22, 61, 64, 66, 86, 90, 91

Stalin, Josef, 71

Strategic Arms Limitation Talks (SALT), 21, 24, 25, 52, 77, 83; effect on strategic balance, 23-25; SALT I, x, 77; SALT II, x, 9-10, 20, 34, 42, 44, 51, 56, 61, 65; Europe and, 61; failings of, 9-10; ratification of, 9-10

Strategic Arms Reduction Talks (START), 2, 6, 9, 26, 29, 43, 66, 83; Soviet reaction to U.S. proposal for, 8; U.S. proposal for, 6-7; verification and, 7

strategic balance (parity), 42

strategic nuclear forces (*see also* ICBM, MX, SLBM, SALT, START), 2, 22; in East Asia, 85–86

submarine-launched ballistic missiles (SLBM), 7, 22, 61, 85–87

superpower competition and rivalry, xii, 69–71; Soviet attitude toward, 70–71; U.S. attitude toward, 71–72

Suzuki, Zenko, 89–90

Taft, William H., 36

technological innovation, x, xiii, 42

terrorism, xiii–xiv, 16, 113, 117, 118, 119–20; increasing sophistication of, 114–16; individual terrorism, 131; nuclear weapons and, 116–18, 119–22, 129–32; "primary" terrorism, 113–14; psychology and tactics of, 118–22; revolutionary and nationalistic terrorism, 114; State terrorism, 127, 129–31; subversive terrorism, 115; transfers of technology and, 127

test ban talks, 38

Test Ban Treaty, x

Thailand, 36, 37

threater nuclear weapons, in East Asia, 86, 89–90, 91; modernization of, xii, 61

Third World, 15, 34, 35, 38; nuclear power intervention in, 96; possible nuclear weapons use in, 96–97; threats to security of nations of, 102; U.S. policy toward (according to USSR), 35–36; war in, 101–02

Thompson, E.P., 56

Tibet, 107

transfers of technology, 11, 127–29; regulation of, 127–29; terrorism and, 127, 131

United Nations, 15, 45

United States, ix, xi, xiii, 18; allies and,

8, 50, 78; arms and arms control policy
in 80's of, 27; arms buildup by, 42; East
Asia and, 83–88, 89; hostility to Soviets
(according to USSR), 41; military
spending by, 21, 28, 38, 42; military
strategy of, 28–29; military strength of,
conventional inferiority, 23; relative
military decline, 21–22, 24, 25; strategic
inferiority, 22, 24; military uses of space
and, 133–43
U.S. Arms Control and Disarmament
Agency, ix, xi

verification and inspection, x, 7
Vietnam, 2, 3, 16, 40, 91, 111

Warsaw Pact, 52
Weinburger, Caspar, 44, 96
"window of vulnerability," 22–23, 28, 29
World Affairs Council of Philadelphia,
viii
World War I, 70
World War II, 11, 70
Yom Kippur War, 16, 77
zero option, 64–65, 66; in East Asia, 90

About the Contributors

ADAM M. GARFINKLE, editor of this volume, is coordinator of the Program in Political Studies at the Foreign Policy Research Institute and lecturer in political science at the University of Pennsylvania, College of General Studies.

COLIN S. GRAY is president of the National Institute for Public Policy and a member of the General Advisory Commission on Arms Control and Disarmament of the U.S. Arms Control and Disarmament Agency.

HIROSHI KIMURA is professor of Slavic studies at the University of Hokkaido, and visiting scholar at the Hoover Institution at Stanford University, 1982–83.

FABIENNE LUCHAIRE is a research associate at the Centre d'Etudes Politiques de Défense in Paris.

EUGENE V. ROSTOW is Sterling Professor of Law at Yale University. Dr. Rostow served the Reagan administration as director of the Arms Control and Disarmament Agency, and previously served as undersecretary of state for political affairs in the Johnson administration.

WOLFGANG SCHREIBER, a retired colonel in the West German army, is on the staff of the social science section of the Konrad Adenauer Foundation, Bonn, Federal Republic of Germany.

K. SUBRAHMANYAM is director of the Institute for Defence Studies and Analyses, New Delhi, India, and the author of many books and articles on Indian foreign policy and security affairs.

GENRIKH TROFIMENKO is head of the U.S. foreign policy desk of the Institute for the Study of the USA/Canada, Soviet Academy of Sciences.

WILLIAM R. VAN CLEAVE is professor of international relations at the University of Southern California, a member of the General Advisory Commission on Arms Control and Disarmament of the U.S. Arms Control and Disarmament Agency, and a former member of the U.S. SALT delegation.

PHILIP WILLIAMS is professor of politics at the University of Southampton, United Kingdom, and a visiting scholar at the Royal Institute for International Affairs, London, 1982–83.